CAMBRIDGE STUDIES IN CRIMINOLOGY XL
General Editor: Sir Leon Radzinowicz

UNDERSTANDING
SEXUAL ATTACKS

THE HEINEMANN LIBRARY OF CRIMINOLOGY
AND PENAL REFORM

CAMBRIDGE STUDIES IN CRIMINOLOGY

UNDERSTANDING SEXUAL ATTACKS

A study based upon a group of rapists undergoing psychotherapy

by

D. J. West, C. Roy and Florence L. Nichols

HEINEMANN
LONDON
ENGLAND

THE BOOK SOCIETY OF CANADA
AGINCOURT
CANADA

Heinemann Educational Books

LONDON EDINBURGH MELBOURNE AUCKLAND TORONTO
HONG KONG SINGAPORE KUALA LUMPUR NEW DELHI
NAIROBI JOHANNESBURG LUSAKA IBADAN
KINGSTON

Heinemann Educational Books ISBN 0 435 82938 6
Heinemann Educational Books Paperback ISBN 0 435 82941 6
The Book Society of Canada ISBN 0 7725 5281 9

First published in Great Britain 1978
First published in Canada 1978

Publishers' note: This title is Volume XL in the Cambridge
Studies in Criminology series. Volumes I to XIX are
published by Macmillan & Co., London, and subsequent
titles by Heinemann Educational Books, London.

Published in Great Britain by
Heinemann Educational Books Ltd
48 Charles Street, London W1X 8AH
Published in Canada by
The Book Society of Canada Ltd
Agincourt, Canada
Printed and bound in Great Britain by
Morrison & Gibb Ltd, London and Edinburgh

Table of Contents

Acknowledgments

D. J. West had the task of actual writing, but the material was produced by Florence Nichols through her work as psychiatrist in charge of a therapeutic programme for sex offenders at the Regional Psychiatric Centre, Abbotsford, British Columbia. The writer must take final responsibility for the way the ideas and opinions are expressed, but they were generated in close partnership with Dr. Nichols and after some months of active participation with her in the therapeutic sessions.

Dr. Chunilial Roy, Medical Director at the Regional Psychiatric Centre, instigated the project by arranging a temporary contract for the writer to work at the centre during a sabbatical leave and by encouraging him to act as participant observer. He also supplied statistical material from official sources, and commentaries on treatment methods elsewhere, so that the observations could be interpreted in a wider context. More importantly, by continued advice, explanation, critical comment and active support at every stage he ensured that the report achieved completion.

The friendly interest and support received from the nursing staff working with the group also made an important contribution. First and foremost, however, thanks are due to the patients themselves who most generously, and with no prospect of personal benefit in return, unanimously gave free consent to the quotation of intimate and often painful details about themselves.

Foreword
by Sir Leon Radzinowicz

This is a moving, frequently horrifying document. At its core is an account of the histories, circumstances and motives of a small group of aggressive offenders imprisoned for grave sexual crimes. The account is based upon their own often painful efforts at self-examination, subject to the searching scrutiny of their fellows and of staff responsible for their custody and treatment. To avoid individual identification, the stories are divided into phases, no single history being followed straight through. Though something is inevitably lost by this approach, much more is gained in terms of allowing free expression and the inclusion of significant detail under the general veil of anonymity. The analysis is skilful, the writing expressive and terse.

My own interest is by no means remote. I had the rather unusual privilege of visiting the Centre where the study was carried out when I was last in Canada, and of conducting a seminar with the prisoners in the company of a perceptive Danish psychiatrist, as well as talking to them individually. I was struck by the fact that, unlike any other prisoners I have seen, they had scarcely a pin-up amongst them: not because of any official embargo but because, as one of them told me, they did not wish to be reminded of the past or to sustain new temptations.

The more notorious sex offences, particularly rape, have always stirred strong public feeling. But of recent years there has been a new questioning of their significance. It started when criminologists began to emphasize the role of victims in precipitating certain kinds of crime, showing a noticeable tendency to select rape as a very obvious illustration. Moreover, studies of selectivity in the recording and prosecution of offences brought out the scepticism manifested both by the police and the courts when faced with complaints of rape. All this encouraged a riposte from the feminist ranks: rape could be seen as a supreme manifestation of male chauvinism, with women not only exploited but blamed for bringing it upon themselves. It is a relief to turn from some of these polemics to an inquiry which seeks by way of painstaking investigation and of scrupulous honesty in recording, to arrive at a closer understanding of at least one kind of rapist.

It is certainly not suggested that those whose stories are told here are typical of sexual criminals as a whole. On the contrary, as the authors make clear, this is not a study of the usual and representative but of the abnormal and unrepresentative amongst those convicted of rape. These were exceptional in the gravity of their crimes, in their progression from minor to major offences, in the persistence of their sexual misbehaviour, in their attacks on total strangers rather than upon women they know, and in their tendency to revert to sexual offences, even after years of apparent stability, with the predictable unpredictability of volcanoes.

The fact that they are exceptional does not, of course, mean that they are unimportant. On the contrary, the elements of savagery, persistence, and randomness in their attacks make them highly dangerous. They also produce very powerful public reactions. A single such case can set in motion waves of fear and vengefulness throughout a community and, by the sheer impact it creates, grossly distort general ideas of what sex offenders are like and of the real threat they offer. To produce such reactions, encourage such distortions, is very far from the intentions of those responsible for this book. It can hardly be too strongly emphasized that the great bulk of sex offenders are nothing like this.

Can we find any consistent pattern even in this small group? Most, but not all, had disturbed, sometimes brutal, upbringings, with problems from the first in approaching contemporaries of the other sex. But they were not sexually timid or sexually starved. They had wives, girl friends, pick-ups, prostitutes. For all their accounts of the frustrations, aggressions, compulsions, leading up to their attacks, something remains unexplained. These men, and the others I saw, combined a deep sense of guilt with a deep sense of helplessness. They asked me, in the course of our seminar, whether they were as dangerous, as abhorrent, as other people thought them, whether it was fair that they could not even be put with other criminals without the fear that they would be attacked.

What is their prognosis? These accounts, in themselves, cannot give the answer though they may raise hopes that some change has occurred. The reader must judge for himself. But at least he can do so with greater understanding after reading this book.

The complaint is very often made that attempts to understand the criminal wholly neglect the victims. In this case the victims were not available for examination, and even if they had been it would have been cruel to seek them out or ask them to relive yet again their ordeals and the aftermath. But the suffering of the women attacked, and indeed of the rapists' wives, who were also in a real sense victims, is acutely recognized.

It is nearly twenty years since I asked Dr. West to join the Cambridge Institute of Criminology. A consistent thread running through all his work has been a thirst to discover, by way of rigorous empirical enquiry, more about the springs of crime, the influences that move or restrain offenders. That was apparent in the first of his books to be published in the *Cambridge Series*, *The Habitual Prisoner*, as well as in the three volumes tracing the development of a large group of juveniles, also in the *Series*. Now we have this, a return to small scale clinical investigation. What binds them all together is the sensitivity, thoroughness and integrity of the approach, the constant and ruthless testing of theories by experience.

I was very much impressed, on my visit to the Centre, by Dr. Florence Nichols, the psychiatrist responsible for initiating and running the treatment group. I realized how able she must have been in freeing and encouraging these men to talk in the way they did.

As editor of the *Cambridge Series*, I particularly welcome the association with Dr. Chunilal Roy. I took to him at once, for he combines qualities of vital importance in this field. He can be firm yet humane; he is ready to experiment yet can accept realistic limitations; he has established a fruitful relationship with his staff as well as with the prisoners; he leads one of the most vulnerable centres of its kind in the world, yet he runs it with confidence and hope.

This volume will stand out in the *Cambridge Series* for its portrayal of a deeply perplexing form of human bondage.

Cambridge
January 1978

Introduction

Rape is a crime of topical interest to psychiatrists, criminologists and the public at large. More publications have appeared on the subject in the last few years than in several decades previously (Chappell *et al.*, 1974, 1977). The incidence of aggressive sexual crimes is reported to be escalating alarmingly in some countries, and this in itself is sufficient cause for increased concern. Another factor has been the rise of the feminist movement bringing with it a new sensitivity to all forms of subjugation of women by men. Rapes are seen as examples of ultimate outrage. The realization that raped women have to undergo more searching and sceptical examination by police and lawyers than do the victims of other forms of criminal violence has provoked much critical discussion. As a consequence, several states have introduced legislative changes to facilitate the prosecution and conviction of rapists without causing the innocent victim avoidable insult or distress.

In this climate of opinion a study that sets out to explore rapists' motives and characters, to understand them as people, and to expose their need for psychiatric help, will not be very popular. To carry out such a study does not mean, however, that one has 'gone over to the enemy'. Discovering what goes on in an offender's mind may promote safer methods of control than years of unconstructive detention, leading to the eventual release of men in a state more embittered and antisocial than when they were first sentenced.

We have made a close examination of the motives and circumstances of a dozen serious sex offenders, as revealed by them in the course of intensive group psychotherapy at the Regional Psychiatric Centre at Abbotsford. We believe that some of the insights gained in this process are likely to prove relevant to many other similar cases. As most of the group are continuing in long-term detention, the results of therapy cannot be expressed in terms of follow-up after release. Nevertheless, from observed changes in attitude and behaviour within the institution, and in the light of the experience of others who have mounted comparable programmes elsewhere, we have ventured some comments on the prospects for this type of approach.

The members of the group lived together in their own ward, and were given the opportunity for protracted self-examination in daily group discussions. In addition to their psychiatrist, who led most of the sessions, the male and female nurses from their ward also participated. These offender-patients proved exceptional in several respects, notably their ability to put their feelings and insights into words, their dedication to the goal of self-exploration, the apparent sincerity of their accounts of their experiences and attitudes and the candour with which they revealed the circumstances and motives of their crimes. With the consent of the group members, this report is based almost entirely upon the material they produced at group sessions, in individual interviews, and in the extensive autobiographies which all participants in the programme were asked to write as one of their therapeutic tasks. The core material consists of an analysis of contributions from the twelve men who were in the group when the writer arrived.

Discretion dictates that the detailed, intimate histories furnished by these men, which included vivid accounts of detected and undetected offences, should not be reproduced in full exactly as recounted. A man might be persuaded to agree for the sake of furthering knowledge, as a contribution to treatment or prevention, or in the hope of promoting a better public understanding of the tragic situation of the serious sex offender who honestly believes he would never commit a similar crime again. To release such a publication, however, might cause distress to relatives and others, or provoke repercussions upon the offender himself. Accordingly, a compromise method will be adopted. Home backgrounds, sexual development and personality conflicts, crisis situations, and crime patterns will all be considered in separate sections, without any attempt to integrate these details into complete, individual case histories. This should permit the general patterns of the group to emerge without the need to link particular crimes, or particular experiences, with an individual, identifiable life story. Except for unimportant changes or obfuscations of too readily identifiable details, this expedient permits the extracts from the men's accounts to adhere closely to what they actually said or wrote.

Given the small size and highly selected nature of the group, sampling techniques and objective methods of statistical analysis were impracticable. No apology is made for this, for the opportunity to learn from such unusually rich material, even though only on an impressionistic basis, was too good to be lost. In any case, there is still a place in clinical research for straightforward descriptive examples of the development of deviant behaviour patterns, especially so in the little understood field of sexual aberrations. The material is being put on record primarily for the contribution it may make towards an understanding of certain kinds of sexual assault, but also as an illustration of a treatment approach applicable to serious sexual criminals.

The advantage of a close study of a small group of these offenders is that their emotional lives and their socio-sexual attitudes can be explored in depth and their significant peculiarities displayed. A small-scale impressionistic analysis cannot establish that the peculiarities discovered will have the same importance among aggressive sexual offenders in general, but it can be justified as pilot work pointing the way to lines of inquiry that it would be profitable to pursue more systematically and objectively with a larger and more clearly defined sample.

The year before the present study, a survey of the twenty-five sex offenders then residing in the institution had been carried out, based upon police reports. The most striking features of these offenders' lives, prior to their last arrest, were unhappy childhood, broken home, aggressive tendencies, numerous indications of psychological instability, poor integration into the community and a variety of antisocial behaviour. Relationships with women had been uniformly disastrous, and those who had contracted marriages had generally failed to maintain them. Many of the offenders were poorly educated and had drifted about the country from job to job. Many of them had committed sexual offences after imbibing large quantities of alcohol or drugs, or both. The victims ranged from under 14 years of age to elderly married women, but females in their late teens or twenties predominated. Many of the attacks were upon victims who had accepted a lift in the offender's car. Rape was usually intended, but not necessarily accomplished. A majority of those who raped females used violence to beat them into submission, and two-fifths made use of some kind of weapon or gun. Contrary to what has been reported of rape in general, a majority of four-fifths of the offenders did not know their victims before they attacked them. Except in three instances, where offenders and victims had been drinking together beforehand, there was no suggestion that the girls had provoked or encouraged a sexual advance. According to the reports of medical examinations, a majority were virgins.

Such was the kind of population from which the treatment group was drawn. They were not, however, a random sample from the institution's sex offenders, because they were selected for their apparent suitability for a psychotherapeutic approach, and transferred out of the group if they were judged not to be responding. Nevertheless, to a very large extent, the personal backgrounds and criminal histories of the group members exhibited the characteristics described. By definition, their crimes were grave enough to have led to penitentiary sentences, several were serving indeterminate detention under the Dangerous Sexual Offenders statute, and two had killed a victim in the course of their attacks. All of them had attacked females, and it was evident that they were of primarily heterosexual orientation, notwithstanding the homosexual experiences or doubts about their masculine activities and performance, that were reported by some of the group.

As will become clear from the accounts to follow, all the men in this group were, or had been, very persistent or very dangerous offenders, and some of them had become progressively more and more desperate and violent as time went on. Their behaviour went beyond the gratification of normal sexual needs regardless of customary social restraints. They seemed more like the victims of an unhappy, alien compulsion that led them to attack female strangers under circumstances that afforded a minimum of erotic gratification and a maximum risk. None of these offenders assaulted their victims in a casual, slap-happy frame of mind. In virtually every case a period of unmistakable psychological malaise or tension, sometimes amounting to a rising crescendo of desperation, preceded the commission of the crimes. In many instances, the outbursts were facilitated by states of self-induced intoxication. Aggravating incidents and frustrating experiences helped to precipitate assaults. In many cases, their attacks upon females appeared to be connected with a chronic feeling of dissatisfaction, real or imagined, with their own masculine performance, social or sexual, and strong and ambivalent emotions towards women, who tended to be perceived as agents of frustration and guilt.

The features of the small group of rapists included in this study likely reflect the predominant characteristics of a limited, but important category of persistent, or potentially persistent, offenders whose criminal propensities are closely bound up with deep-seated emotional problems in the area of their male-female relationships and attitudes. Until their emotional problems can be resolved, such men remain sexually dangerous. The hope is that with psychotherapy, at least in some cases, the emotional difficulties can be resolved and the risk of repetition of offences after release minimized. It would be a pity and a mistake, however, to extend this gloomy interpretation, or this prescription, to all rape offenders.

CHAPTER I

Recruitment and Composition of the Group

At any one time the penitentiaries of British Columbia house well over a hundred sex offenders. The programme described here was much the most intensive form of treatment available to such offenders within the system. The size of the group, partly determined by the number of beds in the ward to which they were assigned, was kept to a maximum of fifteen men. Within the inmate population of the Psychiatric Centre, they formed a self-contained and to a certain extent self-regulating group. They were aware and even proud of their separate identity and reputation. They met regularly for group sessions on five mornings and two evenings each week, in addition to which they were encouraged and expected to have individual discussions with the psychiatric nurses on their ward. Having been drawn from the general population of sex offender prisoners on the strength of psychiatric opinion as to their special suitability and strong motivation for treatment, and having demonstrated, during a trial period, their ability to meet the requirements of the treatment programme, they were clearly a highly selected group.

The psychological processes revealed in the course of this treatment programme are in all probability common to substantial numbers of sex offenders. Nevertheless, it has to be recognized that this was an elitist group who were not typical of the general run of sex offenders detained in the penitentiary system. Imprisoned sex offenders all too often lack the ability to express their feelings and motives or, still more often, have no intention of admitting or revealing the circumstances of their crimes. The prospect of exposing their true thoughts to the institution staff appears to them dangerous and unprofitable. They view offers of psychiatric treatment as a threat and a trap to hinder their release.

This point was brought home particularly forcibly during a visit to Mountain Prison. A series of sex offenders, none of whom had so far been treated at the Regional Psychiatric Centre, were interviewed in order to find out if they might wish to be admitted, should

1

an additional treatment programme suited to their needs be started. It was decided to approach men whose prison records indicated that their sex offences had involved minors under the age of 14. Eleven such men were available in the prison. One refused even to be seen, and not one said he wanted treatment. Only one was prepared to admit to having any particular sexual interest in children. Five of them had been in prison for over nine years since their last conviction. Several expressed great bitterness at being given the prospect of treatment after so many wasted years in custody without it. Most of the refusals to consider treatment were based on a denial of any sexual problem. Three of the men were over 60 years of age. One of these three said he was physically impotent and psychologically uninterested in any form of sex. Another, younger, man, a cardiac invalid, said the same thing. Several attributed their misconduct entirely to their former drinking habits. One man insisted he had no sex problem because he had been wrongfully convicted on each occasion. He spent the entire interview in an aggressive recital of his grievances and in threats of vengeance against the police. Another man emphasized that he was very virile and had no problems, although he was convicted of raping a young girl. Several mentioned the absence of day parole and the restrictions of a maximum security establishment as one of the reasons for not considering treatment at the Regional Psychiatric Centre.

Most of the prisoners expressed scepticism about the benefits of treatment, and several pointed out, with some reason, that men who had been through a long course of treatment returned to prison seemingly no nearer release than if they had never undertaken it. Two men asked if their refusal would 'go on the record' and be held against them. One man was so wildly paranoid in his statements, and so excitable in his eagerness to subject the interviewer to a hostile cross-examination, that he appeared to be on the verge of psychosis. One of the older men was so far advanced in his dotage it is doubtful if he comprehended much of what he was being asked. Some had long histories of convictions for non-sexual crimes. One of these, an Indian, looked upon his conviction for sexual misconduct as an unimportant incident in his continuing war with white authorities. Another man maintained that he was being victimized because he had a criminal record and had been forced to live by illicit car dealing.

Their sexual offences may have arisen from basically similar conflicts and personality problems, but as individuals the members of the treatment group under discussion in this book were very different from some of the sad specimens of hostile humanity languishing in the prisons. As a matter of policy, offenders of below average intelligence, those thought to be psychotic and those known to have epilepsy or other indications of organic cerebral disease were ruled out of consideration for admission to the programme. Also ruled out were those known to have further charges outstanding against them whose expected release dates were consequently uncertain. Except in the early stages of the programme, when admission criteria were still fluid, preference was given to those whose probable date of release was not impossibly far ahead.

In effect, all members of the group were physically healthy adults in their twenties and thirties, the oldest being 39 when he joined. All were of at least average intelligence, some were distinctly bright, and tests given by a professional vocational guidance service identified some individuals as having a variety of potentially superior talents. Far from trying to avoid psychiatric placement, all members had taken some personal initiative to be accepted for treatment at the Centre. Some of them had waged what amounted to a personal campaign, supported by relatives, petitions, lawyers' interventions and recommendations from outside psychiatrists, all directed towards gaining admission.

The prison psychiatrists having recommended a particular sex offender as a candidate for treatment at the Regional Psychiatric Centre, and the Medical Director having agreed to admit him, further hurdles remained. Following admission, each candidate spent some time waiting for a clinical placement conference at which the staff would decide, after having had the opportunity to interview and observe him, whether to try him out in the group psychotherapy programme or in some other treatment programme.

Once admitted as a participant in the group, each man passed through another period of assessment to decide if he would be able to remain as a full member. During the probationary period he had to write his autobiography and also tell his life story verbally during group sessions. After ninety days, members of staff and fellow members of the group would make an evaluation of the candidate's sincerity and suitability. As an aid to this evaluation, each person filled in a sixteen-item questionnaire or check list. This included such questions as the following:

Did this person sufficiently 'open up' (talk freely) for you to understand his problems?

Do you consider that he completed writing his autobiography in a manner that was self-revealing and satisfactory?

Is this person committed and motivated to being treated?

Is this person properly clothed, groomed and well-mannered on the ward? (social responsibility and awareness)

Is this person generally punctual at group events and mentally alert throughout the day?

Is this person developing a feeling of belonging in the group?

A numerical score was derived from these questionnaires by having each respondent rate his own comments on each of the sixteen items on a five-point scale, ranging from one (most unfavourable) through three (average) to five (most satisfactory). A total score of less than an average rating throughout, that is of less than 48, was regarded as inadequate.

In making their assessments, staff and fellow residents had plenty of opportunity to observe and comment upon the candidate's conduct. Within the physical confines of the institution the men were given much more time and freedom to mingle with fellow residents, to participate in work tasks, hobbies, sports and other recreational activities, than is normally the case in a high-security establishment. These freedoms were, however, linked with definite rules. The customary requirements of good order and discipline common to most institutions (such as keeping to the time-table, maintaining a respectful demeanour, keeping themselves and their quarters clean and tidy, avoiding fights, not becoming involved in overt homosexual activity) were fairly strictly applied. In addition, all members of the treatment group had to adhere to an exacting code of frankness, sincerity, trust and goodwill in their dealings with each other and with the staff members concerned with the programme. Regular attendance at the daily discussion meeting was obligatory. It was the rule at the meetings to have an open exchange of feelings, personal concerns and problems, together with critical commentaries on each other's behaviour and attitude inside and outside the group. Mere lip-service to the ideal of self-improvement and self-examination did not suffice. Phoney protestations of innocence of past crimes, distrustful or withdrawn attitudes towards other members of the group living together on the ward, covert rule-breaking when not under observation, declarations of good intentions not backed up by appropriate behaviour, and attempts to play off one member of the staff against another, all aroused adverse comment from the group as a whole.

Activities were organized with a view to providing maximum opportunity for self-improvement, for the control of selfish and aggressive impulses, and for combating tendencies to social withdrawal. Group members were encouraged to pursue behavioural goals common to all, as well as personal assignments geared to each individual's requirements. Emphasis was placed upon developing skills in interpersonal relationships, in recreational activities, in the wise use of leisure time, and in the handling of communal chores.

Job assignments within the institution, educational courses and constructive hobbies were allocated, after discussion in the group, according to each member's interests and particular needs.

In comparison with ordinary prisoners the members of the treatment group enjoyed the privilege of access to a variety of facilities. The hospital, which first opened in June 1972, was newly equipped for clinical examinations and research and provided with comfortably furnished single rooms, exercise yards, school, sports fields, gymnasium and hobby shops. Nevertheless, the patients were still high-security prisoners, and this meant obvious limits to the activities available and the amount of physical freedom allowed. The sixteen-acre site was surrounded by a double fence fifteen feet high, four sentry towers and a mechanically operated double gate. The perimeter was patrolled by armed guards and under surveillance by ten cameras and a giant scope camera for viewing from the central control room.

There was accommodation for 138 patients. The number of security staff was about half that figure, but the number of treatment and administrative staff was roughly the same as the number of patients, and more importantly half of them were women. This favourable staff-inmate ratio, supported by background security, permitted a good deal of relatively informal mingling of inmates and staff during both work and recreational periods, without any apparent loss of control. Incidents of violence were exceptionally rare, even though most of the inmates had come from high security institutions and many had been in solitary confinement on account of their aggressiveness. About a quarter of the inmates were under treatment for severe mental illness, that is schizophrenia, depressive psychosis or organic brain disease. Of those suffering from personality disorders, who were the main participants in psychotherapeutic and social training programmes, roughly a third were under sentence for sex offences. This proportion was large enough to protect these offenders from the discrimination and bullying many of them had experienced in prison.

It was a principle of the treatment programme that disciplinary action to correct poor behaviour would be taken by the group and the staff together, after discussion with the offender. For example, the pay normally awarded an institution inmate for the conscientious performance of allotted tasks might be down-graded to a lower rate. Other sanctions included suspension of hobby facilities, curtailment of telephone call privileges, loss of T.V. viewing, loss of recreation time and confinement to the ward.

If persisted in, poor behaviour ultimately led to adverse assessments and expulsion from the programme. Even after the expiration of the formal probationary period, and approval of full membership of the group, the maintenance of a satisfactory standard was insisted upon. In some cases of doubt probation periods were extended to allow further assessments. In other cases, where members were thought to be making no progress, or failing to modify inappropriate attitudes or conduct, renewed assessments were called for.

The number of men who dropped out of the group prematurely reflects the continual pruning of those who would not or could not conform, and indicates how exacting some offenders found the requirements of the programme. Out of a total of thirty-five admitted to the group since its inception, six completed what was considered an optimum period of around two years, and were then transferred, with favourable recommendations as regards their progress, to complete the remainder of their time in custody in the ordinary prisons. Another three were released into the community, after spending less than two years in the group, because they had reached their date for mandatory release on parole and so could not be allowed to remain longer. One of them, in fact, wanted to do so, but had to be refused. As many as fourteen dropped out, some after having been with the group a year or more. One or two requested their own transfer, the remainder were rejected because initial or later assessments, by staff and fellow members, appeared to show that they were not co-operating or not responding. Half of these drop-outs were given places in other treatment programmes within the Centre, but the others were sent back to prison, usually to the same prisons from which they had come. Even if all the remaining participants stayed the course, this would still mean a rejection rate of forty per cent.

The pressure upon group members to collaborate fully and trustingly was quite considerable, and the stresses produced may have accounted for some of the failures. Everyone realized that failure to meet the requirements of the treatment programme could lead to pessimistic psychiatric reports, which in turn would be expected to have an adverse effect upon the chances of being given parole in advance of the mandatory supervision release date. Some of the present group members expressed the smug view that the drop-outs had been given their chance and had only themselves to blame for the consequences of not having taken it. In contrast, at least one of the drop-outs, whom the present writer was able to interview subsequently, argued bitterly, if somewhat unconvincingly, that he had been unfairly treated and his sincerity wrongly impugned.

Those who succeeded in clearing all hurdles and winning acceptance in the group struck visitors to the institution with their surprisingly relaxed, genial and friendly demeanour. The first impression on meeting them was of a gathering of polite, civilized, orderly young men. They could have been candidates for military promotion rather than a collection of sex criminals. They arranged themselves in a neat circle, one brought out the equipment for the coffee-break and set it up in a corner; another, who acted as note-taker, placed a small table in front of his chair. After the usual exchange of pleasantries and banter expected between persons who know each other, one of the members punctually called the meeting to order and asked for the first item of business. Discussions proceeded in a fairly low emotional key. Life experiences, including criminal offences, were described without histrionics, in a matter-of-fact manner, almost as if in a court-room. Narratives were interrupted sometimes by the doctor or nurse, sometimes by other members of the group, who put probing questions, but in a kindly exploratory fashion, like a physician eliciting descriptions of medical symptoms. Only gradually did it become obvious that this well-controlled discussion was no trivial club room debate, but a deadly earnest analysis of each man's personal tragedy, and a slow but searching exploration of some truly horrifying crimes. In the course of time, the pain and distress and shame which accompanied some of these semi-public disclosures became all too obvious. Also obvious was the discomfort of the 'hot seat', when one member would be singled out for exclusive and critical attention from the whole group, and confronted with evident contradictions and irrationalities in his attitudes, his version of his life and problems, or his conduct within the institution. With longer experience of group sessions it became clear how much effort was being demanded of these men to withstand the emotional stress of continued self-questioning while maintaining reasonably equable, co-operative social behaviour. It also became more understandable why so many had dropped out and why those who persisted with the programme were exceptionally determined and dedicated to the treatment philosophy. As the author's observation period was drawing to a close, one of the more unhappy members insisted upon leaving the group, was transferred back to the penitentiary, and subsequently killed himself.

CHAPTER II

Adversities in Early Life

A phrase in a psychologist's report on one of the men in the group referred to a problem of 'troubled masculinity'. It was a theme that ran through all their stories. Regardless of differences in upbringing and social circumstances, or of the contrast between those who were boldly aggressive or seemingly inhibited, or of the varied modes of their sexual aggressions, all seemed to share to some extent one salient characteristic, namely, their feelings of inadequacy, confusion, anxiety or discontent about their fulfilment of the social or sexual requirements of the masculine role.

Men fail in heterosexual relationships in a variety of ways. Their erotic interests may be elsewhere, emotions of resentment, suspicion or plain fear may colour their attitudes to women, or they may have doubts, often unjustified, about whether their personality, social skills or sexual performance will meet a woman's expectations. Men suffering from such difficulties are commonly found to have been exposed in childhood to defective parental attitudes and emotional turmoil in the home. A great deal of evidence points to early family influences as crucial factors in the genesis of the sexual problems of adult life. One need not search far to discover reasons for this.

Our culture remains prudish towards children, with the result they are deprived of the natural sexual learning experiences enjoyed in so-called primitive societies. Moreover, sex remains the only social skill in which no systematic practical instruction is given by adults to young children. After puberty, adolescents find themselves exposed to confusing pressures, to the official public morality of continence till marriage, to the peer group values according to which sexual conquest is a necessary qualification for manhood, and the notorious double standard whereby the ready seducer gains status while the readily seduced loses it. The high valuation upon sexual freedom and variety seems irreconcilable with the pursuit of romatic love and the assumption of marital responsibilities. To add to these confusions, the culture, and more especially the working-class culture, defines masculinity not merely in terms of sexual virility and copulatory expertise, but also expects males to display assertiveness and com-

8

petitiveness as well as physical strength, courage and willingness to stand up and fight. Males who lack the social skills or temperamental qualities to produce a satisfactory display of this kind have low status among peers and many suffer tortures of self-doubt and despondency. In efforts to weave a reasonably straight path through this maze of contradictions everyone experiences some difficulties and anxieties. The task becomes particularly difficult for those who have lacked the support of a secure, unbroken parental home, for those who have passed through critical phases of development without contact with confidently masculine and feminine adults, and for those who have been subjected to early life situations or attitudes conducive to a permanent sense of guilt about their sexual feelings. Psychologists nowadays believe that a sense of gender identity, a feeling of belonging fully and unquestioningly to the category of boy or girl, becomes firmly established in the first few years of life, even before an infant comprehends the essential anatomical differences between males and females. Confident expectancy from the parents, and a quietly automatic encouragement of behaviour appropriate to a child's sex, plays an essential part in the development of gender identity. In extreme cases, where mothers have treated their boys like girls, and kept them dependent and clinging, and weak fathers have done nothing to prevent it, the result has sometimes been transsexual deviation. The unhappy male thinks and feels feminine and in his heart believes himself a woman, trapped inside an unsuitable male carcase (Stoller, 1968). The commoner forms of parental mishandling are not of a kind to induce such extreme cross-sex identification, but they frequently so undermine self-confidence that a boy never feels completely at ease about his masculinity or completely satisfied with his performance as a male.

Among this group of rapists peculiar and unhappy upbringings were the rule. Only two, at most, out of twelve men, described parental homes that could be classed as anything like normal or average. Only four of the twelve had lived consistently with both natural parents from birth to adolescence. Most of them recalled very unhappy and peculiar upbringings, some of them amounting to conditions of manifest physical brutality or severe emotional rejection. The following accounts of the early years of these twelve rapists are arranged in roughly ascending order from the worst to the best of the backgrounds to be found among the group.

Example 1

His first hazy recollections are of the years from 3 to 6, which he spent, together with his younger brother and sister, in a foster home in the country. 'I remember the exciting car journey when we were all three taken home, then the disillusionment on arrival. The cold reception from the people I was to accept as my parents.' During the next ten years spent with his natural parents he was treated with extreme harshness, his movements were restricted, he had no love or attention from his parents and was kept in isolation from children outside the home.

'My mother was a mean-looking woman. She was easily controlled and manipulated by my father, to the point where one wondered if she had a mind of her own. She had once been religious, but had been swayed into accepting my father's atheism and fanatical communist beliefs. She was sloppy in dress to the point of embarrassment, and bitchy, moody and uncommunicative—only just tolerating my existence.

'Father was slim and tall and most people thought him handsome, but a withdrawn, antisocial, friendless person, and given to senseless outbursts of anger. My parents were my keepers, the bedroom was my cell and home. The bed had to be made at a certain time, the floor swept at a certain time, meals taken cold and in isolation, while authority was kept up just as cold and impersonal as any prison guard.'

He remembers savage beatings from both parents for the most trivial reasons. 'Coming home late from school, dirty clothes, worn shoes, whatever the excuse the result was the same, a clenched fist over the head. I remember being strapped by my mother for some similar reason and ending up cowering on the floor being punched and kicked. Another time, as I was the last of the three children due to get the strap on that occasion, I got panicky and attempted to run from her after the first few hits. She caught me and pushed me hard into the corner of a door. My face struck and blood spurted from a cut near my eye. She followed me up to the bathroom and kicked me from behind in her anger when she saw the mess of blood everywhere. Then I was made to clean up the bathroom and to go bed with no treatment for the cut.'

He remembers that when he was around the age of 6 or 9 he and his brother and sister were subjected to group beatings. 'The parents having worked out a rap sheet against all three of us, they would begin by listening to music and drinking. Then they would strap each of us one after the other. One of them would hold the arms and the other the legs and they would lay on the strap hard and often while we were suspended in the air between them. The whole session would last from evening till the early hours.'

There were times when he tried to establish some rapport with his parents, less with his mother, for whom he had only feelings of disgust, than with his father, whom he looked upon as clever and knowledgeable. Each time he thought he had made progress he was rapidly disillusioned. For example, he was delighted when his father took him on occasional car trips to visit a relative, but he was soon put off by the shameless way his father behaved towards women as they passed, and he came to feel that he was being taken only as a ruse to allay his mother's jealous suspicions.

At the age of 15, he gained courage to steal a bicycle and run away from home. He was charged and brought before the court, but with his father sitting right behind him, he did not dare to tell what had been going on at home. He was put on probation. 'For the first time I was treated as an individual, their son, but only for very obvious reasons, to pacify the probation officer with good appearances. I was bought, bribed. I got a bicycle. I got some old furniture for my room. Through necessity, I was allowed out socially and for the first time I could come and go from the house without much restraint. But I was not allowed to bring anyone home, and it was made clear I was just being tolerated.'

After the period of probation, things became worse again. He was told they could not afford any more schooling for him. 'When I turned sixteen, I wrote them a note that I was now of legal age and wanted to leave. In turn, I was presented with a paper, with a legal firm's letterhead, stating that I was being disowned by the family and could by no right come back for anything as they could no longer be held responsible for me.'

Example 2

When he was about 3 or 4, his father was busy on a job that involved a lot of driving about. 'I remember he would pick me up in the afternoons and take me out with him on his rounds. He would take the sleigh for me and I would slide down the embankments while waiting for him to transact his business.' By the time he started school, however, the home atmosphere began to deteriorate. 'There were five other children by this time, and father had taken to drinking more than he usually did. He would come home from work drunk. I suppose it affected mother, because the two of them would usually end up arguing about it. I think she was afraid he might get fired. By the time I was 7 my father was in an almost perpetual state of intoxication. Arguments went on over Christmas, and I was glad to get back to school after the break. The arguments at home got worse and more violent. It got to the point where all the kids were jumpy. I knew for sure that I could not concentrate. My school work was beginning to show the effects of the home situation and the fact that

I wasn't getting sufficient sleep.' His father became ill as a result of the drinking and lost his job, so his mother had to go out to work to pay the bills. 'Father was forced to put the family on welfare. He could not work, and as soon as mother departed for her work he would get restless, go out, and start drinking again.'

By the time he was 10, his father was becoming violent after drinking. 'I started to feel an active dislike for my father. My brother and I would be awakened at night by our parents screaming and yelling at each other. Those fights would last well into the early hours, with little or no sleep for me. I would lay there listening, wishing there was some way I could get up and stop it, but I realized if I did get up it would only result in a beating for me as well as my mother. Then father changed his tactics. Now he would beat my brother and myself, leaving my mother alone. He would do this while she was out, and she would only find out by the bruises that were constantly appearing on our bodies. Then he took the money we had saved from a paper round, calmly telling us it was time for us to help with the expenses.' The brother left home after a fight with the father, and the family was forced to move out of their house for non-payment of rates. 'Then I started to enter houses of paper-round customers, taking money that had been left lying about.' He was caught and taken home. 'I cannot remember if father even asked an explanation, he just beat me. I do not know for how long, it just seemed to go on forever. I am sure that if mother had not intervened he would have beaten me to death. I was stiff and bruised for weeks after.'

At the age of 13, he recalls a temporary improvement following his father's committal to hospital for a few months, but things soon became as bad as ever. 'Father took all my savings again. All I can remember is a feeling of great deadness.' He resumed his stealing habits and got caught again. 'I had resigned myself to a beating, but when I got home, the fact that I really did not care much what happened to me must have been evident, for my father just took one look at me and told me I was on my own (as far as the court proceedings were concerned). The age of 14 was the most violent period in my life. I was constantly fighting, if not with someone at school, then with my father. At first, my fights with him were all one-sided, due to my lack of knowledge of self-defence, but that soon changed and any restraints I had had about fighting with my father seemed to dissolve. Mother could not stand this fighting, and intervened whenever she could do so safely. It proved too much for her, and she departed taking the younger kids. I had to try to see that the remaining kids got taken care of. By the age of 15 I was on the verge of nervous exhaustion. The welfare agency stepped in and got my parents to agree to unite again. I was sent to a summer camp, but on my return mother was gone again and father was drunk. I left then and told the welfare to see to the kids.' After this, the parents were divorced.

Example 3

'My earliest recollections are of sleeping with my brother and sister all in a bed together in the living room. It seems that we were always locked out of the house and waiting for mother to come home. We seemed to live mostly on peanut butter, and there was never much food in the kitchen. On many a night, mother brought home some "uncle" or other, and we would hear her with him in the next room, moaning and groaning. I was scared, thinking she was being beaten and I would cry in bed with my younger brother and sister, all three hugging each other. Then, a few moments later mother would come out looking happy. It was confusing.

'When I was about 7 the three of us were taken away to a children's home and then to a foster placement. Mother visited us once, with a strange man, but I felt no emotion. It was just sort of "Hello-got-to-go-good-bye." Then one day they told me that some people had taken my sister to live with them for good (as an adopted child). I cried, heart-broken, and begged to be told where she was, but was told they were not allowed to say.'

By the time he was 8 or 9, his brother had also gone. 'I never felt happy after that and was always running away. The police were nice and would often feed me before bringing me back to the home.' There followed a whole series of temporary placements, with intervening periods in a detention home. 'I had to stay longer in that place than expected. The welfare officer kept telling me they had still not found a place for me. It made me feel bitter, sad, unwanted, rejected.'

At about the age of 10, he spent some time in the home of a woman minister. She had three other wards from different places. 'I always felt we were on display for her just to show us off. The ladies (at church functions) would remark, "What wonderful boys you have there." How I hated her! One day, I think because I swore, she stripped me naked in front of everyone and strapped me viciously with a belt. It hurt so much I thought she was never going to stop.'

At another placement soon after, 'the couple had a young adopted boy as well as their own children, and they were always running down his natural parents. The foster mother would often beat him cruelly, and I mean cruelly, so that I was terrified. I must have left there three to five times. Each time they would forgive me and take me back. I was a beautiful actor. I'd fake tears and ask the Lord to forgive me, but it was done just to satisfy them.'

Example 4

'As an infant, I seem to remember being unhappy a lot of the time, and my parents continually arguing. My mother moved away from home and took a live-in housekeeping job with some guy. After that my parents were often separated.' They divorced when he was 8. 'Father was a no-good boaster and philanderer.

'When I had just started talking I had a bad accident. From the time I got out of the hospital till the age of 4, I didn't talk again. I was told it was my father's fault, and I guess I have hostile feelings to him because of that.

'At the age of 7 I went to my first foster home. I used to visit mother at week-ends, and always hated to go back. Not that the foster parents mistreated me, but I felt I did not belong there, and they kept me only because they were paid to do so. Father came to visit a couple of times. Once, he spent the whole visit arguing with the foster parents about how much they charged to keep me.

'Somewhere around my tenth birthday, I went to my second foster home. The first couple said they didn't want me to go, but they couldn't afford to keep me, and my father wouldn't pay any more money. It was a strict household, this second foster home. We all had our household chores to do. I can remember the foster father would come home drunk. Then everyone would hide and he would charge around the house yelling and breaking things. I think my foster mother used to get thumped regularly when her old man was on these drunken rampages. He gave me a beating only a couple of times, after that I learned to stay out of his way. I used to wonder what it was like to come home from school to one's own mother and father and home. I remember asking some of my friends about how they felt.'

After three years he was moved to yet another foster placement. 'It was a sad time saying goodbyes to foster mother and the kids. The next place was on a farm some distance away. I went to a different school and can't remember making any close friends. I could never understand why my father had to pay for me at this place, for I am sure I worked hard enough, milking cows and other chores, to earn my keep.

'When I was 13, mother remarried and I went to live with them. I would call my step-father dad and he would call me son, and he was very easy to get along with, but later he took to drink and the marriage failed. Father came round yelling and making a fuss, trying to make me go to live with him. But he never kept his word. His word was worth two cents, his mouth a million dollars. I told him I didn't want to go with him.'

Example 5

When he was 5, his father was jailed for a serious offence. While his father was serving this sentence, his mother obtained a divorce. 'Mother told me he was in a hospital and I couldn't see him. I cried when our old housekeeper went, because we couldn't afford to keep her. Mother had always gone out to work, and this housekeeper had been just like a mother to me, played games with me and told me stories. Up until then, we had a good relationship with father's relatives, spending Christmas with them but after this we hardly ever saw any of father's side of the family. My maternal grandmother took the housekeeper's place looking after me. She spoilt me all the time, against mother's wishes, but I didn't mind.

'When I was about 9, father got out of jail and moved into his parents' place. I was sure happy to see him after so long, and wanted to go around and see him all the time after that, although my mother didn't like the idea very much. My life at home with mother was happy, except that I felt out of place at times. My mother seemed a lot closer to my older sister than to me. They used to spell out words to each other so I wouldn't know what they were talking about.'

At the age of 11 or 12, he became aware that his mother had boy-friends who would come back home with her at a late hour. He never let on that he had heard them, but 'I hated the guy for just being there, and my mother disgusted me also, because I felt she should have taken him somewhere else.'

His loyalty to his father remained firm. As soon as he began working, he started trying to help his father, who had by this time become an alcoholic, and increasingly irresponsible, socially and financially. It took him a long time to realize that his efforts were futile and that they were interfering with his own way of life and marriage prospects.

Example 6

His parents remained physically together until he was 15, but from an emotional standpoint he had a chronically deprived upbringing. His childhood world was largely bounded by the attitudes of his mother and older sisters, which he came to perceive as cold and hurtfully rejecting. The family was materially very poor, and he tried to accept many of his deprivations as 'the way things are', but certain experiences left him with deep resentments that rankle to this day.

He had a chronic habit of bed-wetting, which persisted well into adolescence, in spite of the harsh measures taken to control it. 'When I was 4 or 5, my parents would give me spankings for wetting the bed. They would try every way they could think of to make me quit, but I didn't know how to quit. I was afraid to get up at night by myself and walk in the dark to the pot. The other kids were allowed to sleep with my parents once in a while, but if I tried to get in their bed, I was kicked out as if I was taboo. I had to sleep in a wet bed all the time. I used to hate to go to bed because it was so cold. I had a rubber cover on the mattress and I wasn't allowed to wear pyjamas and I can't remember ever having sheets. My mom wouldn't let me drink at all after supper, and sometimes I would have given anything for a little drink of water, I got so thirsty. In the winter, I used to lick the frost off the window.' Washing facilities were sparse, the mattress was left damp, his bedroom always stank, and he recalled painful incidents when other children remarked upon the smell he carried around.

It seemed to him that women were particularly cruel about his problem. 'When visitors or relatives came over, the women would sit around the kitchen and joke about me wetting the bed. I would be really hurt and ashamed. To me, women always seemed so cold and hard to talk to. They were always making fun of me. I always wished they would like me as much as the other kids.' His sisters also used to tease and taunt him about his wetting and stinking.

He was punished frequently as a child by severe beatings, often for conduct he did not see as being wrong. 'Our family was always financially poor. Us kids didn't know what it was like to get gifts for our birthdays. One time, when I was about 10, my cousin and I went hunting pop bottles. We took them to the store and sold them and I spent all the money on candy. I was sure happy because now I thought I could give the rest of the kids a real treat. I was really going to be a good samaritan, but when I got home Mom was really mad that I had spent all my money so foolishly. When Dad got home from work he gave me a heck of a good beating. They took all the candy away, locked it up in a cupboard. They gave us kids a little bit at a time, until it was all gone. I felt really hurt at being beaten for doing something I thought was a good deed.'

He blamed his mother, rather than his father, for the severity of these beatings. She used to get mad at him, and tell his father about it, and insist upon his father administering some punishment. She would nag at his father for not beating him hard enough. That would make his father lose his temper and punch really hard, knocking him across the room and leaving him bruised for days. Then his mother would scream to stop, but his father would get madder still and beat all the harder. He never held these incidents against his father because he felt that his mother instigated them, and it was at her that his father's rage was actually directed. At other times, his father used to sympathize with him, because he was the underdog, the one who got blamed more than the other children. 'I forgave my father for the beatings because he was kind to me in other ways, but I never forgave my mother because she was always so cold towards me. I could never have a happy conversation with her. It seemed like she hated me.'

He used to love doing things to try to help his father, for instance, when his father was working on the construction of an extension to the house. But there was always the fear of doing wrong and being punished. One day, when his father had left the construction site briefly to get something, he and some other children were playing, and he sustained an accidental burn from some hot roofing tar. It was a nasty, painful, burn, but he went home and tried to conceal it for fear of the licking he would get. His parents discovered it and took him to a doctor. 'I could never understand why I didn't catch heck for that.'

When he was 10, his mother took a job working outside the home, and it seemed to him that from then on her interest in cooking and housework and doing things for the children gradually lessened. After a time, she started going out with other men. 'After work she would go out drinking and come home late. Most of the time she was drunk. Some of the time she would come home with men she had met at the bar. I remember seeing her parked down the road from the house necking with strange men. My father found out and was really hurt by her actions. He beat her up a few times for it, but that didn't stop her.' Finally his father employed a detective to obtain evidence for a divorce. In this conflict, he sided with his father. He remembered his father confiding to him in later years, that his mother had been sexually cold and that he had had to 'fight' for anything from her.

Example 7

This man recalled no active parental cruelty, but seems always to have regarded his father as a distant, frightening, punitive figure. He thought of his mother as loving and helpful, but frequently pre-occupied and overworked. He was born in wartime in Europe under circumstances of considerable stress, with bombings, food shortages and father away fighting. When he was around 3, his mother was forced to evacuate their home and go to live with his father's relatives, who were from a middle-class background, superior to her own. 'Grandmother had a beautiful, large house, but bitterly resented having to share it with penniless refugees. She was a stingy woman who I felt resented us children. At this time, there was no word from father, and he was practically given up for dead.' When his father did return, he was obliged to accept work beneath his previous status and training. 'I believe this likely rankled him.'

A bright, quick-learning female cousin of his own age lived in the grandmother's house. 'I have the impression that she being so bright, and also cheerful, she would be given most, if not all, the attention and love. I could not compete, so I would misbehave to get attention, even if the wrong kind.' At this time he recalls father 'as a tired man coming home in the evening. Mother I also recall only vaguely as a very kind woman who seemed to be busy almost all the time.' At the age of 4 he was hospitalized for a serious illness which left him weak. 'Before then, father had been very proud of me, but I have the feeling that after that he changed his opinion of me. This I cannot ascribe to anything memorable except he never seemed to have any physical contact with me, barring the odd licking in later years.'

At the age of 8 he remembers 'working in grandmother's garden the odd time. I remember mother being used like a servant by my grandmother. She seemed to be kept busy from sunrise to sunset. At the time, I merely thought that this was the usual course of events. I tended to stay away from father when he was home. He seemed to be quite irritable, and I feared his wrath would come down on me. We were sometimes warned by mother to be especially quiet on his account.'

When he was 10 his father emigrated. 'I was glad to see him go, for he had been more than usually irritable. He criticized me more than ever about my school grades. Before he left, I got a licking. We had been tossing stones in grandmother's cherry tree, trying to knock the fruit down. One of the stones bounced off a branch onto my brother's head and he was knocked out briefly. What I didn't know then was that father had been gambling and lost a substantial sum. I don't know how much, but it was all the passage money he had been saving to have the whole family emigrate together.'

In the years following, he was repeatedly punished for occasional stealing, unsatisfactory school performance, and various acts of mischief. When he was 14, he and the rest of the family emigrated to join his father. 'I trod carefully around father as I was not sure whether he knew of my misdeeds.' A little later 'the resentment against father I had felt earlier came back when he made me turn all our paper-round money to him, receiving in return only a dollar a week pocket money. If we argued, he would shout at us. I began to cheat him on the paper-round money.' Not long after this, his father took suddenly ill and died after a painfull illness. 'His suffering prompted some guilt in me, for I had wanted to hurt him, but these feelings did not last long. When he died, I pretended to feel sorrow, but really felt more like "so what?" At his funeral, I couldn't feel sorrow for him.'

Example 8

He described his parents' marriage as 'difficult'. They never got along well. After many years together, they started the process of divorce. His father was self-employed with an income barely adequate for necessities. In his view, the main cause of the trouble between his parents was his mother's desire for a better social status and his father's unwillingness or inability to provide it. He blamed his mother for the situation. He thought she was a weak personality, dominated by her relatives. She let them interfere in their family life. As a boy, he used to resent her for this. He never cared what she thought, but always strove to win father's good opinion. He felt she was over-emotional and doted on him whether he did right or wrong. Whenever his father remonstrated with him she would try to stick up for him, but he did not thank her at all for doing that. He wanted to make his own relationship with his father. Even in prison, he does not relish visits from his mother.

His father had a violent temper and was a 'strong man', physically and mentally, dominant in the home and over-fond of alcohol, but never violent with it, so drinking was not the cause of family problems. He recalls one incident at about the age of 10, when he was caught for 'borrowing' a neighbour's rifle. 'My father, in a temper, proceeded to blacken my arse to the point where my thighs were swollen and bruised for days. This was about the worst spanking I had ever received. I can't remember hating my father for it, then or since, but I was scared of him afterwards. The incident caused real hard feelings between my father and my mother and my mother's relatives. I did not share their point of view as I felt I had deserved the punishment.'

He referred several times to disappointment at being unable to win his father's good opinion. He recalled feeling extremely cut up at his father's comments on being told of his plans to marry. His father told him that the girl was too good for him and that he could never make a good husband.

Example 9

This was one of the few members of the group who claimed to have had a happy childhood. Nevertheless, there were some odd features about his background. His father was a distinctly shadowy figure in his life. 'In my parents' marriage, my mother was the dominant partner, but they were both happy with that arrangement. Father was a quiet man, a very steady worker and a non-drinker. He had the same travelling job for thirty years, and was away five or six days of the week. As a result, I really did not know him all that well. He allowed my mother to handle all the finance. I can remember receiving a spanking from him only once, and that was on mother's instructions.' When he was 14 his father died.

'Mother was aged thirty-six when I was born.' He was the youngest by ten years in a family of four. His elder brother was already married and away from home when he was born. They occupied a large house and 'for as long as I can remember there were many other children living in our home, both boys and girls. My mother was very fond of children, and she simply took in and cared for unwanted children.' Being brought up in a close proximity to older children, his contacts with sexuality began at an early age, and generated considerable guilt. 'I can remember my mother telling the kids that playing with each other or ourselves would make us crazy. She referred to it as "dirty tricks". Although sex as such was not discussed, we all knew what she meant.'

He thought his mother tended to favour him in small ways above the other children, occasionally giving him extra candy and so forth, on the side. She would seldom say no to what he wanted. Basically, however, there was little to distinguish him from the foster children, some of whom he believed, at the time, to be his actual brothers and sisters. A psychiatrist, commenting upon his history, noted that with so many children in the home at one time, he was unlikely to have had much attention or supervision from his mother.

Example 10

In his written autobiography, this man reported very little about his parents. He described them more fully during interviews. In his recollections of infancy and school years, his parents were rather distant figures, the important people in his life were his older brothers and his friends. His father was nearing 50 when he was born, and communication with him was not so easy. His father was a big, well-built man, nervous, with an explosive temper. 'Like me in that way! He had a hard time showing any love, but he would show it in an indirect way by worrying about us children. I was really afraid of him. I remember once writing "I hate daddy" on his truck (inconspicuously) and then being terrified he would see it.' He knew his father had some love underneath the tough exterior. He recalled an incident when he was 17. In a fit of temper, his father shouted at his mother in front of some visitors. In a rage, he got up with the intention of fighting his father. They went out of the room together, but having gone that far, they both broke into tears. They remain on good terms to this day.

Mother was easy-going and sentimental, but a somewhat distant figure also. He tended to take her for granted, someone who was always there to cook and wash. She managed the house efficiently and there were never any money problems. She seldom showed anger or love. There was a period when she indulged him to some extent. In his teens he could get round her for some money any time, but he always had to ask her secretly. As he did not feel close to either parent, he tried to tag along as much as possible with his older brothers. They were bigger and more powerful than he, as well as being older, and he used to get beaten up pretty often. He often felt in the way and unwanted.

Example 11

In outward appearance, and in his own estimation, this man's early upbringing was not particularly bad, but neither was it altogether satisfactory. In recalling his childhood, he several times mentioned his father's continual absences, first while serving in the forces, later while engaged in transport work and away from home almost all of the time. He remembered one incident that took place when he was about 5, and was staying with a couple who were friends of the family. He had been sent there possibly because his mother was away having a baby. 'While I was still staying there, I was outside one afternoon and noticed my dad's car at the shop across the street. I don't believe he noticed me at first, for I stood on the curb calling out to him and I was crying and hollering my head off. He immediately told me to stay where I was and not to cross the street, and he crossed over to me. I then went out with him. This seems to be my first memory of doing something with my father.'

At the age of 9, 'I was going to ball games and hockey games on my own. I knew the man at the arena, so I usually got in the back door. I can't remember if Dad ever made it to any of these games. I saw very little of him. It seemed that if any of us children saw Dad it was late on weekends when he came home, but even then he would still be involved with his work.' When he was 10, the family spent a year with his paternal grandparents. 'That Christmas was the best one I had. I received all kinds of toys and games as so many relatives were there. Even Dad was there. While we were there, Dad usually stayed at my uncle's house, which was near where he worked. He would be away a week at a time, but us kids were used to that.' Years later, when he was serving time in a mental institution following sex offences, 'Dad came out there visiting on a regular basis, and we started a relationship. I thought to myself, what a way to get to know one's father—through being in a bug house.

'Mother was warm and loving, always doing a lot for the kids. She always saw to our material welfare and kept us clean. But there was a gap. As long as she had girls to raise, she was okay. She found it harder to communicate with boys. At the same time, I rejected her. I felt that, being a woman, she wouldn't understand boys' things, what boys have to go through. I rejected her so much it is hard to say what she was doing when I was a kid, I would never be around to find out.'

In later years, 'I hated staying at my folks' place, because Mom seemed to fuss over me to make me happy, or to show concern or something. This turned me off. It is as if she felt guilty for something and was trying to make it right. She likely blamed herself for the trouble I had already been through with sex crimes, but her efforts just pissed me off. She said she should have been firmer with me when I was young. I think she was right on that. I was always able to go out where I wanted with whom I wanted. It got so she couldn't have stopped me because I went and did just what I wanted if she liked it or not.'

Over the topic of sex 'she was no good at all. She got educated by me. Up till my teens, if I spoke to her about sex, she would tell me I knew more about it than she did. She was interested, I suppose, but she would change the subject, as if she didn't want to get involved.'

Freedom to go his own way as a child, combined with precocious development of physical sexuality, led him into frequent sexual experiences and experiments, about which he came to feel guilty as he grew older. In adolescence, normal sexual relations had become fraught with inhibitions and difficulties. By that time, however, his independent ways and unwillingness to confide his inner insecurities to anyone led him into ever deeper involvement in deviant sexual substitutes for the loving heterosexual relationships which he desperately wanted but could not sustain.

Example 12

This man's account of his parental background was in startling contrast to that of the majority of the group. 'I feel I had a happy normal home life. My dad's job was driving, and I really enjoyed the experience of going out with him whenever possible. I've always admired and respected him as a person of trust. Whenever I had a problem, I went straight to him. If I misbehaved he would warn me the first time, and if I repeatedly misbehaved, I was disciplined. I was never mistreated or neglected by either parent.

'I think of mother as a happily married housewife. In my opinion, she was the perfect mother and homemaker, well-respected, kind-hearted, affectionate, open-minded. Above all, she understood and cared about people.

'I can only remember one argument of any significance that my parents had, because generally they always got along very well. This happened during a summer vacation from school when I was about 7. I don't recall what the argument was about or how it started, only that there was a little shouting back and forth and then Dad walked out of the house. I ran after him and asked him where he was going and what was wrong. He said that he was just going for a walk. I told him that wherever he went I was going with him. He seemed to cheer up then. He took me to a grocery store, bought some groceries, and some candy for me, then we went home. Mom had been crying, but everything got back to normal again shortly after we got in the door.

'I admit I was jealous of my older sister. She always got good school reports, had very few problems, got along well, studied hard, got good marks, had a good personality and could do almost anything that I couldn't. She could swim, dance, play the accordion, she took ballet lessons, and she joined clubs such as Brownies. At school, I became timid, didn't mix with many classmates and didn't like the teachers as they always seemed to be comparing me with my sister. They had been my sister's teachers before they taught me.'

In spite of the statement that he could take his problems to his father, his extreme timidity and inability to communicate his feelings evidently interfered even with his dealings with his parents. He rarely reported to them, until long after the event, the difficulties he had at school with his teachers. He thought he was letting his parents down by not getting on well at school. He recalled one incident at the age of 9, when he turned on the light in the garage. The electric wire started burning and the place went on fire. 'I spent the rest of the night in my room still frightened from the fire. Dad came in and asked me what had caused the fire, so I told him briefly what I remembered. I didn't think he believed me. I got the impression that he thought I'd set fire or was responsible for it in some way. It was not until many years later when I discussed this incident with my parents that I found I had been wrong all along and had never been suspected.'

These stories have little in common save for the general picture of unhappy childhoods. The families varied from middle class socio-economic status and outward respectability to the poverty-stricken, outcast mother bringing up her children on the proceeds of prostitution. Three out of the twelve had spent a substantial part of their childhood in foster homes or institutions. In some instances conflict between parent and child manifested itself in brutal beatings, others experienced more subtle forms of emotional maltreatment. In some cases, a feckless, violent, or alcoholic father dominated the scene, in others a faithless, neglectful or rejecting mother was the worst feature.

This high incidence of abnormal upbringings, and the extreme nature of some of the situations described, leave no doubt of the significance of disturbed family backgrounds in the development of these rapists. In itself, however, the fact provides no sort of explanation for sexual crime, since similar observations have been made about the backgrounds of other categories, including persistent recidivists who have not been convicted of sexual crimes, psychopathic personalities who have no criminal convictions at all, the parents in problem families, behaviour-disordered dullards and some schizophrenic parents. Moreover, as in all these instances, one sees that a few cases come from backgrounds which, at least to outward appearances, fall within an acceptable range of normality. Mac-Donald (1971, p. 138) demonstrated very neatly the need for caution in evaluating the significance of rapists' disturbed parental upbringing. He compared homicidal offenders with non-homicidal hospital patients and discovered an equally high incidence of reported parental brutality in the histories of both groups.

Knowing the diverse family stresses experienced by members of the treatment group during their formative years one could predict that they would develop in adult life a variety of disturbances, such as personality disorder, delinquent or antisocial tendency, neurotic symptoms or sexual maladjustment. In fact, every one of the group had problems in one or more of these categories, but to understand why they should have also become rapists calls for a more detailed study of each individual's personality development. Classical psychoanalytic theory suggests that seductive and over-possessive mothers, by provoking incest fears, tend to produce guilt-ridden sons vulnerable to sexual deviation. For example, Abrahamsen (1960, p. 165) reported that the rapists he examined had frequently been exposed to abnormal seductive and sexually stimulating behaviour by their mothers. One woman went so far as to seduce her son into actual incest and then to press charges against him and have him arrested. In Abrahamsen's view this was merely an extreme example of a general tendency on the part of rapists' mothers to alternate between sweetness and harshness in a confusing and frustrating manner calculated to foster in their sons permanently embittered, distrustful and aggressive attitudes towards all women.

The twelve cases in the treatment group certainly did not conform to any such simple pattern. Active rejection or marked lack of warmth on the part of one or both parents was the main characteristic of their backgrounds. Adverse early experiences prepared the way for subsequent lack of confidence, anticipation of further rejection, and the development of feelings of hurt or damaged masculinity. These attitudes led to inhibitions about making contact with the opposite sex, to an unwillingness to treat women as equals for fear of revealing weakness, or to anxiety about the adequacy of sexual performance, effects which in turn were liable to hinder acquisition of the social skills necessary for normal courtship. It has been observed by authorities familiar with imprisoned sex offenders that many of them appear awkward in social situations with women and that very often, in spite of their experience of copulation, their knowledge of the sexual physiology of the female remains at a primitive level.

CHAPTER III

Impaired Masculinity

The family disturbances endured by these men in their early years left them ill-prepared to cope with later stresses, oversensitive to rejection and singularly diffident in their approach to life. Some of them found early sexual experiences traumatic, others found it difficult to adjust to a school community, and nearly all of them found it particularly difficult to deal with the crisis of adolescence. Difficulties and frustrations in establishing their first socio-sexual relationships, which more confident characters might have overcome, served to aggravate their problems. The examples which follow illustrate the malignant course of events.

Example 1

Having had no close relationship with any parent figure, his social and sexual attitudes were greatly influenced by interaction with his peers. The outstanding feature of his later childhood was an incestuous attachment to an older half-sister. The situation provoked intense guilt, fear of rejection by respectable girls, and hostility towards the kind of female who could exert power over him by means of sexual temptation.

'Her name was Doris. She started the thing going. I can remember the very first time. She was going upstairs to the attic, and she looked down at me and asked if I wanted to come up. I just knew from looking at the expression on her face what was going to happen.' This took place when he was just about 11. He was already familiar with sexual activity and sexual arousal from covert peeping in upon a young married woman and through secret games with other children.

'With Doris, the sex between us was simply that, there was no feeling otherwise. For example, we would never kiss each other or show any kind of affection.

'At this age, I was also having sex thoughts about some of the girls at the school. Except for some kissing, I never made sexual advances to girls at school because I had the idea the girl would think me dirty or bad.'

26

At the age of 12, he also had guilt feelings about masturbation. 'Every time I had a climax from masturbation I had a strong feeling I was taking a human life, but even so I could not resist doing it. I got that idea from what I had learned at Sunday School. There was a lot of hell-fire being preached at the church we attended.'

At the age of 12 to 13, 'my relationship with Doris was the outstanding reason for a feeling of insecurity. I know I would have rather died than have someone find out what was going on between us. The guilt feeling which my conduct caused me retarded my ability to communicate with other girls. I had very real and strong feelings that I could not carry on a conversation with a girl, the thoughts of having to do so gave me nausea.'

At age 13 to 14, 'the desire to be with girls was very strong, but even more strong were my feelings of inadequacy. A number of times I had the chance to invite a schoolgirl to come with me to a skating party or something, but I never did so. I had a fear of girls outside.

'I was still having sex with Doris as frequently as once a week, but by this time she wanted to do it only when she felt like it. Otherwise, I had to pay her, beg her, or even blackmail her, to get to have sex with her. When I had sex with her I would pull out prior to ejaculation to avoid her becoming pregnant. This I did on my own initiative. After I had pulled out, she would want me to put it in again, as she was still sexually aroused. I found these requests most aggravating and frustrating. It made me angry that I should pay her so that she should enjoy herself. I despised the hold my sex desire gave her over me. I longed to have a normal relationship with a girl, but I couldn't bring that about.' Even after the incestuous affair ceased and Doris departed, his inhibition about making dates with other girls continued as bad as ever. He remembered one instance when he had got so far as to arrange to take a girl to a film, and then panicked. He watched the girl from across the road as she was waiting for him outside the cinema, but had not got the courage to cross over and talk to her. Next day, he made some feeble excuse and after that had no more to do with her.

By the time he was 17 he acquired a large, if elderly, car. This gave him a sense of confidence he had never known before, and enabled him to have a number of sexual experiences. Nevertheless, he still felt very uncomfortable when he was in the company of a strange girl, unless she was a very casual pick-up. In addition, his habit of 'peeping', which began as a small boy, now led him into nocturnal wanderings in which he would roam round the neighbourhood spying through windows. When he had a large car available, however, the urge to go peeping was less. He enjoyed much more the chance to pick up strange girls. 'It was like being real. I can see now that I needed material things to make me feel confident.'

As time went on, he became increasingly promiscuous, but always with women he felt were of an inferior caste, young Indian hitch-hikers, or women he found hanging around beer parlours. He had short-lived affairs with a number of loose women or near-prostitutes. In between affairs, however, his peeping activities continued more recklessly than ever, and he started actually breaking into houses where he knew he would find a woman on her own. Although it was not very apparent to an outsider, he still felt uncertain with women he admired, but in his deviant peeping activities, and with his casual pick-ups, he could let himself go. It was a repetition of his childhood situation, when he felt driven by his sexual impulses into situations he despised, while unable to sustain relationships with the kind of female he really wanted.

As with so many of the men in this group, his marriage, instead of solving his problem, served to make matters worse. He was only 16 when he met his future wife, then a schoolgirl. For once, his pressing sexual needs overcame his social inhibitions and he started taking her to dances. For a time, 'I respected her as a good girl. We did some heavy necking and touching but nothing more.' Then he got so frustrated he told her they would have to break up as he needed someone who would have sex with him. 'I thought that I was in love with her, but I can recognize now it was only the sex that I was in love with. She was not enjoying the sex we had every week-end, she was just doing it to maintain the relationship.' When she became pregnant, 'we both felt pretty sick and scared about it. Neither of us was ready to marry or to settle down, especially not me. She claimed to be in love with me, and I told her also that I loved her, but I was not ready to settle down with one woman for the rest of my life.' After a bid for abortion failed, 'I just wanted to get lost, but I couldn't bring myself to do it. I think the reason I couldn't leave her stranded was a combination of caring for her and concern about what other people would think of me. I treated her badly all through the summer, because she represented a ball and chain I could not shake off.'

During this engagement, if that is what it could be called, his drinking, already quite heavy, increased considerably and he would leave the girl behind and go off drinking with friends. He recalled with some shame one incident when he brought a drinking buddy home, and after having sex with his fiancée, who was also quite drunk, encouraged his companion to do the same. As the pregnancy progressed, 'I was drinking very much, and I felt things were closing in on me.' He married just before the baby was due. He and his friends were drinking heavily. At the ceremony, 'I was quite impaired, but I knew what I was doing.'

This state of affairs continued after the marriage. The situation was not helped by the fact that his wife, who was still a school-girl when she became pregnant, herself came from an insecure background, with an alcoholic father and with elder sisters who had also been forced into marriage by unwanted pregnancies. Although he tried, he could not bring himself to remain sexually faithful to his wife. There were many unhappy arguments about his long absences during drinking sprees and his suspected infidelities. On one occasion he infected his wife with venereal disease. Another time she found him drunk and unconscious inside their car, which he had parked nearby, with one of the girls he had picked up still with him. Their marriage was punctuated by various moves, supposedly due to changes of job, but largely dictated by his sexual needs, which required changes of scene for peeping, and opportunities for cruising around by car looking for girls. There were also repeated separations and reconciliations, due to his inability to find fulfilment either in his deviant sexual escapades or in his marriage. There were times when he made a determined effort, as for instance, when both he and his wife joined a stern religious sect which imposed a strict moral code and public confession for any wrong doing. After a few months, he failed to live up to the religious precepts, having secretly gone with another woman and then found himself unable to confess the fact to anyone. Now he felt a double pressure, not only the sex urge, but the weight of hypocrisy as well. There were times when he deliberately provoked rows with his wife in order to have an excuse to walk out and be free to indulge in sexual escapades. On one occasion, by threatening to leave her if she did not tell him the truth, he bullied his wife into confessing an incident of infidelity during one of his many absences. 'When she did tell me that, I cried like a baby for a good half hour. My ego was really damaged. I felt then I must leave her. There was nothing special with her any more. She begged me not to go and to forgive her. I found it hard to leave, but I was excited about being free and the thought of the new sexual adventures that I would be able to find.'

But it was not long before he was once more dissatisfied with a life of sexual freedom and let her come back. 'I made her crawl back, and it was cruel.' But once again, after only a few weeks, 'I felt cornered again. I would start fights to get away alone, and drive to the nearest town.' His sexual escapades became more and more reckless. The peeping and the pick-ups led to break-ins and sexual assaults. In a mood of guilt and remorse, feeling he would never change for the better, he made an altruistic gesture to release his wife from the situation. 'I wrote to her from prison and told her not to visit me again. I told her that I did not want her any more and to find someone else. I did want her really, but I could see no other way out of it.' After his release, when she had in fact gone to live with another man, he regretted having let her go. He resumed his deviant sexual activities ever more desperately.

'I was feeling bitter against the law, but even more bitter against myself. But ego prevented me from trying to go back to my wife after everyone knew she had been living common-law with someone.' Before long, he was imprisoned again for repeated sexual offences.

In this example, it is easy to see the connection between inadequate parental upbringing, the development of unhealthy sexual guilt centring upon an incest situation, and the resulting feelings of masculine deficiency and social inhibition. Good and desirable women are viewed as unapproachable and unlikely to allow the gratification of his 'dirty' sexual needs. His unfortunate wife finds herself at one moment the evil, unfaithful seductress, who has trapped him into marriage and is unworthy of his love, and the next moment a symbol of cramping female virtue denying him sexual freedom and forcing him unwillingly into marital conformity. The conflict is exacerbated by the unwise early marriage, by the retreat into alcoholism, and by the vain attempts to reach some unattainable satisfaction through the increasingly reckless pursuit of deviant sexual habits.

Looking back on his marriage, he thought that he had needed his wife for sex, but had not really respected her as a person. It seemed that the only women with whom he had been able to communicate were types he at heart despised. Although he had never lacked confidence in his ability to perform the physical acts of sex, he always felt himself at a loss with decent women, not good enough for them and expecting to be rejected by them.

Example 2

As in the previous example, there were ample reasons, in the conflicts between his parents, why this man should have developed some childhood anxiety about male-female relationships. There were other factors to add to his concern about his manliness. He was of relatively slight physique, which was of course some handicap in physical competition. As a child, he was made to wear glasses. 'I remember this as being quite awful. I got into a number of fights because of guys calling me four-eyes and similar names. This did nothing to help me make friends, although I should point out that I did eventually make a lot of good friends at school with whom I spent many pleasant hours playing and fighting, as well as getting into childish mischief.'

Striving to keep up with what he conceived to be appropriately masculine standards became a major preoccupation. He was bright academically and obtained good marks at school as a matter of course with little effort. From the age of 12, however, 'I started to feel the other guys were avoiding me to a certain extent because of this. At this point, rather than lose my class grades, which I was proud of, I started to rebel against the school system. I felt that if I were in some sort of minor trouble with the teachers the other guys would overlook my surpassing them in academic standing.' Another example of his need to prove his manhood arose out of his participation in a school drama group and in a training course for survival in the wild. He liked both activities, but deep down he got special enjoyment from the plays he took part in, although at the time he deliberately gave everyone the impression that the survival course, which involved all the so-called masculine activities, was much more important to him.

The one unmasculine feature which he failed to overcome was a certain degree of sexual shyness, not sufficient to make him conspicuous, but enough to make him doubt himself. About the age of 9 or 10, he came into contact with two neighbourhood children. 'These two were brother and sister, the brother being slightly older than me, and the sister slightly younger. They were both to a high degree preoccupied with sex, and it was through them that I first came face to face with sex. The sister had numerous relationships with a large number of boys around the neighbourhood, but her main partner was her brother. I observed these two in the sexual act on numerous occasions, even though I was never myself involved. My most vivid recollection is of going to their house one day and finding their parents were away. I called out and they told me to come in. When I entered the house they called me up to the bedroom, where they were in the process of having sexual relations. I just stood by the door and waited for them to finish. I remember the brother getting off his sister and her turning to me and asking if I wanted it too. While I really did, I was too embarrassed to say so, and I turned her down. After that, there were times when I fondled her, but I never actually had intercourse with her, the main reason being, I think, that I was too modest to expose myself to anyone. In spite of being so exposed to sex, I was more inclined to sports and soccer. By that I mean while I had ample opportunity at this stage to further my sexual experience, I can't remember ever going out of my way to accomplish this. But I did at infrequent intervals proposition my friend's sister into fondling sessions, when I would play with her but never the reverse. More often than not, I wanted to play cops and robbers with her brother than have to have anything to do with her.' From age 11 onwards, 'I started to masturbate as a regular habit, at least two times a week. I was reading all the books I could get hold of on various matters, including sex, preferably with pictures.' At the same time, he began to experience strong, but largely platonic, sexual attachments to girls at school. There was one girl in particular. 'All I could think of at that time was being with her to talk and hold hands and kiss. We often went on picnics and hikes together during summer months, but we never went further than necking, we never explored each other's bodies. I was extremely jealous of her, and had a number of fights with other guys over her, but I can't remember having any sexual fantasy about her. This happy love affair lasted three years, and I really felt bad when she went away and we broke up. I cried a lot at night for quite a few days and I felt a real sense of loss.'

It was not until about 14, after breaking up with his first girlfriend, that 'I started to think in terms of sex with girls rather than just dating. It came about through a girl who had just moved into the town. Through her actions and talk, she had developed a certain reputation, the idea of which excited me. I was still delivering newspapers, and this girl's parents were among my customers. She was a year ahead of me at school and fairly aggressive, by which I mean she actually started every one of the necking sessions that we had. Her parents were often both out at work and she usually enticed me into the house by taking an extra paper or taking the collection book and running inside with it. When I followed she was always sitting on the couch and she would tell me if I wanted the book back I'd have to start necking with her. This I was extremely willing to do in spite of some playful avoidance. During these sessions, I was quite often able to undo her blouse, but I had to fight every step of the way. On the rare occasions when I went to undress her further she would chase me out of the house, on one occasion with a knife, but the next day she would start the same process all over again. I never did manage, from my point of view, to accomplish much with her. But on these occasions I was at the very peak of excitement, and they provided me with a vast amount of material for sexual fantasies during nightly masturbation sessions in which this girl was the central figure. The fantasies were about always of an imagined extension of that day's activities.'

This state of affairs continued up to the age of 16. He indulged in repeated necking sessions with this girl, and occasionally with other girls she introduced to him, all of whom behaved in a similar way. 'This led to a great deal of frustration, only partly eliminated by sexual fantasies and masturbation. The fantasies now began to take the form of rape, for I felt that was the only way I would ever be able to have intercourse. This girl and her friends were the only contacts I had with girls at this period. If I wasn't with them, I was making it on my own. I did not have any emotional feelings with any of these girls. It was strictly a sexual thing. I never took any of them out on dates. All the incidents took place either in their homes, when parents were away, or else outdoors in summertime.'

These unsatisfying relationships came to a halt when he was 16; he obtained a driving licence and took to going about with other youths and drinking heavily. 'On these occasions we rarely had any girls with us. If some were present I concentrated more on drinking than on them. I wanted to do something with them, to neck or kiss or do almost anything, but I never did. I think this was because I had been turned off by my previous experience with girls. At this time all my activities centred around booze and pool halls. Almost my only sexual encounter at this period involved the same brother and sister mentioned earlier. We used to get permission to have nights out, using the parents' cars, by pretending we were going to shows or dances, when in fact we were busy driving around drinking or playing pool. Once we were forced by his parents to take the sister along too. The brother got drunk, and slept in the back of the car. I asked the girl to sit in the front seat with me and the other guy who was with us. Once she had got into the front seat, I drove off onto a side road. When I finally stopped, my friend and I started to drink some more beer. When we finished the beer we started talking very suggestively to the girl. I can recall asking her to have intercourse. She refused us, so we decided to try it anyway. This was my first experience of forcing myself against a girl who was in no way willing. I can recall feeling very excited at the prospect of maybe having intercourse with her. The other boy and I forced off her blouse, bra and panties. We then started to fondle her body, exploring all parts. I can recall being very excited about feeling her breasts and vagina, the first that I had ever been able to touch. This carried on for about fifteen minutes, until she really started to cry. Once she started that, we both quit and let her get dressed. We all thought she would never want to go out with us again.' In fact, she did ask him to take her out, saying that she thought what happened had been all the other boy's fault. 'I did not really want to take her out at all. She rated so low in my opinion that I never wanted to be seen with her.' He did in fact take her out in the car, but she behaved very primly and irritated him by wanting to drive from one place to another. 'Once we had parked, she refused to indulge even in some kissing.

By this time I was real mad at her and started to drink quite heavily.'
He went on drinking without bothering to talk to her or to make a
move towards her. 'It was simply a battle of minds. I never once
the entire night touched her. When all the booze was gone, I started
up and drove her home.'

These youthful escapades, an unhappy foretaste of things to come,
revealed all too clearly a deep feeling of inadequacy in the male art of
wooing, an expectation of continual refusal, a bitterness against
women, and a willingness, in fantasy or while intoxicated, to establish
masculine dominance by force.

Following this early incident of near rape, his drinking persisted
and led to a driving conviction and other brushes with the police. A
further insult to his masculine aspirations occurred when he was
rejected as an applicant for the regular army and advised to finish
his schooling. At about the same time, when he was 18, his sensitivi-
ties were again hurt by a failure in a sexual encounter with a young
woman who showed very plainly that she would like to go to bed
with him. They did so, but in spite of a good erection, he could not
penetrate. 'The evening ended up a complete exercise of frustration
for both of us.' He believes his failure was due to inexperience and
the fact that she was only partly undressed, with pants still round her
calves, which prevented him from separating her legs.

Then an important change occurred. He met and fell in love with
his future wife. Normal sexual relations were established, and for
some time his sexual inferiority feelings were quelled. Unfortunately,
as with so many of these men, the early wounds were very deep and
never completely healed. In this instance, after years of seemingly
normal marriage, his emotional reaction to a vasectomy revealed
how easily his apparent confidence in his masculinity could still be
undermined. 'A few years ago, I felt this operation was the answer to
my wife's and my own birth control problems. However, much as I
knew intellectually that I was still as good as the next guy when it
came to sex, all the stories and ribbing I took became to me more of
a reality than reality itself. I seriously doubted my own virility, based
not on my actions, but on what doubts were in my mind, placed
there by continual ribbing.'

The same sense of inferiority came out in other ways. 'The
strongest feeling within me prior to my crimes was that of inferiority.
I continually sized myself up physically against men who were larger
and stronger than myself. I could only see my weaknesses and
ignored any of my assets. I irrationally ignored the fact that there
were some things I could do that my friends could not. I was quite
aware of my spontaneous emotions, though I tried to control them.
I would, and still do, get emotionally moved to tears by various

things. This left me with the feeling of being a sissy, or at least, not much of a man.'

Example 3

So many traumatic episodes occurred in this man's early life, any one of which might produce anxiety about masculinity, it is difficult to know where to begin. One of his earliest recollections of infancy was of an incident in an outhouse, when he was detained by two men. 'They stood just inside the exit door. One kept watch while the other, with his pants down and his hand on my head, forced me to take his penis in my mouth to the point of ejaculation, at which time I became sick to my stomach.' During his early years, this kind of experience made all the deeper impression because 'there were no counter relationships of any sort from any male, never any closeness, companionship, normal attention, or understanding.'

At school he made hardly any friends. 'A great many times I was subjected to humiliation and aggravations from school bullies, by reason of my poor, ill-fitting clothes, my skinniness, my shyness, and being a loner on top of it. I got into a number of fights which amounted to me being a punching bag. One time, when I was about 13, I was in a particularly bad mood when I was challenged again. While on the ground under my aggressor, I sort of flipped out. I pushed him off, and picked up a rock, and began hysterically striking him with it. I was pulled off him after two or three blows and ran home. I can recall seeing a lot of blood and getting a lot of satisfaction seeing him like that. After that, I was shunned as much as before. In fact, nothing changed for me except that I was not molested again.'

His early sexual experience consisted of solitary fantasy and masturbation, during which thoughts of cross-dressing and being a female came up. Between the ages 8 to 13, 'I spent hours peeking out of the bedroom window watching neighbourhood girls playing in the street. I would become aroused at the sight of upper legs, underpants and so on, to the point of masturbation. I also explored my sister's room for dresses and underclothes to use for masturbation. I also had visions, in my fantasies, of my own body being that of a girl. I recall having a quite intense feeling for one girl at school. It was both emotional and sexual involvement. She was one of the persons most used in my sexual fantasies, but it was out of the question for me to confront her or any of the other girls I had an interest in. I was definitely self-conscious about my person. I felt inferior to them, not good enough for them, and perhaps guilty on account of my sexual thoughts about them.' His only contact with a girl was a short-lived, semi-incestuous affair with his sister. 'We somehow got into a make-shift love affair. It was a case of kissing and holding hands, with talks of marriage and so on.'

At around the age of 10, he was subjected to further sexual trauma, this time by his foster father, who used to indulge in sex games when he was alone in the house with the children. Under the threat of a beating, he would be made to strip and forced to fellate his father. At a somewhat later age, about 13 or so, the father instructed him in making love and forced him to attempt intercourse with his sister. The first time 'I was too far gone in bewilderment and panic to make anything of it, and was allowed to go. The next time, I went through the steps of foreplay, as I had been told, and completed the act, but climaxed inside her, which scared the hell out of me because he had told me not to do that. As I left I had a glimpse of her lying nude, a glimpse that I can clearly visualize to this day, and that has formed the subject of numerous fantasy trips ever since.'

The feelings produced by these experiences were an unhappy mixture of guilt, rage and inadequacy. Not surprisingly, his first attempt at a heterosexual affair turned out a miserable failure. It happened when he was 16, when he was just starting out on his own, working to support himself and to pay for his lodgings. 'I became involved with a girl about my age who used to come around the place where I worked. Probably because of her loose, flirting ways and character it wasn't too difficult to get to know her.' He became very attached to her, and spent a great deal of his time with her. Her parents wanted her to break off with him, but instead she ran away from home and hid in his room. 'I quit my job and for about a week she stayed in my room, rarely going out.' Attempts at love-making were a failure. 'On the first night I was nervous as hell, completely unsure, and climaxed within seconds of entry, which made me feel like an idiot and a fool. I felt depressed, sorry I failed her, and guilty at having hurt her, as she was a virgin. She was crying and carrying on and I felt totally responsible. I felt I had to make it up to her and prove my potency. But I didn't get that chance. She was too distraught and didn't want to try again.' After a day or two her parents and the police came around and caught them, and after some angry and violent scenes he was finally forced to give up seeing her.

After that, he went on 'a three-year criminal binge' which involved petty thieving, taking cars and house-breaking. At the same time, he developed further his passion for stealing and hoarding women's underclothes, and an increasing desire to see women naked. 'I became gradually but unashamedly a peeping Tom—not too frequently at first, and more on an opportunistic basis than by deliberate searching out.' This stage of his life was interrupted by periods in a reformatory. There he experienced further insults to his masculinity. 'I was cornered into becoming indebted to one group, and after some beating was forced into a prostitution affair in one of the dormitories I was in.' A few years later, while he was serving a prison sentence, a big powerful prisoner who had started off by being merely friendly, 'began showing signs of possessiveness and jealousy. Soon he was around me all the time, telling me how he loved me, wanting me to live with him when we got out, promising me everything—my own car, a home, money in the bank, etc.' Terrified of the way things were turning out, 'I made up my mind it was my suicide or his death. I lifted a cold chisel out of the carpenter's shop.' It was discovered on a routine check and he was sent to solitary. During solitary confinement 'there was a great deal of masturbation, averaging two or three times a day.' On these occasions he re-experienced, during masturbation fantasies, the clothing fetishism and the peeping episodes as well as love-making scenes. Outside prison, his occasional heterosexual affairs all proved abortive. At the age of 18, he acquired a second girlfriend. She mixed with the same group of social dropouts as he did. 'She was 16 and on a bout of leaving home. There was a mutual attraction and a need for each other, for some mutual loving and caring and attention. Sex with her was good and there were no problems.' Imprisonment brought this relationship to an end. She wrote him encouraging letters to prison, but when he finally got out 'she was pregnant and apparently not sure who the father was. Also, she didn't want to carry out the promises made in her letters.' He had sex with her just once 'that night on the bathroom floor. It was an animal copulation, and I walked out on her while she was still on the bathroom floor. I was greatly disappointed and angry at her, and I got some satisfaction out of using her as I had.'

After this disappointment, 'my habit of collecting female clothes began again in earnest. For the first time, I started satisfying my obsession for seeing nudity with a full swing into window-peeping.' At the time he was living in a big city, which he found 'greatly depressing and monstrously big and inhuman'. At this point 'I met a person who was homosexual. He showed concern for my welfare, where I had been and how I was doing now. After a couple of days he propositioned me. He set me up with clothes and money and the use of his car. He did his sex thing, which I allowed by reason of the goodies I got in return, but as it always had been for me I found it difficult to tolerate. It turned me off to the point where I had to use considerable concentration to make it.'

After this, he teamed up with another man. They were both basically heterosexual in inclination, but together they mingled with hippies, slept out in the park, smoked dope and 'hustled ourselves around parks, gay clubs and bars. We did it to make ends meet mainly for food and the cost of rooms to which we would take our tricks.' At this point, he was also 'heavy into the female clothes thing, out and about dressed in them till all hours of the night. I was always afraid of actually being confronted so dressed, but I would take untold chances walking long distances along back streets.'

There was not much scope for heterosexual adventures at this point, but the one incident which did occur proved even more disastrous than usual. He encountered a girl staggering on the street, obviously high on drugs, and went home with her. She encouraged him to stay the night and have sex. Her lack of inhibitions stimulated him to put some of his private fantasies into action. While she was deeply asleep, he was able to move her legs about and explore her nude body just as he wanted. 'I completely lost myself in look, touch, feel and kiss.' When he left, he took with him some of her clothes and wrote a goodbye and thank-you note. This encounter left him with a bad and painful dose of gonorrhoea, which did not respond to treatment initially, and which he was warned might cause sterility. He felt enormous anger against the girl. He felt sure she must have known she was infected, and was just using men for her own purposes. He went looking for her, with murderous thoughts in his mind, but never found her again. 'I spent the better part of a month searching, getting more and more infuriated, with hate for anything in a dress building up all the time. These thoughts still surface on occasion to this day.' The venereal disease made him feel 'worthless as a man'. The fear of sterility destroyed his dream of having children and being able to bring them up so much more happily than he had ever been.

At the age of 22, he made a considerable effort to change his way of life. At the same time, he began another intense love affair with the inevitable unhappy ending. He was staying with a friend whose parents made him more or less one of the family and helped him into a steady job. He was trying hard to live up to these new standards. He met a young girl, only 14, but physically very mature. Her parents were very broad-minded, accepted him fully, and did not seem to mind their daughter having a sexual affair. In spite of being so young, she took a dominating, leading role. She liked almost any form of sex, exhibitionistic dressing and parading in the street, nude photography, and intercourse out-of-doors. She had an ever-sweet personality with a free and open manner of expression. All the love and attention she showered on him 'was something new and alien'. He found it difficult to live up to the whole situation. 'Though I had a beautifully convincing front and act, it was difficult not to show the turmoil underneath.' His urge to expose himself in the street dressed in erotic feminine attire became more compulsive. 'I also got into peeping more extensively. This was tied up with breaking and entering activities. Mostly they were for sole purpose of stealing women's wear, but sometimes for goods like stereos, which all too often ended up in the pawn shop for money. As the habit of peeping through windows into girls' bedrooms progressed, the satisfaction of merely looking at nudity lessened and an obsession to feel and to touch the nude body took over.' In spite of the satisfactions of an active sex life with the young girlfriend, 'it still somehow seemed necessary to be, anonymously, this other dominating, forceful person, cross-dressing, peeping and contemplating sexual assault. Whereas previously a relationship with a girl had brought these moonlighting activities to a halt, now it seemed to make no difference.' Matters came to a head when he was caught by the police while having oral sex with his girlfriend in a car. A conviction for 'contributing to juvenile delinquency' followed, and brought to light his past criminal record. The girl's father, shocked by this, told him to keep away. Much to her disappointment, he gave her up without much of a struggle, feeling that in any event he could not have kept up with the affair very much longer. In spite of all his feelings of inadequacy and futility, his bitter experiences with women, and his repertoire of substitute sexual gratifications, this man fell in love yet again and contracted a common-law marriage. For a time he kept up a successful work routine and apparently settled down to family life. Then, as happened with all the men in the group, stressful events supervened, overthrew the precarious balance, revived the masculine self-doubts and the grudges against women, and unleashed a desperate sex criminal.

Example 4

Athletic, sport-loving and fiery-tempered, a hard-drinking type with a reputation as a fighter, a man who married and produced a baby while he was still in his teens, this was to all outward appearances the last person in the world to be suspected of harbouring feelings of insecurity about his masculinity. And yet, according to his own frank admissions, doubts of this kind, and a compulsive need to prove himself in acts of physical aggression, had influenced his conduct from early childhood.

Emulation of a bigger and more powerful older brother played some part in this. His brother used to beat him up quite frequently. He recalled one occasion in particular at the age of 13 when 'my brother got me on a bed and beat me till I could not breathe any more. I thought I was going to die and was really scared. To this day, I love my brother a lot, but sometimes I think I would like to show him a thing or two. It bothers me that he probably thinks me a coward, but I believe I could knock his head off if I wanted to. I know there is a tremendous feeling of aggressive competition in me. For example, if I am out running, I force myself to the point of sickness.'

From early childhood he was uncomfortably aware of being small and skinny. He remembered hearing that when he was born his mother had been expecting a girl, because he was a small baby and the pregnancy had not shown much. When he was about 10, some women at the bathing beach commented upon how thin he was. He felt he had to make some excuse, so he told them he had been sick, although that was not the case.

At school he over-compensated. 'I became aggressive to the point it made me dangerous. I learned to be vicious, to fight to hurt people. I got a feeling of strength out of being able to hurt. In earlier years, when I was small, I was afraid of people and often got the worst of it. When I learned to fight effectively, I was out to make people afraid of me.' He had one particular buddy with whom he was always fighting. This friend was very obstinate, and however much he beat him, he could not make him give in. Sometimes he got punished for fighting at school, but that made him more respected. On one occasion, at about the age of 10, in the course of an argument, he kicked a boy on the head and then punched him while he was on the ground. Another boy who had witnessed what happened told the headmaster, and his victim was found still lying in the snow outside. At that point a lot of the other children claimed that he had beaten them, and he was strapped severely for what he had done.

During his whole school career he was much more interested in and concerned with sports and physical activities than academic matters. By the time he reached the age of 16 he was able to hold his own in a scrap with anyone. The boys he went around with were a heavy-drinking, fast-living crowd, mostly a couple of years older than he was, but his fighting reputation helped him to win acceptance among them.

He was adventurous in other ways besides fighting. He was not generally inclined to the delinquent way of life, but at the age of 11 he joined up with some other boys in a house-breaking enterprise, taking money, watches and antiques and selling the loot at a second-hand store. He was caught and convicted and also punished at home. From the age of 8 onwards, he took part in many exploratory sex games with other boys and girls. At the age of 11, he and a friend got so far as to undress a girl they knew, lay her on the ground with her legs apart, and attempt penetration. They did not succeed because it hurt her too much, and they did not try again. At the age of 12 to 13 he enjoyed some homosexual experiences with a friend of the same age. They used to stay at each others homes overnight occasionally, sharing the same bedroom, and indulging in mutual masturbation and body contact. At the same time, they swapped fantasies of sex with girls, read sex magazines together, and enjoyed looking at pictures of female nudes, so their association did nothing to interfere with heterosexual orientation.

Not withstanding his early-acquired familiarity with sex, his hetero-sexual relationships did not develop nearly as satisfactorily or as confidently as his bold social front. He could not compete so well with his other male companions in respect to sexual conquest as he could in other ways. He was considerably discouraged by disappointing experiences and episodes of impotence. He recalled an unsuccessful attempt at sex with a girl when he was 14. 'She wouldn't let me undo her pants, and I had a terrible time undoing her bra. I attempted to finger her with her pants on, but the whole thing was very awkward. I remember being very ashamed of myself afterwards for being awkward and clumsy.' During the year following he devoted himself to male pursuits and had little sexual experience.

At the age of 16, boredom with school routine and the urge for fun and excitement led him on impulse to quit school and to join up with other boys to go searching for work in the lumber trade. He teamed up with an older friend with whom he went to numerous parties. They were often without work and 'often got drunk and generally did little'. He recalled one party at the home of an older woman whose husband was away. She let them take turns having sex with her. He took his turn, but it did not work out too well. 'I was going at it with her for about ten minutes. The guys in the next room were yelling at me to hurry up. So I tried to go off, but couldn't. They started pouring beer over the two of us and laughing.' This infuriated him. 'I grabbed her bra and tore it off. I think I almost bit her breast. I finally had a climax, but it was nothing too great.'

At this age he was sensitive about being too young and in-experienced for the girls they met, and concerned about his sexual potency. 'On a couple of occasions my friend's girl told me never to try anything with her because she wouldn't be able to control herself. I knew this was a hint, but I was afraid to make a play because I might not get an erection.' He described a few occasions on which he had been humiliated by failing to get an erection. Usually this happened when he was with a girl in a car, and it was too cold and the circumstances were not right. But even in more propitious circumstances sexual relations did not always work out satisfactorily. He recalled one occasion when he was with an older girl in his car. 'I was pretty drunk and drove up on an old road into a gravel pit. After I stopped and started necking she got pretty worked up and I took her clothes off. This girl had everything and knew what to do with it. I tried to back out in a roundabout way, because I was afraid I couldn't get an erection. I told her I was only 16 and had only been to bed with one other girl. She was nice to me, she said I must be lying because kids of 16 didn't kiss the way I did. So we kissed for a bit and then she said, "Let's do it." I told her I might not be able to get an erection. She said she would take care of that.' All went well at that point, but back at the motel early the following morning 'There was a tap on the door and she came in. She wanted it again right now. She seemed awfully impatient. I had a bit of difficulty hitting the right spot, so she helped me put it in. She seemed like such a bitch to me. She told me to do this and to do that. She was ruling me completely, but I couldn't control myself and I climaxed. She made it quite apparent she was disappointed. I felt like a fool for going off too soon. She just left and went off home.'

During the subsequent year, when he briefly went back to school to try to complete more grades, 'I had little to do with sex. At weekends I went to parties and drank and once in a while fooled around with the odd girl, but it was just necking.' He remembered one occasion, when he was 18, staying overnight with a girl at a friend's place. 'In the middle of the night we started necking again. I was going to take her clothes off, but then felt disgusted with myself, I didn't want to go through all that and then not get an erection. So I just rolled over and went to sleep.'

His restraint with girls was not paralleled by restraint in other directions. His drinking sprees became excessive and he was also indulging occasionally in hallucinatory drugs. He remembered one incident when he took some acid. 'It wasn't long before I became stoned and was hallucinating. As I drove along the road, signs turned into big beasts that jumped out on the road at me. There were little green fluorescent butterflies in front of the car. Every time I drove over the centre line it felt like a three-foot drop into the other lane and I had a hard job getting the car back into the right lane.'

While still 18 he met, among the people he was going around with, a girl who liked drinking as much as he did. They would drink together and then move off into the park to have sex, but she had a routine that caused a gradual disillusionment. 'She would always pretend to fall asleep. I could take her clothes off, but if ever I tried to take her pants right down to have sex with her, she would push me away. What she really liked was to be licked out. She was a very clean girl and I enjoyed doing it. She was so cute and beautifully built I would have done anything for her. But I was stupid. I did not realize she was using me for her own pleasure and to hell with me. She was also going out with another, older guy. That really bugged me.'

Although he himself had these doubts about her, he reacted very violently when a man in conversation with one of his friends mentioned her name and commented that she looked like a slut. 'I lunged at him at once, slugged him three or four times, and he fell to the ground. This guy couldn't see or hear when they got him to his feet. My friend said reprovingly "Look what you've done now." I told him to shut up or he would be next, so he shut his mouth. Then someone yelled that the cops were coming, so we beat it.'

By this time his tolerance of frustrations with girls was decreasing. He recalled one incident with a girl he knew well. 'I was driving down a back road with her. She was holding my penis in her hand. I think she liked to do that as much as I liked her to do it. I said to her "Let's do a few body presses." She refused and I felt angry and said, "I should give you a good fuck and afterwards throw you out on a snow bank." I don't know how serious I was, but the idea did flash through my mind.'

He was 18 when he first met the girl he was to marry. She was only 14 at the time, and because of that she perhaps made fewer demands upon his masculine self-confidence than the older, more experienced women he had known. He met her in the company of her sister, who was a little older. 'Daphne kissed well, but she was a little frigid, as if she wanted to kiss but wasn't quite sure how to do it. Her older sister was very gentle and soft. When I kissed her, I could feel the heat radiate from her. She was very passionate, but it was "hands off". I began taking the two of them out, one on one night and the other the next. Her sister was the more attractive, but Daphne seemed to fall in love with me more, so I tended to bend my affections more towards her in the hope of getting a little action.' After a while 'I stopped taking her sister out altogether and took Daphne out every day, but our sex life never got beyond fingering, and playing with breasts.' She was completely inexperienced and when first he got her to masturbate him 'She couldn't believe it when I went off. She didn't know what to expect.'

He was restless and unsettled, uncertain what to do with his life, and his love affair did not deter him from looking for other sexual outlets. He thought of joining the services, but very quickly became homesick. On the train journey home, he had an encounter with an older woman. 'She said, "Let's go to your room." We went in, closed the door, and lay on the bed and started necking. Without a word, I released myself and started to take my clothes off. She did the same.

I had no trouble entering her. She then went crazy on me. I had a hard time hanging on. I thought she was going to tear me apart. I climaxed a few seconds after she did. I was truly exhausted. She treated me like a little kid. She got me to lie beside her and rest my head on her arm. She told me to rest and take it easy. I gathered she wanted to do it again and I became afraid I wouldn't get another erection, so I told her I had to get off the train.'

Soon after this he met at a party his former girlfriend, the one who had been selfish with him in her sexual requirements. 'She said she was sorry she had been so mean and she wanted to pick up where we had left off.' This put him into a state of confusion. He went to see Daphne the next day. 'I told her I was mixed up about her and the other girl and I gave her her ring back. Daphne was crying and I just had to escape—the pressure was too great.' He evaded the situation by quiting his job and going off to the city, leaving both girls behind. A short time later, after some unsatisfactory adventures in the town, he returned and took up with young Daphne again. But he was not satisfied. 'I was drinking a lot. I was angry with Daphne because she wouldn't have sex with me.' He took out his temper in furious driving. 'I would slide around corners and knock out stop signs and keep going. She was greatly scared. Once I saw a cop-car following, so I just put the gas pedal on the floor and went off onto a side road at about eighty. When the car came back to the ground it hit with such a bang everything stopped . . . so I grabbed Daphne and we hit it through the bush.'

Eventually he persuaded her into having sexual intercourse and all went smoothly. Before long she became pregnant. At the time 'she was working in a cafe and I was not working. So a lot of her money went into my gas tank and in supplying me with cigarettes. One day she said she wanted to break with me because I wasn't responsible enough. I went out and got drunk and thought about killing myself.' In his angry, despondent mood, he went so far as to slash himself, later pretending he had been attacked, but looking back it seemed that all he wanted was pity and attention.

His affair continued to run its uneven course. He would drop Daphne off home and then visit an all-night cafe where girls used to hang around waiting for pick ups. Several times he went with one of these, but again had trouble getting an erection. 'Then I found out that Daphne had gone out with some other guy. I was very angry. I would go out with the guys all the time smoking weed and getting drunk.' He started taking another girl out, one he had always looked upon as 'an old whore'. 'We had intercourse lots of times. I was mean to this girl. I didn't care about her. All I wanted was to stick it in, go off and pull out . . . I felt she was a tramp . . . The only reason I could get an erection with her was that I was accustomed to being around her and the first time we had sex it was warm and comfortable and I had been OK.'

In the midst of the violent quarrels and reconciliations over Daphne's infidelity 'she told me she would like to smoke hash. She had never smoked it before. We went out and smoked and had intercourse. The next day we decided to run away together (she being still under age). For some reason her nerves and the hash caused her to be constantly stoned. We went to a motel, and at about one in the morning she flipped out on me. She was crying and yelling and saying her baby was going to miscarry. I took her to the hospital. They said she wasn't going to loose her baby, but she was stoned.

'As the effect of the drugs wore off, Daphne started to be more responsible. She started to think about me and the baby more. We decided to keep the baby no matter what happened.' They managed to obtain the agreement of her parents and they set up house together. 'The next night after moving in, about seven or eight in the evening, Daphne started crying. She said she wanted to go home to her mother. I was really set back. I told her I'd kill myself if she did. I drove her half way there to her mother's, but she changed her mind and decided to stay with me.'

This example highlights some features common to the life stories of a number of these rapists. They include the neglect of work and education in favour of a life style that was an aggressive over-compensation for imagined masculine inferiority, the dismay when sexual conquests failed to attain to the exacting ideal of male efficiency and dominance that the boy had set up for himself, the shifting of anger at his own supposed deficiencies onto the girls with whom he came into contact, and the juvenile eagerness to rush into a marriage that looked from the start like a prescription for disaster.

Example 5

This rough, powerfully built, aggressive man, who could hold his own in any fight, was, like the last example, not at all the kind of person to fit the popular concept of an individual with masculinity problems. Nevertheless, ever since childhood he had found great difficulty in communicating with girls, and had harboured massive inferiority feelings about his ability to win acceptance from females. His adolescent attempts to establish heterosexual contacts swung between extremes of ridiculous and paralysing diffidence and out-right sexual assault.

His earliest remembered experiences of sex, at about the age of 9,

were of a commonplace kind. 'We had made a little playhouse under
the front steps of a neighbour's house. We would go in there and
play with each other and look at each other's private parts. My sister
got me to perform cunnilingus on her, and after doing it a few times
I got to like it. We would do it whenever we could get to a private
place, but somehow the novelty wore off and after about two or
three months we stopped doing it. We didn't see any wrong in it,
except for the fact that we knew we would get a beating if we were
caught. At this time, around 10, I seemed to get on much better at
school with the boys than I did with the girls. They seemed to be
little sissies. I never liked to be called a sissy, and I preferred to play
boys' games like football and cowboys.'

Among other boys he achieved some kind of status. Owing to
having started school late and failed to pass first grade, 'I was
usually older than the rest and the biggest kid in the class. I was
fairly aggressive and the other kids would choose me as the leader of
the games or the captain of the team. Pretty well all through my life
I felt comfortable making decisions and telling other kids what to do.
It seemed to me that that is how life should be. A good part of the
time I was able to pretty well have my own way, either by force or
because the other kids felt threatened.' At the age of 13 his aggressiveness got him into trouble. He had hit a boy who had been annoying
him on the way to school by splashing stones into a stream to stop
him from getting across. 'At recess time he told me he would get me
after school. He turned up at the place and we started fighting. His
friends were with him and were teasing me about a hole in the seat of
my pants. I knocked him down and jumped on top of him. The
more they teased me the madder I got and I beat him up real bad.
The janitor from the school had to come over to stop the fight and
call an ambulance to take the boy to the hospital, where he was kept
for three weeks. The police and the welfare agency got involved and
explained to me how wrong it was to fight. The next day I got the
strap fifty times on each hand. For the rest of the term I had to stay
in the classroom and hold the door for the kids to come in and out
at recess time and as they were arriving or leaving school. This
severe punishment really had a bad effect on my interest in school
and on my marks in class, which went down from honours to a
bare pass.'

From the age of 14 onwards, he was masturbating regularly,
having many fantasies about girls and an urgent desire for sexual
contact. 'At this age I didn't have the guts to make a pass at a girl,
I was afraid of them turning me down. I sure wished I could make
my fantasies come true. It seemed that having sex with a girl would
be a way of showing each other affection. That is what I had hoped

for all my life. I wanted to have girls like me, and I wanted to be close to girls.'

Unfortunately, he met up with a number of discouragements. His elder sister, towards whom he directed some of his early erotic fantasies, was distinctly discouraging. 'She would tell me that I would never amount to much, that no woman would ever marry me and that I would stay living off Mom and Dad all my life. She said this many times. I decided to prove her wrong and to get married at the first chance I got, which is exactly what in the end I did do!'

At this time, he had a stammer and he had a great difficulty in talking to any girl. He and a friend used to walk the streets with a certain girl. 'He would do almost all the talking. We would take her into her father's garage and then take turns kissing her. I remember this very clearly because it brings to mind how hard it was for me to talk to her. She and my friend had no problems talking, but I never knew what I should say to her. There was a girl who lived next door to us. I had been told by my sister, who knew her, that she had a real crush on me. I felt really good, but I didn't know what to do about it. I thought she was about the nicest girl that ever walked the earth, and I would have given anything to have her for a girlfriend. One day her mother asked me to go round to keep her company while she was baby-sitting for her baby sister, as she was afraid to be in the house alone.' He was tremendously excited, got dressed up in his best much too early, and waited behind her house for the moment to come to knock and go in. 'She sat on the chesterfield watching the T.V., and at first I sat as far away from her as I could. Every once in a while I would get up and go to the bathroom. Each time I came back I would sit a little closer until finally I was sitting right beside her. Then I finally got up enough nerve to put my arm over her shoulders and she leaned her head back on my shoulder. I had an erection and I was afraid she might see it. Finally, because I couldn't stop being so embarrassed, I told her that I had to go home. She didn't want me to go but I went anyway. After that I couldn't face her. Whenever she came over I would keep out of her way as much as I could. I didn't have anything to do with her again.'

He often thought that if he had been a girl he would have escaped the things he found so difficult. 'I had no trouble getting along with men. I longed for affection from somebody and I felt that if I had been a girl, I would always have had companionship. I would not have had to find a way to talk. Men would do it because they are the aggressors. I always had great trouble in talking to girls. I could never find the right things to talk about. I always thought that if I had been born a girl that would have been the answer to all my problems. I thought that if I was a girl, I would have been a prostitute.

That way I would be getting all the sex I could handle and I would even be getting paid for it.' His extreme shyness with girls did not prevent him from developing some covert and deviant sexual outlets. From the age of about 15 he began a habit of peeping at girls, first into the bathroom at home, watching his own sister, later on peeking into other people's bedroom windows. 'At the age of 16 to 17 my friend Tim and I were doing this. We had about ten different basement suites that we would watch each night when we thought people were going to bed. I would fantasize all the more after I had been peeking. I would imagine myself in the bedroom with one of these women. It really enriched my desires for sex relations. I would masturbate and when I was done I would feel really ashamed of myself. I felt I had degraded myself and my family and the people I had thought about. But as time went on, I realized I was going to keep on doing these things, so I did my best to get rid of the shame and to convince myself that these thoughts were not so bad as I had first understood them to be.

'During the same span of time, from about 15 to 17 years of age, I would steal women's underclothes off clothes-lines and take them home and masturbate with them. While masturbating I would picture a woman wearing them. She would always be friendly to me and we would always have a good sex relationship.'

At this time there was one girl with whom he was able to have sex. She was something of a social outcast and he did not feel inferior with her. 'She was a very simple girl from a poor family. Her parents were alcoholics and they had thirteen kids. She was the first girl I had sex with. I enjoyed being with her because she was willing to go to bed whenever I wanted to. I had sex with her because I wanted to see what it would be like, but I didn't have any great emotional feelings for her. She didn't push me and she never once turned me down, but our relationship was strictly sexual. When I was through with her I wouldn't have anything to do with her until the next time I wanted sex. We didn't talk much to each other. We mated like two dogs in heat. Our relationship lasted about six months, until I moved away to work elsewhere. I think this affair a good illustration of how I could not relate to girls except in a strictly physical sexual way. Sometimes I thought that sex was all some girls were good for, but in reality I think that was only an excuse for my inability to talk to them.'

He was scarcely 17 when his sexual frustrations led to an incident amounting to assault. 'Jane was a girl that I had always admired. She was a little younger than me. She was in the playground, playing on the swings and I had been talking to her there. When it got dark she decided to go home. I followed her and when she went down a back alley, I jumped her and tried to feel her up. She started scream-ing and I got scared and let her go. The next day I heard kids talking about it and I felt really cheap. I wanted to apologize to her, but I didn't have the guts.

'After this incident I was still mentally disturbed and lonely. I was still peeping into bedroom windows. One night I watched a woman who was alone at home going to bed. I waited until I thought she was asleep and then went to her house and broke in and tried to rape her. She resisted a lot. She tried to masturbate me to make me desist. She fought whenever I tried to take her bedclothes off. Finally, after a couple of hours trying, I gave up and went home. I had threatened her life if she told the police, but the next day I saw the police were there. Every time I saw her or the police in the vicinity I felt like crawling into a hole. I was tempted to turn myself in, but I did not do so.' Instead he managed to bring himself under control and for many years his deviant activities ceased. '(In recalling this attack) I remember the loneliness I felt in every bone in my body. I needed somebody so I went looking at women and hoping that I could be with them. I knew I couldn't, but I wanted them so badly that I tried rape, hoping that even a few minutes with a woman would get rid of the loneliness, if only for a time.'

After this, he managed to secure a regular girlfriend, but she was only 13 years of age, and the affair ended in disaster. 'I had a car and I would take her out every night. Whenever I wasn't working or sleeping I was with her. . . . She was very mature for her age. She asked me to marry her and I promised I would. We decided to wait till she was out of school and I had saved enough money to finance our marriage. Our sexual experiences were very uninhibited. We loved each other very much and had a good rapport. We liked the same things and her mother agreed completely to our marriage plans.' Then her parents suddenly changed their attitude. He never fully knew why, but the mother was unstable, a former mental patient and at one time a prostitute. Having become angry with her daughter about something, this was the mother's way of hurting her. 'They complained to the police who picked me up and charged me with contributing to juvenile delinquency. I admitted having had sexual relations with her, and pleaded guilty in court and was fined $150.00. All our plans were in vain and our relationship was over. . . . We both felt guilty and we knew that if we tried to make it work her parents would have put me in jail.'

From the age of 18 onwards, he overcame his difficulty in talking to girls to the extent that he was able to date and to have sex with a succession of girls. None of these relationships proved rewarding. He caught gonorrhoea from one of the girls, and was terrified at first, 'I had all kinds of illusions of it falling off or rotting away.' The longest-lasting affair continued for six months. 'I fell in love with her and we had sex many times. But she had been married before and she had a little boy. Her ex-husband would come and visit and take her home with him. She would stay a few days and come back. I was very jealous and argued with her about it, and at one time I tried to beat up the husband, but he got away in his car. Finally she started to show her true colours. She would go to the bar and pick up old men and take them home with her. She would sleep with them and the next night she would have another one. I gave her up then. . . . At this time I was seriously looking for a girl suitable for marriage.'

Another girl 'tried to make me marry her because she was pregnant. Her father tried threats. But I told him to sit on it. If he had not butted in, I could quite possibly have married her, but after my earlier experience I wanted nothing to do with a girl whose father was threatening me with legal troubles. She had an abortion and married someone else a year after. In some ways I regret how things turned out.'

His attitude to women was intense and complicated. Those he could make contact with seemed easy game and not worth having, others seemed elusive and unattainable. He had a need to idolize any woman he became attached to, but at the same time he was fiercely possessive and domineering and quick to suspect infidelity. The girl with whom he finally fell deeply in love and whom he married was one he had previously rejected because she played around with other men. Indeed she already had an illegitimate child. 'I have never been so happy and self-confident as I was when I first got married. . . . It was Utopia for me!' It was unfortunately a precarious Utopia. When stresses came along, as inevitably they must, his turbulent love-hate feelings for women, and his desperation at his own imagined masculine inadequacy, revived as acutely as ever and led to the sexual attacks for which he was currently under sentence.

This example illustrates particularly vividly how sensitivity about his own imagined inferiority and disadvantage can transform a man from a shy, tongue-tied wooer into a dangerous aggressor. One moment he is a miserable supplicant and the next a violent avenger. One moment he idolizes his fiancée and the next he finds her a miserable, faithless bitch. Even more clearly than the previous example, this history shows how a propensity for sexual assault may reveal itself at an early age, though it may not be till many years later that the full force of sexual aggression breaks out. Although the escalation of minor into major sex crime is relatively unusual, this case also shows how peeking and stealing of women's clothes may sometimes form a prelude to sexual violence.

Example 6

Unlike some of the more diffident members of the group, whose withdrawn attitudes or tongue-tied efforts to overcome their social inhibition were painfully apparent, this man was a fluent extrovert who coped smoothly with most situations. In fact, he was suspected of hiding his real feelings behind a smoke screen of flamboyancy and play-acting, and on occasions was unkindly accused of wanting to be a loud-dressed, loud-mouthed, show-off. In spite of these outward appearances, in spite of being a proud father, and in spite of having had sexual adventures as extensive as any in the group, in his autobiography he revealed the same sense of sexual guilt and masculine inadequacy that pervaded all the other stories.

At school he disliked most of the subjects that were taught. Although intelligent, he never applied himself to lessons and frequently failed to pass his grades. He did not worry about that at the time and his parents did not try to push him. Since coming to the institution and attempting to take some educational courses, he found he still had a distaste for lessons, and an extreme difficulty in applying himself. In contrast he had always enjoyed active pursuits such as sports, music and manual tasks like woodwork. At school his devotion to sports, and his love of displaying his abilities in games, had been almost an obsession. 'I can remember every Saturday morning getting up very early to go skating, because up to nine o'clock, when the juniors took over, the younger classes had the ice to themselves. I can remember some of the older boys coaching me. I was fast on my skates and I could out-skate all the boys that were in my class.'

As a child, he was venturesome and curious in matters of sex. His inhibitions in that regard came about later on. One time, at the age of 8, while the boys and girls were changing clothes after a swim, positioned on opposite sides of a very large tree. 'I was dared to go in the nude round to the girls' side. I did this and the girls were plenty mad and told me to go back. They all hurried up changing and headed home faster than ever before. When I arrived home I had a few questions from Mom to answer, but it seems that I got out of it quite easily.'

At age 8 or 9 he had a sexual relationship with a slightly older girl. 'We played ball games together. I found I could easily do things with her, without questions. The first time we went all the way we were in the wheat-field playing house. We made a kitchen and what have you, and one thing led to another, until we were in our all-imaginary bedroom. She initiated what happened from then on, and I followed along. I am sure I was surprised at what was happening but I went along and carried out the act with guidance. I didn't know what erection or ejaculation was, but the excitement was there. We masturbated and I entered her as well. These incidents became quite frequent, and then I began looking forward to them . . . One time in the middle of our sexual acts we were noticed by some boys hiding in the bushes . . . I was embarrassed and didn't like the kidding I got from these guys . . . I don't remember carrying on with her after that, it seemed to scare that attraction and excitement out of me. In any case, she left the district soon after.'

It was not long afterwards, however, that he found another co-operative girl. 'She was a year or two younger than me, about 8 years of age. It didn't take much to persuade her at first, as we would be playing house. When we pretended to go to bed, while playing the game, I told her what to do and then I would carry on and on. This continued for a year or more, till she took a really firm stand and wouldn't do it. I didn't feel guilty about this at the time, only if I heard someone approaching, then we would have to rush for our pants, and pretend we were doing something else.'

Up to the age of 13 he had some problems with bed-wetting at night. Although this is often a sign of insecurity, and a difficulty that causes much embarrassment and distress to the child, he referred to it as if it were of little consequence. 'I remember I was still wetting the bed when I was 11, on the average two or three times weekly. I don't know if there was ever any discussion on this, as I never knew of any. Mom would take precautions by not giving me anything to drink after a certain hour, and by making sure I went to the washroom before I went to bed. This did help, but I still continued having a lot of accidents. I can't remember any real fuss being made the times I did wet the bed, as I had a rubber sheet and no mattress just in case of accidents.'

By the time he was 14 he was quite sociable with girls, but his early sexual contacts had ceased. 'It was an exciting time as we had dances at school and somebody usually had a hop party at their home on Friday evening. I always looked forward to these. I was always very active in sports and made all the school teams. I had two special friends in school. We were always together, took our girlfriends out as a three-some to shows, skating, school dances, house parties, etc. Lindie was always my partner at these events. She would let me copy her school work. She knew I had problems with that, and she tried to teach me things and help me to keep up. I must say she sure was determined with me in school work. I gave her my knowledge in return, in sports and in teaching her different dances, as the latest dances came naturally to me. Masturbation had become a regular outlet at this time, as I wasn't having physical contact with girls. Although I did have my share of petting with Lindie, I never did try to make a further advance with her. She seemed too nice a girl for that kind of thing, and nice girls didn't do that anyway.'

This pattern continued for the remainder of his school life. The last year 'I was on the school committee as sports convener. I helped the school principal to organize school events, as he was also the sports teacher. I played more than ever before and toured the countryside by using the thumb.' He and his friends 'once in a while went stag to a hop in town. A lot of kids hung around there from all parts of the city, especially the bobby socks and sweater-on-backwards type. We used to have white shoes, white stripes on the sides of our pants, and black leather jackets . . . I worked part time at a bowling alley, so I was able to have money to take a girl out on the weekends. I spent a lot of time during noon hours as well as after school with a girl called Carol . . . We had a favourite shop where most of the kids went, we had a favourite booth which was at the back. The waitress had to remind us continually about the noise. We always ended up at the coffee shop if we were out on Friday and Saturday nights.'

During this somewhat feverish social round, sexual activities went through a curiously dormant phase, being limited to masturbation and occasional deviant acts. 'When I was fifteen, my sister had a girlfriend stay overnight. I woke up during the night and went to her bedroom which was next to mine. I went in to her room and climbed into the bed where she was asleep. I was fondling her vagina and trying to remove her pyjama top when she awoke. I hit the road and returned to my room. She woke my sister who checked to see if I was awake. I played the ass and made it look like I was sleeping. At parties with school friends Friday nights we had necking sessions which went to some length. With Carol, my hands always wandered, but she would stop me at a certain point. There were others in the same room in a dark corner, also necking. Afterwards, when I had taken Carol home, I would be sexually aroused and wonder what to do to satisfy this strong sexual urge. I thought of peeping, and I started doing it at this time. I felt it wrong, but it was hurting no one, and it satisfied my sexual needs, so I soon forgot about the right and wrong, and it became a regular practice.'

It was at the age of 16, when he was working on a farm, that he began stealing female attire and dressing up. 'The family went out and I stayed behind. The neighbours were out and I went over to their house with sexual thoughts in mind. I knocked at the door and hollered to see if anyone was at home, but there was no response. I checked the door and entered. I found a bedroom, but with no women's clothing in it. I was really wound up, so I went upstairs and found a bra, girdle, slip, etc. I took all these and left for home. I arrived back with all these things stuffed in my shorts and around my shirt. I knew no one was in, so my attention turned to sex. In the house I put these things on. I was very wound up sexually and I ended up masturbating. I soon turned around and I thought I must get rid of this stuff. There was a stove in the house, so I took them in there and put them inside, and I put in some fresh wood so as to make sure there was no evidence left.'

At the age of 17, he had a car and a girlfriend. 'I see now all kinds of problems starting. I never stayed home, I was out to the lakes on weekends, besides driving around the town every evening of the week. We visited places where pop groups were playing. Her parents always knew where we were going, and only asked us to drive slowly. We got sexually involved many times. Many times she told or asked me to love her all the way. I wanted to, but I was afraid to go through with what I had started. I felt sexually very inadequate with her. I dared not even take my pants off to penetrate her. I didn't want to get her pregnant, and I had heard about V.D. I was too shy to go for a contraceptive from a drug store, I felt that if I did people would know what I was doing. At that time everybody trusted me, thought I was a nice boy.' He recalled that his father had warned him against sexual intercourse before marriage, because the girl is always someone else's sister, and how would he feel about anyone else behaving with his own sister that way? This talk had such a strong and lasting effect he became to be incapable of making love, though he had the physical desire to do so. His feelings for his girlfriend became very strong, but this produced another difficulty. 'I loved her, and I could not handle it. I was scared to get too involved, I didn't want the responsibility of marrying, it meant being absolutely true, and staying in one spot, and having to support her. So I told her exactly how I felt. She couldn't understand why I wanted to break our relationship, if I was in love with her, but we parted. She left my car running away and crying. I felt really bad, but I never tried to contact her again. I felt too much of a heel.'

These thoughts prevented him from having sexual intercourse with any of the numerous other girls he took out, even when they obviously wanted it. He would manipulate the situation and make excuses to avoid the necessity for outright refusal, but even so some girls declined to go out with him again on account of this behaviour. One girl became very emotional. Her mother was divorced and had become very promiscuous. This greatly upset the girl. She played on his sympathies and tried her best to seduce him into sexual intercourse. She would become so excited that her pants were soaking wet, but she never managed to overcome his resistance.

After declining these opportunities of sexual gratification, he often felt very aroused and frustrated. He turned to deviant sexual practices. During the time he was going with these girls without having intercourse he did a lot of peeping. 'I'd say about two or three times a week. The routine involved getting the attention of a female through a window, then masturbating in her presence. I was always on the look-out for a basement suite with a girl inside. I also spent a lot of time at swimming pools watching girls and becoming very sexually aroused by my fantasies. I was also raiding clothes-lines, taking women's undergarments by the handful, bras, panties, slips, anything of a silky material. I would handle these things, wear them and run them over my genitals causing great sexual excitement, until I ended up masturbating.'

Although arrested on various occasions by the police for these activities, and advised to accept psychiatric treatment, he could not bring himself to confide to anyone the full extent and nature of his sexual obsessions. 'I couldn't tell anybody how inadequate and inferior I felt. At work I felt that way as well, because it seemed that other people could learn easily and do things better, and I hated to see them superior to me. I also hated the superiority women have. A woman who wants sex can get it whenever she pleases. A guy has to ask for it and perform all the way through to satisfy the woman.'

He married at the age of 21, believing that this would solve all his problems. It did not do so. Before many months had gone he had fresh grounds for discontent. He no longer feared to have intercourse, but he complained that his wife was unresponsive, that she was not interested in having sex as often as he would wish. She frustrated him by her insistence on a narrow, set sexual routine. She rarely achieved a climax.

Except when both had been drinking, their sexual relations remained unsatisfactory. He felt that he was using her like a sex machine. She told him to take her whenever he needed sex, but he was not happy about that, not knowing what to do to satisfy her. 'She must have hated me for the way that I took her, just for my own satisfaction.'

There were other problems. Financial circumstances forced both of them to work in jobs that kept them apart most of the time. This he resented, and it added to his frustrations and boredom. Before long, he was caught again for an indecent sexual act. 'I cried myself to sleep, hating myself for what I had done. But still I wouldn't say a word to anyone. I was sent to a psychiatrist, but what could he do when I would say nothing at all, or very little.'

This history shows once again how external appearances, in this instance sporting accomplishments, sociability and poise, can conceal inner insecurity. The origins of this man's feelings of sexual inferiority were less clear than in some other examples, but the seriousness of his handicap was obvious enough, and marriage and copulatory experience had failed to overcome it. This was another example in which anxiety and frustration in achieving sexual contact with girls had led initially to relatively harmless substitute gratifications—fetishism and peeping—and, only later on, to aggressive crime.

Example 7

For this man, discomfort and shyness in social contacts, especially with members of the opposite sex, inability to assert himself effectively, and the stubborn attitudes that developed from this situation, were already quite apparent during school-days. 'I feel that the first few years at school contributed to my present character faults. During my second and third years at school we had a female teacher who took pleasure in punishing boys. She used to strap the palm of the hands with a yardstick. I was considered a slow learner, although I got good marks at that time and kept on trying my hardest. I didn't feel that any of my actions were deserving the kind of treatment I was getting from that teacher. From that time on, all through my years at school, I never got along with any other female teachers. I became very timid and scared of most of them.'

It seemed to him that girls had an easier time at school than boys. They usually got better marks than boys, and they were punished less severely if they did wrong. A girl would be sent out of the classroom for bad behaviour, but a boy would be humiliated in front of all the class. He remembered one nervous boy, with whom he felt some sympathy, who was too shy to ask to be allowed to leave the room, and would wet himself as a result. He blamed the teacher. She must have been aware of the boy's need from his expressions and restlessness. One day he told her so, but the only result was that he was punished himself. That experience turned him against the school. He used to daydream a great deal in class, mostly about cars and things that interested him, instead of paying attention to the lessons.

At age 11 he was kept back a year for failing to pass grade five. 'I felt uncomfortable and out of place for part of this time because I was a year older than everyone else. I didn't like the fact that I had done most of the school-work once already, but it gave me a chance to study the things that I had not learned. I developed an interest in spelling and was given some coaching in it. My spelling teacher entered me in a special contest between students in grade five and six.

It took place in the school auditorium, near the end of the term. I remained in this elimination competition until there was only two of us left, myself and a girl. She was an "A" student from grade six. I had known her from the previous year. I began to feel the pressure mounting up inside me. I had never been in a situation like this before. I felt self-conscious and tense and had difficulty concentrating. We were each given the same word to spell. I knew the right answer, but through nervousness I misspelled the word, and she got it right. I felt relieved that it was over, and I also felt disappointment that I had been beaten by a girl.'

The recognition he gained from this event helped him to develop new relationships at school, but the improvement was only temporary. 'By the time I was 14 I was becoming more and more disinterested in school. I never really set any goals for myself, so I began slipping out of classes, showing up late for school and playing hooky from school with a friend. My parents didn't know about it because I always wrote my own notes, saying that I had been sick. My lack of effort resulted in my failing again. I intended quitting school, but could not do so because I could not get my parents' consent, and I didn't have a job to go to.'

At school he sympathized with the underdogs amongst the teachers as well as amongst the pupils. 'There was one teacher who was somewhat strict and had a raging temper. He had been hit on the head with shrapnel during the war and had to have a steel plate inserted in his head. He often complained of headache and would let the class fool around whenever this happened. I think he was a little shell-shocked too. I remember some guys in our class used to bring a bag of buttons to school and as a practical joke they would dump the buttons into the heating fan. It would make a sound like a bunch of machine guns going off, and the teacher would stretch out on the floor covering his ears. Most of the guys thought it was funny, but I hated them for their sick sense for hurting people. It was just the same feeling I would get myself whenever someone teased or humiliated me.'

He remained at school until he was 18. 'Towards the end at school was the most difficult time for me. I developed a couldn't-care-less attitude about furthering my education. I got only average grades, but I reduced my studying time. I felt that it was just a waste of time. I hadn't set any future goals for myself other than wanting to complete the year and find a steady job.

'English was one of my problem subjects, and I didn't get along very well with the English teacher, who was a woman. She seemed overly critical, sarcastic, quick-tempered, and strict. I just never seemed to be able to talk without her threatening to kick me out of the class. I often spoke to my counsellor about her, but he didn't seem to understand. He just told me to try to discuss the problem with her. Near the end of the school term the class was given an assignment to write an oration. When this was completed the teacher asked me to read mine in front of the class. I turned in my written assignment but refused to read it to the class. She approached me, dragged me from my desk and told me to read or to leave the class. She told me that, if I walked out, I should fail the English course and just have to go through the same situation next year. I tried to read but the words would not come out. I felt a lump in my throat and my stomach was in knots. I walked out of the classroom and went to see the counsellor. I was crying and my nerves were shaking as I tried to explain what had happened. I told him that I was quitting school and then I went home.'

Throughout his school-days he was very much a loner, and particularly shy of girls. 'The only involvement with females I had at school would be either during lunch, or when we got to dancing lessons in the gymnasium, which I hated. I was always afraid to approach the girls that I liked, so I usually ended up with the fat girls that I didn't like. I developed a lot of jealous feelings, but kept them bottled up inside me. Generally I lacked self-confidence, and couldn't communicate at all well with females as a result. . . . I received some information and sex education while I was staying with my cousin when I was about the age of 12. My cousin had an older brother who was married. His father was dead, so his brother explained the facts of life to him. I happened to be staying at the house at this time. I heard his talk and it seemed more like a lecture of do's and don'ts. It was all about contraception and descriptions of venereal diseases. From this, I became afraid to experiment with sex, I had fears of causing pregnancy or spreading a disease. This could be one reason I didn't even begin to masturbate until I was about 15 or 16 years of age.

'I do not recall exactly what age I was when I had my first experience with sexual intercourse. It must have been between the age of 18 and 20. I had known the girl for quite a while. We had met accidentally through some telephone mix-up. After we had been seeing each other for a few months, I was invited over to her place to meet her parents. She was sexually experienced and had had a baby, but she had put it up for adoption. When I got to her place her parents were both in bed drunk, and she was drinking quite heavily herself. We were drinking beer and watching a movie on television. We began kissing and I fondled her breasts for a while. She took off her panties while I took off my pants. Just as I penetrated her, we heard a noise, then her father walked into the room and noticed what we were doing. He was as embarrassed as we were and it was fortunate that he was drunk, because he never said anything except that, when he staggered out of the room, he said the movie on T.V. must not have been worth viewing. This incident made such an impression on me that I refrained from having any sexual involvement with women for a while after that.'

At the age of 20 he was out one evening with a male friend at a pool hall when two girls came up and introduced themselves. They wanted to have a game. He became friendly with one of these girls. 'I began dating her on a steady basis over the next year. She had a job as a secretary during the day, and I was working nights, so we had very little time together. I used to phone her from work and meet her for supper during the week and then take her out on the weekends. We had planned to get married, but we never discussed a date. I still did not have a car and I wanted to find a better job. I spent all the money I had buying things for her. It seemed too real to be true, and I feared to lose her. We never had sex during our relationship, although we both wanted to. We felt that we should wait until we got married. We had planned to go to a night club at Christmas, but that had to be postponed because I got called to work. Instead we made reservations at a club for New Year's Eve, but the place caught fire and closed down before we got there. I decided to take her to another similar club, but she wanted to go to a different place. The place she wanted to go to was a sort of paradise for drug addicts, prostitutes, and hippies, so I told her that I wouldn't take her there. I explained what I thought of the place and told her that if she wanted to go there she must go without me. She decided to go home, and I walked her to her door, and then went home myself. I spoke to her on the phone afterwards to clear this up, but we both decided to split up for a while. After that I got a car and I often drove past her house wanting to go in and talk to her and take her out, but I never got past the point of parking in front of the place. I always feared that she would be out, or with someone else. Driving home at night usually at about two in the morning I used to drive at high speed. This seemed to take my mind off my problems. When I thought about the girl during this time I sometimes considered committing suicide to escape the hurt I felt, but this thought only lasted a couple of seconds, because I realized that I would be accomplishing nothing.'

This case was an interesting example of the so-called passive aggressive personality, an individual who appears subdued most of the time, whose hostilities break out explosively and unexpectedly on those rare occasions when he seems to behave out of character. This man's problem of miserable unassertiveness, of feeling crushed and helpless in his dealings with the opposite sex, anticipating rejection at every turn, led to depression and thoughts of suicide. It must also on occasion have led to bitterness and anger. Although he expressed few hostile feelings verbally, except in oblique references to girls having a better deal than boys, his hostility revealed itself in action, in the shape of repeated sexual attacks upon strangers.

Example 8

A shy, unassertive person in most situations, but irritable and obstinate in some, this man had personality problems which had been evident since school-days. 'I had a bad speech problem in my younger years, and I would get a hard time at school from some of the other kids. Most of the time it was easier for me if I didn't speak at all, and this would be the same at home.' He developed the same defeatist attitude about his appearance. 'I got a tooth knocked out with a stone when I was around 9 or 10. I never smiled after that because it made me look funny. In fact, I never smiled for about twenty years, not until I got dentures.'

He never liked schools, went only because he had to, and often used to suffer from headaches when he got there. He liked neither sports nor studies. 'In high school nothing much happened to me. I had few friends and no girlfriends. I had my one and only fight at that school. One of the guys kept needling me every day and kept wanting a fight. I was not interested in fighting him, but he kept at it. In the end I fought him and knocked him down the school steps. I didn't want to, but he kept on riding me until I did. I got no feelings of satisfaction that I had won.'

He quit school at the early age of 14 and went to work on a farm. His relationship with his own father was distant and hostile, but the farmer 'soon became a father image to me. He became my hero, and when I talked to him my speech problem was practically non-existent.' Under this influence he became more self-reliant and independent and especially proud of his growing ability to handle machinery and do a man's job. In spite of his shyness he developed a strong machismo image, an inner conviction that real men don't betray weak feelings, especially not where women are concerned.

'When I was 15 I met my first girlfriend. She was 13 and I was very fond of her. From time to time we would go in for some heavy petting, but we did not make love fully. I spent all the time I could with her and gave up hanging around with the guys to be with her. Her mother kept a close eye on us. It seems the last boy the girl was involved with had been caught in the act of making love with her. I guess her mother thought that I was trying to do the same thing, which I was of course, and I guess I would have done so if I had not been so shy about it.' This friendship lasted a year, but then he became disillusioned. When his place of work closed down, 'I stayed around to be with her. I got a job on a farm with room and board. I had a lot of work to do and I was at it seven days a week. I could usually get Sundays off, but even then I had to be back in the afternoon in time for the milking. I had a motor cycle with which I could go to see the girlfriend in the evenings. But by this time she had started to go out with other guys. I got tired of her flirty ways, so I quit the job and went back to stay with relatives.'

Soon after this he joined the armed forces. At this time he developed a highly cynical attitude towards women. 'I started going into the town which was a few miles away from where we were stationed. At a show one night a girl sat next to me and I started talking to her and went home afterwards to her place. She was the first girl I made love to and she was well experienced. She sure loved sex, and I never missed the opportunity to enjoy my new-found pleasure with her, but I never loved her. She had such a bad reputation she had been banned from the base. It was not long after meeting her that I got a car. In the evenings and at weekends my friend Larry and I would drive around the country and pick up girls. We were both shy talking with girls, but Larry was very shy, except when he got drunk, then Wow! All he wanted to do was to go and pick up girls day and night. . . . In the two years I was there I must have had about thirty girlfriends, and most of them I made love to. I don't think I satisfied any of them though, looking back on it. I worried very little about how they felt. I had so many different girls I did not worry about trying to keep any one. When I was going with my first girlfriend I had nothing to do with any others, although I had lots of opportunities to do so, but that had not stopped her from going with other guys. Now it was the other way round. I told every girlfriend that I had when I was in the forces that she was the only one in my life, but I cheated on every one of them. It seems I went out of my way to make love to some other girl behind their backs. One time I had three different girls going at the same time. I would take each of them out on different nights.

'As far as I was concerned, being in the state commonly referred to as being in love was too painful to let happen. One thing I found out about girls while I was in the service, if they thought you were crazy about them, they would start playing up, flirting with other guys, being bossy and so forth. I caught onto their act. If I phoned up for a date and one started saying she wasn't sure, or any of that stuff, I would bang the phone down and call someone else.'

While in the service he obtained some engineering training and was pleased to be put to work on machine repairs, but before long he fell foul of authority. He felt that a particular sergeant was picking on him, giving him all the most boring jobs, looking for faults, not recognizing his abilities and accusing him of being lazy. In point of fact, his long-standing habits of working in isolation made it difficult for him to adjust to the give-and-take of a crowded workshop. The conditions irritated him. He was something of a perfectionist, and if he could not do things in his own way at his own pace, he would respond with passive resistance and apparent laziness. More and more of his energy went into his nightly sexual adventures. 'My work started to go downhill even more than usual, much to the sergeant's delight. I started sleeping late in the mornings, and would get extra duty for that. This would make me still more tired, and I would fall asleep in the workshop and get more extra duty with confinement to barracks.' At one point he went absent, after which 'my name was on every extra duty list they had, but I did every job they gave me with ease and went out chasing girls twice as much.' Finally, he was told he did not take the service seriously enough and was discharged for 'insufficiency and unsatisfactory conduct'.

At the age of 21 he met his future wife, but his attitude towards her was scarcely more trusting or tolerant than his attitude to the other girls he had known. She was a few years younger and she was in fact the sister of a girl he was currently dating, but at that time 'I had the morals of a tomcat. She worked in an office and was well educated and could talk on any subject.' In those respects her personality was in marked contrast with his own rather morose and unsociable attitude and his difficulties in self-expression. 'After a few dates I made love to her. She claimed to be a virgin, but I had no difficulty in making it with her the first time. I used that thought to ease my conscience when I cheated on her in later years, but deep down in the back of my mind I'm sure she was as she said. Her sister seemed to accept it without fuss when she told her about us, and I still made love to her sister on occasions the same as before.

'She soon moved in with me and it wasn't long before she became pregnant and we decided to get married.' Looking back he realized that he resented being forced to marry her. On his wedding night he went out with friends and got very drunk, which was most unusual with him, and became aggressive, kicking in the door of a police car and wrecking the furniture in a hotel room. Next morning a friend had to bail him out. He found a small place in the country to live. 'She seemed pleased with it at first and for a little while took good care of the inside. She hadn't wanted to move out of town, because she loved going to clubs and dances and all that, but I wasn't interested. I guess she only came with me because she was pregnant and more or less had to. I was working pretty hard at my job, and when I got home at night all I could do was to sit for an hour and get my strength back.'

Soon he began to feel that his wife was neglecting him. He noticed it especially after the baby was born. 'She started to let the house-work slip. We always seemed to have dirty dishes and diapers lying around. I told her one day that if she wouldn't do her job then I would quit mine. She would work for a few days, then let things go again, so I did quit. Then she went out to work and I stayed home and took care of the little boy. This arrangement suited her, but she did not earn enough to keep up payments on the house and I did not find another job for four months. So we lost the house and I felt it served her right. We then moved in with her parents and I helped her father in his business. I did not like living in their house and was miserable most of the time. I started going out by myself in the evenings and I would pick up girls in coffee shops or walking along the street. If I could I would make love with them, but I never had anything lasting with any of them.'

Several years went by, another child was born, and they had a place of their own again, but the marriage remained unhappy. 'She kept the house like a pigpen, and I stayed out as much as possible. She refused to wash the clothes most of the time, so I had to do it. I was on regular night shift and had a hard time sleeping with the kids around, so I built myself a small cabin and slept away from the rest of the house. I dreaded any relatives or visitors coming and seeing the sloppy way she kept the house . . . I blamed myself for the way she was. I was firmly convinced that if I had been able to give her a real nice house things would have been different. As I think back on it now, it would have been the same anywhere. She was just not cut out to be a housewife.'

Matters came to a head when he developed an infatuation for the young daughter of an old friend and neighbour. 'When I visited there she would ask me to drive her into town. As soon as we were out of sight of her home she would snuggle up beside me. I realized what a precarious position I was putting myself in, but the harder I tried to keep her at arm's length, the more persistent she became . . . One night she phoned me and said she was lonely and wanted to talk to me about some problem she had. When I got to her room she wanted to be kissed. I wouldn't do so and told her I had come to talk. She got mad and started taking her clothes off. I turned my back and she said if I would not watch her she would scream. I watched her and when she got into bed I made love to her. I think she had been seduced a few times before, but I'm not sure.' After that sexual intercourse took place many times.

At this point 'my wife was getting suspicious and started to become demanding in bed. I made love to her more often to try to assure her that I was not doing it to someone else. I was also under pressure at work. My foreman was making me fit more and more jobs into my schedule. I was not eating right and my nerves were shot. I tried drinking but I didn't like it. I began losing weight. I just wanted to be away from everything, so I quit the job, though I had been there four years. I borrowed some camping gear and set off in the car for parts unknown. I stopped on the way to say good-bye to the young girl, but she said she would run away by herself if I wouldn't take her with me, so I did.'

The inevitable happened. The girl became pregnant, her father found out, and he was jailed for contributing to juvenile delinquency. 'They tried everything to get her to give the baby up for adoption, but she wouldn't, but they convinced her to give me up. She even wrote to ask me for the baby's pictures back.' When he got out of jail he went to see her, pulled her into his car, and tried to get her to tell him where the baby was. That escapade cost him a further stay in jail. Meantime, his wife had moved into an apartment in town and was prepared to have him back. He visited the place, but disliked it instantly, and couldn't face her style of life in town. He went off to live on his own and secured a driving and delivery job which brought him into contact with many females. 'I would drive fast and use the car to attract girls. Most of them I made love to and some of them I would bring out to my place. I was not interested in forming any lasting relationships . . . I never had any trouble making love to a girl even if I did not love her, but unless I had strong feelings bordering on love I would not or could not try to satisfy them, for instance, by taking my time so that they would reach climax at the same time as me.'

So far, hurt male pride, and inferiority feelings stirred up by repeated failures in heterosexual relationships had resulted in nothing more serious than lapses into a disillusioned promiscuity. But the groundwork was laid for worse to come. His next relationship, though he entered into it cautiously, became the main focus of his life, more so than ever before. The greater the commitment to a love relationship the greater the shock when things go wrong, especially if there is no one else to blame but oneself.

'I noticed a girl who ate at the same cafe. I made a point of being at the lunch counter at the same time each day. After about a month I was getting a light smile from her. Strange as it may seem I was still as shy about talking with girls as I always had been. In most cases I never spoke unless I had some good excuse for doing so, or unless they spoke first. I found out later that she was shy too . . .' Eventually he managed to invite her out and before long they were having a serious affair. He lost his driving job at this time 'but I did not mind because I was no longer interested in meeting with other girls. I did not know at the start whether I loved her or not. I had strong feelings for her, that I do know, but it was not a wild, hurting kind of love like the others had been. But over the years it continued to increase in a way that never ceased to amaze me . . . I told her about my past and about having been in jail. Somehow she got me agreeable to marrying again. I still don't know how she used to get me to do things without nagging. That turns me right off, and my mother was famous for it. I guess I realized that I really did love her when she was coming down the aisle at the wedding.'

This man's possessive and domineering attitude to women was clearly an overcompensation for inner insecurity. No girlfriend could please him for long because his ideal mate was little more than a female slave. As soon as a relationship began to deviate from that model, as inevitably it did, he became sulky and irritable or tried to withdraw. Much of his anger he directed against himself for having failed to keep control of things as a real man should. His extra-marital escapades, and later on his actual crimes, were ways in which he tried to avenge his hurt masculinity.

Example 9

Like the case before last this was an example of the quiet, withdrawn type of man whose depth of feeling remains unsuspected until a sudden explosion of violence, which seems totally out of character, calls attention to his state of mind. On the ward he shut himself up alone in his room as often as he was allowed to do so. In the group he maintained an ostentatious silence about himself, giving curt, sarcastic retorts to questions about what was going on in his thoughts. He professed detachment from his crimes, alleging that they were committed on sudden, meaningless impulses that caused him to act contrary to all his conscious ideals. On one occasion, when pressed to describe his feelings, he declared a complete lack of concern for himself or others. Another time, he remarked that he could kill someone whose behaviour he disapproved of without the slightest hesitation or regret. His supposed aloofness from all human feeling was exemplified in a statement he made to the effect that he was present in the group in body, and was aware of what was going on, but that was about all. From time to time, as treatment progressed, this defensive mask dropped away and he was able to describe some of the hurtful experiences and dreadful inferiority feelings that had kept him from revealing his thoughts to anyone. He was also able to convey something of the intensity of his positive feelings for the one and only person in the world he cared about. It was evident how he would have viewed any threat to that one inflammable relationship as the worst possible calamity.

His habit of social withdrawal had been with him since infancy. He recalled the year his elder brother started to go to school. 'This made me feel sort of left out, because he had all these new clothes and books and everything. He had all that new stuff as well as more new friends, while I had no friends of my own age. Even at that age I found it difficult to make friends on my own.' He remembered a joint birthday party with his brother. 'My mother had invited some of his friends from school over for a small party. I knew them from the times they came over to play with my brother, but I realized they were his friends, not mine. I felt pretty well out of things. That was the last party that I shared with my brother, mainly because of this left-out feeling.' His parents must have recognized the existence of a problem, for they made attempts to get him to associate with neighbourhood children. 'I did not really push myself into these relationships. I thought that having a couple of friends of a sort would satisfy my parents so they would stop trying to introduce me to every kid in the neighbourhood.' On going to school 'I did not get along well with my schoolmates. Even then I could get along better with the teacher than with the pupils. I kept to myself and didn't make friends. I would not invite anyone to my place to play and very seldom went to theirs.' He had no particular childhood nervous symptoms, but was always very much a loner. He spent a lot of his early days on farms and liked to be with animals.

He remembered his earliest sexual experience was around the age of 5. 'There was a girl a couple of years older I didn't mind playing with because she was as good, if not better, than me at anything I could play or do. One day she and I were playing in an abandoned house about a quarter of a mile away. I am not sure how it came about, but we decided to undress. Since neither of us had ever really seen a member of the opposite sex nude before, this was an opportunity to examine each other closely. This we did in a sort of detached manner. Her elder brother saw us doing this and reported it to his parents. Needless to say we were both spanked when we got home.' Some years later he reacted to a similar situation with near panic. A 16-year old girl, daughter of a neighbour, was in the house acting as baby sitter. 'One evening she started drinking some liquor. We were all fooling around. I am not sure who instigated it, but she started to remove her clothing. As she had an attractive body, I should have been excited or something, but I became frightened. The memory of the time before when I had been caught with a naked girl, and the knowledge of what my father was like in a temper was sufficient to frighten me.' When the girl saw how frightened he was, she gave up the game and got dressed again.

His later years at school were blighted by unhappy and poverty-stricken home circumstances. 'I soon discovered the humiliation of being on welfare. The agency took a long time to pay the money for the school bills, during which time I was repeatedly asked when the payments would be forthcoming.' As he grew older, he began working off some of his frustrations in frequent fights at school. At the age of 15 'I was suspended for a week for punching a fellow student in the head during a school period. I was very upset about it, because he had started it and didn't have the guts to admit the fact. A couple of months later he made the mistake of climbing onto a boxing ring with me. I got my revenge on him—and revenge it was! I had been in training for over a year. After that I was ignored by, and in turn I ignored, almost everyone else in my class or age group.' When he left at the age of 18 his unsociability and alienation from school life was underlined by his reluctance to attend the graduation ceremony. 'I stayed till the scrolls were handed out, then left. I thought the whole exercise a bit ridiculous and an unnecessary expense.'

He spent the next two years training and serving in the forces. He took his work and his courses extremely seriously, worried about his progress, and was concerned to obtain his promotions on time. In fact, his performance and progress were above the average.

Judging by his descriptions, his first love-making experiences, which took place at this time, were somewhat cold and clinical. 'I picked up a girl downtown and ended up in bed with her. I was a bit disappointed over the brief affair. I had been sort of clinical in my way of reacting to the situation, trying to observe her and my reactions. Because of this attitude I did not allow myself the pleasure I should have derived from the encounter.' It was not until more than a year had passed that he ventured to repeat the experience. He was living alone in a rented apartment at the time and became friendly with a married couple living next door. They asked him over to supper and without telling him asked a girl over at the same time. 'I could not leave because I had already accepted the invitation. I found the girl to be friendly enough and easy to get along with. I obtained her phone number and address before leaving and made a date for two days later. We found each other mutually attractive, and after a couple of dates we went to bed together. This time I allowed myself to enjoy the girl without trying to analyse any of the feeling. Just before I was due to go away on a posting for six weeks she lost her apartment. I let her have the apartment during my absence.

When I got back she told me she had started an affair with the young man who lived below. That solved the problem that I had developed while I was away, wondering what I was going to do with her, how I was going to be able to kick her out of my place without hurting her feelings too much.'

Soon after this began his first and only love affair. As with so many lonely, inhibited people, his feelings, once aroused, were intense, possessive and beset with anxieties. The woman of his choice, a neighbour, had recently left an unfaithful husband and was looking after a small child on her own. Her depressed and unsettled frame of mind at the time may have struck a sympathetic chord in him, but in the long run the complications of the situation had anything but a calming effect upon his already taut emotions. At first they slipped into each other's company with little effort. 'After a couple of nights we just sort of came together. I found her very comfortable to be with. I was not nervous with her in the way I normally was no matter who the woman I was with. I must have been aware even then of the difference between my feelings for her and for other women for that first night we had sexual relations I found myself trying to satisfy her as best I could. But the first year of our relationship was shaky at best, with numerous problems . . . We both agreed she needed a friend more than a lover at that time, so that is what I tried to be. She just wanted to be left alone with the child. I could understand this, so I left them alone for a couple of weeks. When I did drop in on them again I deeply regretted ever having left them alone, for she had been drinking almost constantly and had been at it every night. This carried on for a couple of months, during which time we had numerous arguments.' She left the apartment and disappeared for a few weeks. When he saw her again, 'I do not know which feeling was the more predominant, I was angry and happy at the same time.' After they started living together, her husband started making difficulties about the divorce and custody of the child. This goaded him to a pitch of murderous but impotent fury.

By means of social withdrawal and expressions of cynicism and aloofness this man strove to assert his independence of all other human beings, but his behaviour was obviously a device for protecting himself against fears of hurtful rejection derived from unhappy experiences in earlier years. Only with difficulty could he bring himself to admit any positive feelings or commitment to a sexual partner. Once having done so, however, his love became frighteningly intense and possessive, the only meaningful feature in his entire existence. Any upset to that relationship was liable to release all his dangerously pent-up feelings of aggression in a cataclysmic emotional reaction.

Example 10

This was yet another example of the outwardly quiet but inwardly seething type. On admission to the institution he was described as 'a quiet, soft-spoken young man, polite and respectful'. He was reported to be 'apprehensive'. These descriptions did less than justice to his extreme shyness in certain situations. He confessed to uncomfortable feelings, amounting almost to a phobia, about having to eat in public, especially with members of the opposite sex. During group discussions he would sit silent, taking in what was going on, but intervening hardly at all. When questioned directly, he would look unhappy, shift uneasily in his seat, play nervously with his cigarette, and reply in a way that implied he had no important unresolved problems worth discussing. He admitted that the thought of coming to a group meeting and having attention focused upon him put him into a state of great anxiety, and he was always relieved when a session was over.

He had shown signs of a nervous disposition as a boy. At kindergarten age 'I was still wetting the bed every night, and if I woke up late at night, which I always did, I used to crawl into mother's bed. The kindergarten teacher said I wasn't settled enough for passing Grade 1, and she was right, I failed it. I used to get along pretty well with the teachers, especially the male teachers, I liked them a lot better for some reason.' At home he was tied to and dominated by a forceful mother and an elder sister. 'My sister was good at school and I felt bad because I was losing marks and letting my mother down. One time I tried to sign my mother's name to a school report and return it to the school without showing it to her . . . I used to steal change from my mother so I could go and buy pop and candy from the store. She always gave me spending money, but I guess I was greedy . . .' At the age of 12 'owing to lack of space I still had to sleep in the same room as my mother. I didn't like the arrangement because there wasn't any privacy.'

For a boy so inhibited in other respects his practical sexual experience began early and was surprisingly extensive, as if the assertiveness he could not express elsewhere found a secret outlet in covert sexual adventures. It was one way in which he could rebel against the maternal domination that troubled him. When he was around 12 he made friends with another boy of similar age. 'We started having a few sex feelings for each other. We used to masturbate each other quite often when we could get to be alone together. Sometimes I would sleep over at his house and sometimes the other way round. We were both looking for something, but were not sure what it was. We never felt embarrassed or had bad feelings for what we were doing. I kind of knew that it wasn't right, but even so it didn't bother me at the time. It never went any further than just masturbating each other . . .' After a year or so 'I quit having sexual experiences with my friend because now we both had lots of girls to go out with.

'At about this time, when I was 12, I met my first real girlfriend. She lived in the apartment behind us and was quite good-looking and the same age as me. We went skating together quite often at weekends, and usually just stayed over at her place or mine. By this time I finally had my own room in the basement and there was also a small built-on recreation room. She and I used to go in there a lot and play records and sneak a beer in there. We used to take each other's clothes off and touch each other and do everything else but actually have intercourse. I'm not sure whether I actually knew how to do it at that time, or if I was just too scared to try it.' This relationship came to an end because the girl and her family moved away.

'By this time I'd started smoking and drinking behind mother's back. When she found out she said it was up to me if I wanted to ruin myself. I had three or four close boyfriends who always came over weekends and we all drank. We used to stand outside the store and ask people if they would buy us some booze. At that time it was the only way we could get any. We used to hide most of it when my mother came round to check on us. She didn't realize how much we drank. We all got pretty sick at times.

'When I was 13 one of my friends asked me over one day to his mother's place. She and another woman were there. They were already drinking before we arrived and we all ended up getting pretty drunk. The subject of sex came up and one thing led to another. . . . It ended up with me having sex with his mother. I felt quite good about the whole thing, knowing that a grown lady would want to have sex with me. I was a bit scared at first, but being drunk it didn't bother me as much as it otherwise would have . . .

'After this I started dating girls pretty steadily. I was having friends, boys and girls, over most weekends and we'd end up having sex. At most of the parties we had at home, or at neighbours' places, we would get pretty drunk and damn sick, but I was lucky enough to keep out of trouble. By this time I was getting into an endless routine of booze and sex at weekends. By the age of 14 I was tired of school and started skipping out once in a while with friends. Some of my friends started getting their driving licences and that gave a bigger choice of parties to go to. . . . At home I still felt out of place a bit with just women around all the time.'

At 15 and 16 'I had quite a few girlfriends, but never seemed to stay with any for very long. I usually found someone better and dropped them, or else they did the same to me. All the sex experiences were primarily for my own needs and wants with no regard for their feelings or what they wanted. Maybe it was because I didn't know any better. They never really said anything to me about it to make me feel any differently. I never had any guilt feelings about having sex, even if the girl was drunk at the time. I remember that there was one girl at this time who wouldn't have sex with me. I told her I would find somebody else if she didn't, so she changed her mind, and I ended up going with her for a year or more, off and on. . . . One weekend I asked her to come back to a hotel with me. We were in the phone booth opposite the hotel. I was ringing up the friend who worked on the desk to find out if it was all right to bring her in and take her to the room with me. Then a police car stopped outside the booth. They found us both stoned drunk and took us to the station. I got a fine. That was the first time I had any trouble with the police, and it was because of the booze, but it didn't stop me from drinking the same way afterwards. We had some pretty wild parties, and at this age I didn't think I was doing anything wrong, just having a good time. All my friends were doing basically the same sort of thing. I stayed away from stealing cars or breaking in, I just didn't want to get involved with anything like that. My mother never came downstairs when I had friends around. We hid a lot of the liquor and kept a close eye out most of the time, especially if we were having any sex.

'I was about 16 when I started having sex with other girls at the hotel where my friend worked. One that comes back to my mind was a girl of 12 who was living there. I would meet her in an empty room and have sex. I had other girls I was taking out, but I liked this one for sexual reasons. Finally someone told her mother who blew up and was ready to call the police. . . . After a month or so our relationship began again. We ended up getting caught by the police as we were shacked up in another hotel. I was scared as hell at this point, but her mother was talked out of laying charges and the police decided I was scared enough and they wouldn't do anything more about it. All my other experiences were with girls older than this. I probably would have had sex with every girl in the place if they had been willing. . . .

'The same partying and drinking scenes continued until I finally got fed up with school and decided to pack it in. By this time I was skipping out every second day and my marks were getting worse. I couldn't get along with the teachers, they all seemed to have their own special pets and didn't bother with the other pupils, such as me. I wanted to get out and make some money. I was told I was crazy to quit, and was nearly thrown out of the house . . .'

He saved up and bought a car, but within three months he had lost his licence for speeding and possession of liquor under age.

His happily irresponsible conduct and seeming freedom from inhibition when among his old drinking cronies and their easy-going girlfriends was only one side of his nature. At other times he was an anxious, worried individual, concerned about his mother's poor opinion of him, ashamed of his family history, conscious of his defective education, and tongue-tied and ineffectual among respectable feminine company. When he became engaged to a girl whose standards he admired but found hard to live up to, his inferiority feelings were aroused and a period of stress and conflict became inevitable. The more he tried to live up to the girl's expectations, socially or otherwise, the bigger failure he felt. He could not dominate her as he had done with his casual sex partners. His failure to do so conflicted with his image of what a man should be and revived his painful memories of previous maternal domination. He reacted with the sulky, withdrawn behaviour that, in the passive aggressive personality, is often a prelude to some violent outburst.

Example 11

This young man's history was one long succession of seemingly inexplicable failures, at school, at work and in all his personal relationships. Phases of rebellion alternated with periods of hopeless despondency. Both stemmed from a massive inferiority complex. He was highly intelligent, but ridiculously over-sensitive. He was consumed with anger one moment, full of self-blame the next. He was afflicted with a mild but noticeable physical deformity. He suffered tortures from this as a child, and it still troubled him far more than he liked to admit. He was suspicious of people's attitudes and motives to the verge of paranoia. At times he was depressed to the point of being actively suicidal. He spent a large part of his time in the group arguing why he should leave it, even if that meant a return to the deadening routine of protective custody in the penitentiary. His relations with the opposite sex had always been particularly disastrous. He blamed his own sensitiveness, exacerbated by his mother's discouraging attitudes, for effectively preventing any sexual affairs in his youth. In later years, his unstable work habits, his moodiness, his sadistic sexual fantasies and his repeated criminal convictions combined to preclude any satisfactory or lasting heterosexual relationship.

The first indication of a tendency to react badly to stress came when a childhood illness necessitated admission to hospital for investigation. 'Apparently I acted rather oddly. I threw things like thermometers out of the window and tried to escape from the hospital room, which was normally locked, by way of the visiting intern's open legs. For these antics I was labelled a psychiatric case . . . I remember little about it now.

'I recall crying a lot on my first day at school . . . I got good grades at first, but I believe my behaviour outside class was not exemplary. Kids would make fun of me at times, and I would end up in a few fights . . .' This 'teasing and insults' about his deformity continued for some years, as did the fights. 'I had no particularly close friends. After school we would sometimes kick a soccer ball around and at times form scrub teams. I was only fair at the game and would usually be picked in the middle, rarely at the end, and even rarer was I captain.' On changing school at the age of 10 'my grades were good, but outside the classroom I had to establish myself again. This being a different school I would get a certain amount of name-calling and be involved in a few fights. It is possible some of these I caused by my defensive attitude. It seems I was called Einstein because of my quick answers. I liked this yet did not like it, because it set me apart from the others. Another thing I sometimes resented was my dress. My clothes were often worse than other kids' . . . I recall complaining about it, but I knew it couldn't be helped because money was short.'

By the time he was 11 he was becoming more disobedient and doing less well in his grades. One teacher 'who had an authoritarian approach to his class reported that I was disrupting his class to such an extent he wished my folks would pull me out.' 'During this year I met a neighbour's boy. He would be a year or two older, but of the same mischievous and devious turn of mind. We became friends and soon were together most of the day. . . . We stole fruit together from neighbouring gardens. He would also steal money, cigarettes and candy from his uncle's store. I began to steal money, too. I don't know who turned whom on, it seemed spontaneous. In school my grades continued to slip, so that I failed part of my courses. Because of this, coupled with the loss of friends I caused myself by acting irresponsibly, I was no longer wanting to go to classes. My friend fitted into this pattern beautifully. With him I could steal fruit, shoot animals with a pellet gun, and do other minor pranks. I looked up to him and wanted to prove myself with him. . . . By the time I was 13 I was stealing more and getting caught and getting lickings, causing me to tearfully repent. I even meant it, but somehow or other I continued after a few weeks . . . I remember stealing a bayonet from a deserted boat shack. Strangely enough, I fixed this to the handle-bars of my bike. The owner recognized it and the predictable licking followed.

'The most important incident that occurred at school that year was that I was given a dare for a fight, over what I don't recall, and I accepted it for after school. What has greatly bothered me ever since is that I didn't show up. The boy was bigger than I and I was afraid knowing I was going to get quite a beating . . . I was glad to leave because of the humiliation regarding that fight cowardice.' Ever since then he has felt very badly if ever he failed to assert himself. 'Out of this I feel I have developed a line of thinking that causes me to view non-assertion as serious personal failure.'

He recalled that it was about this time he experienced his first intimation of the dangers of sexuality. 'I went mushroom-picking in the woods. This was something I did periodically on my own. I had few friends now, as my former friend was attending a vocational school and my few other acquaintances were all from the class where I had dropped out, and I was ashamed to see them. On this occasion I asked my young sister to come with me. This was against mother's strict orders . . . I believe her refusal was partly caused by sexual fears over us. I didn't think of my sister in a sexual way, though. She was only 9, I was 13, and hadn't yet strong urges. Mother's fury though was tremendous. I had let my sister go into the house first, wisely, through cowardice, and when I heard her crying while she was being slapped, I turned and ran and didn't come home that night. I slept in the open, but got the licking anyway in the morning.'

At the age of 15 he was finally convicted of shop-lifting, put on probation, and placed temporarily in the care of some relatives. He was, however, more concerned about a sexual incident with a neighbour's daughter. 'We became friends and would spend much time together during the summer. There would be a certain amount of petting, but no more. A day came when we were alone in her house. I tried the kissing and petting routine, but instead of stopping when she resisted further advances I tried to take her clothes off. She resisted so that without hurting her I could not possibly succeed. A wrestling match ensued during which she began to cry. Since I had thought of forcing her I felt very guilty. I was so ashamed I would go out of my way to avoid her, for I felt that the terrible thing I had done to her, if she were to tell anyone, would bring hell and damnation down on me.'

Soon after this he began to play hooky from school more and more until finally he quit altogether. He spent a lot of time wandering about on his own. 'In the summer I was fired from my job for not calling in over an absence or too many absences. I had run out of goodwill either way. I began prowling around the shore hoping to steal from deserted beach blankets. I got forty dollars once, but usually there was nothing . . . I soon tried a purse snatching on a woman of 30 late one night. I had a small pocket knife with which I tried to scare her into coming into an alley with me. When she refused and threatened to start screaming I ran. After I calmed down I blamed myself for not using the knife in a more threatening manner. I called this a purse snatching, but I feel it was only a prelude to a sexual assault . . . In my thoughts I had the idea of committing rape, or what I thought was rape. I still was not quite certain of the sexual act at that time. Rather than relief for not having carried my plan out, I felt blame for having failed.'

He was caught, convicted, and sent to a reformatory. On release he was befriended by a professional couple who took him into their home as a boarder. He started attending school again, but he had a hard time making friends. 'In school I had no problems passing grade eleven in good standing, but I had no close friends, and only a few casual acquaintances. I was beginning to meet more people though, at a downtown club where there were periodic dances and parties. I attended most of them, but felt unable to talk to girls unless I had a few drinks inside me. It seemed very difficult for me to be at ease with girls under social conditions. Drinking at this time was a rare occurrence, but if enough liquor was available, I tended to end up becoming drunk. To illustrate, I had a couple of beers and then went to a party. After a couple more I got up the courage to ask a girl no one seemed attached to for a dance. She agreed, and bit by bit we began to neck. I tried to lure her into a bedroom, but with no luck. The evening ended for me when I staggered to the cabin where we were put to sleep . . . Next day I couldn't recognize the girl until she said hello. I am no prize for looks, but I was ashamed of this girl. When people teased me about her I got defensive. It was an uncomfortable few hours, for I had nothing to say to the girl, felt like leaving, but stuck it out.'

At this time, his knowledge of sex was rudimentary, his experience nil, and his sense of guilt acute. He felt terribly inadequate and uncomfortable with girls. He feared they would see through him and comprehend the dirty sex thoughts that motivated him. The daughter of the house where he was staying was just a few months older than he was and he developed something of a crush on her. He was very hurt and offended when he found she had reported him for being absent from some classes. He turned very cold towards her and the situation in the household became tense. 'I started to have rape fantasies about her, where I would beat and even kill her. At one point I went up to her bedroom with a knife. The house was deserted, but had she come just then, I think I might have attacked her . . .' Prior to this incident I would go to the odd party and drink a little. I still felt quite shy with girls, in fact, I had taken only one girl out for a date to a school dance. After this incident I was still shy, but I also became spiteful. To explain, I wanted to have the beautiful girls that seemed unattainable, but the girl who came with me to the dance I treated in a shoddy, insulting manner.

'When I was 18 and 19, I had no dates with girls. I would cruise the city when I could get a car, but only once succeeded in picking up a girl off the street. She was only about 13 or 14, and I came very near to forcing her to have sex, but a premature ejaculation in my pants stopped anything from happening. I felt guilty over what might have happened and drove her home . . .' At 20 he got a room and a car of his own. 'My life changed dramatically. After a week or two I picked up a girl of 17 while I was cruising for just that purpose . . . She gave in after four or five hours. By this time I couldn't get an erection. The following day, though, we met again and had inter-course in the car. I began to date rather than to pick up girls after that. The relationships lasted anywhere from one date to three months, usually two to four weeks. I had sexual intercourse with most of them. The common denominator was my uncaring or mere surface feeling for them.' In short, his newly acquired success in obtaining intercourse did little to improve his feelings towards women. He still had guilt feelings about sex, and once the act was completed, he had little use for the woman concerned. 'For me sex seemed to be an indication that the relationship was soon to be over, for a girl often seemed cheapened to me if I had sexual relations with her.'

Over the next few years, he drifted from one job to another, depressed and aimless, continuing his promiscuous sexual habits without satisfaction to himself, and sinking ever more deeply into delinquent ways. 'I was getting more and more into debt. I had good intentions of paying them off, but it seemed I was too weak or too dumb to stay away from gambling and girls. So I gradually stopped payment on all of my debts and left without a forwarding address . . . Very seldom did a period of more than a few days go by when I did not have sexual intercourse. The trouble was that I did not particu-larly like these girls. I always seemed to be lonely and dissatisfied with myself. Also, I began using the technique of telling the girl I had picked up off the street, once we were in some isolated spot, that she had a choice of walking home or having sex with me. Thus, the possibility of rape came nearer . . .

'One girl I became very close to for about three months. I was thinking of marriage, even of going to the university, for that was what she was doing. I loved her till the end came. I believe the love was a two-way effort for about two months. Then she was told by a girlfriend about my past and that I had been in a reformatory. That likely was not the determining factor in the break, more likely it was my seriousness and possessiveness towards her.'

Following a further conviction for robbery (again of a female victim), there was a brief attempt at reinstatement in the community. But 'despair and depression' set in, he went on the run from parole, took an overdose of sleeping pills and was unconscious for three days. After various spells of detention, prolonged by fruitless escapes, he finally regained his liberty and was once again befriended by a sympathetic family. He resumed educational courses and a part-time job, but again began inexplicably to fail. 'I had hoped that a different setting might help me in going straight. Life with these people was good, but as I seemed to be failing in school I began to feel guilty. I did not want to disappoint them because of what I felt to be their expectations of me, and of course because of the debt I owed for their kindness. I did not tell anyone what I was feeling. I rented a car, bought some camping supplies and set out on the highway. I had no clear destination or purpose in mind.' He had not driven many miles before he picked up a girl hitch-hiker, drove off the road, pulled a knife and raped her.

As in a number of these cases, this man's attitude to sex was notably inhibited and guilt-ridden. During his youth he had found girls, especially desirable girls, intimidating and unapproachable. This was extremely hurtful to him because, driven by over-sensitivity about his appearance and by other inferiority fears, he had a great urge to excel physically, intellectually and socially in order to prove his masculinity. He never could reach a level of performance that quelled his anxiety, and in any event the neurotic intensity with which he pursued these goals was self-defeating. His failure to establish himself in an independent career, criminal or otherwise, and above all his failure to achieve a satisfying heterosexual relationship, angered and depressed him to the point of suicide. It was against this background of emotional turmoil that rape became a real possibility.

Example 12

All his life he longed for love and acceptance. He rarely found it because he was for ever testing goodwill to breaking point by troublesome, attention-seeking behaviour. 'At school I was always showing off, pulling girls' hair, dropping things on the floor in order to bend down and peer up skirts and smoking in the classroom. I guess I wanted attention, or to try to impress Dennis, one of the bigger kids in the class. I was scared of him and didn't want to appear a coward in his eyes . . . The guys all used to call me by a derisory nickname and it hurt real deep inside. I felt the girls didn't like me on account of that.'

The earliest sexual incidents he recalled were all associated with violent misbehaviour, guilt and rejection. At age 8 'I can remember playing with two little girls in a hole we had made underneath one of the houses. I believe I made them take off their panties by grabbing them and choking them.' Soon after this 'one time in the gym in the basement a kid who was bigger than me made me suck him off. I was frightened and disgusted.' When he was 12 or 13 a good-looking blonde girl at school showed some apparently sympathetic interest, but when he plucked up courage to ask for a date, she turned him down. 'I had thought she liked me, and I felt real hateful to her for leading me on. One Sunday, when her family was all at church, I walked into her house and smashed everything in her room. I ripped some paper money to shreds and then lay on her bed and smelled her panties and bras. Everyone knew I had done it. A few days later I was sent to a psychiatric ward.'

In the years that followed he spent various periods in psychiatric institutions and children's detention homes. He ran away time and time again. He discovered at a very tender age that he could find a refuge with male homosexuals. 'On the run from the hospital I was hitch-hiking and got picked up by a Roman Catholic priest who was a homosexual.' This man was kind to him and gave him food, clothing and shelter. 'I stayed there a few days. He bathed me every night and sucked my penis later in bed. I enjoyed all the attention . . .' On various subsequent occasions he returned to this priest. 'I enjoyed being bathed, fondled and fussed over again.

'I often felt so lonely and unloved and I so much wanted to go to a woman and cry on her breasts and be hugged with love and warmth. A lot of young student nurses in the hospital felt sorry for me. That was how I became aware I was good-looking. I was a real good actor looking for attention from these nurses, and when I was ignored I would start swearing or smash a window. When I was 15 I went to live in the home of one of these nurses and I worked at a filling station. After a few weeks I just up and took off. Maybe I felt I couldn't handle the job. I do know I was never given anything responsible to do. That hurt me and made me feel small.'

Soon after this he began to have encounters with homosexuals for money. 'I stood outside of a bar and was picked up by a man and taken to his hotel room. I wanted to hurry to get there because I felt so ashamed and disgusted with myself. He sucked me but couldn't make me come, even when he hand masturbated me. While he was doing this I kept one of my arms over my eyes because I was so ashamed.' Although he soon got more used to the routine, he never lost his sense of shame. 'I spent my money foolishly and began regularly to sell my body to homosexuals. I would just stand in front of a bus station and wait to be picked up. A lot of times I would get fifteen dollars or twenty dollars, but I always felt ashamed and disgusted with myself. When some of them wanted intercourse with me in the anus, or wanted me to suck them off, I would always refuse, but there were times when I would enjoy the necking and kissing part because I felt I wanted to be loved. When I made money from a queer I would go down to where all the hookers hung out, hoping perhaps, to become a pimp, or at least to be accepted by someone.'

At the age of 17 his attempts at heterosexual relationships were anything but satisfactory. He was staying in a cheap lodging-house. 'The only washroom was opposite my door. A retarded girl called Elsie lived in the place. She was about 12. When Elsie came to the washroom, I would scare her, be right behind her and grab her. I would throw her on the bed, pulling her by the hair and grabbing her throat, pulling up her dress and pulling her panties down. I did this quite often. Sometimes I would make her suck my penis, or I would try to put it up her anus or vagina, but I never really knew if I ever entered her because I would come off so quickly. I was scared of being caught, but I think I also enjoyed the danger part of it.

'At about this time there was one girl who came to be the nearest thing I've ever had to a steady girlfriend. She would come down to see me every night after work, and she would give me most of her pay cheque. Even though I had her initial tatooed on me, I don't believe I really loved her, I just used her. We would often go up to my room to neck. She let me fondle her and suck her breasts, but nothing further. I believe I was happy with the arrangement, for I never manhandled her . . . I finally persuaded her to have intercourse, but it turned out to be a failure. I just couldn't get an erection. After that our relationship went downhill. I began hitting the cheap wine, playing the queers, sleeping in parks and flop houses . . .'

After that 'I got bored and disgusted at what I was becoming.' He returned to the homosexual priest he had known. 'After a week or so I was sick of him and planned to rob him. I took his Sunday collection money, threatened to expose him, and made him drive me to the town where there were plenty of whores. I wanted to be part of the action. I wanted to be noticed, I wanted to be a big-time criminal.' Instead, it was not long before he was back at the priest's house 'hoping he would forgive me. But by nightfall he hadn't shown up, so I broke into his house, helped myself to something to eat and fell asleep. When the housekeeper arrived and found the back door smashed open she reported it to the police and I was woken up and arrested for breaking and entering and sent to prison.

'I was dead scared with all the stories I had heard about blood on my knife or shit on my boots. I knew I was no fighter, more like a coward. Fortunately, I met Fred, an old solid convict who became, in jail slang, my sugar daddy. Not once did he touch me in any way. At first he may have wanted to, but he got to like me as a person, or maybe like a son.' Even this relationship came to a sour end. 'At the time I got parole he was making me a present. Through childishness I told him to shove it. The morning I was to go out I stood before his cell and called him, but he didn't answer. I cried when the guard led me out to get dressed. If it hadn't been for Fred, I know for a fact that I would have been a frightened coward and given in to a different kind of sugar daddy or else been raped.'

On release from prison, he drifted along much as before, making his way by petty crime and selling himself to homosexuals, associating with prostitutes and pimps, finding little satisfaction anywhere, feeling worthless and hopeless and dulling the impact of reality with heavy drinking. The following description of a sexual encounter when he was 21 typifies the cynical, aggressive and exploitative attitudes towards heterosexual relationships he had developed:

'She was a whore for a rounder called Joe, who was buying the drinks all the afternoon. Finally Joe told her to go turn a trick. I left something on the table for Joe to get some more drinks and said I'd be right back. I went after her and asked her why bother to pick up a trick? I could give her twenty dollars and a room. We went to a hotel and I made her strip naked. She wasn't bad looking and had nice breasts and I must have come into her three times. After I had come the first time, she thought that I was going to get up off her, but I pulled her roughly by the hair and finished my business. As I got up she mentioned the money I had promised her. I told her to go fuck herself, and threatened to kill her if she said anything. I said that Joe wouldn't believe her anyway. I walked off down the street still a little drunk and laughing my head off at what a sucker job I'd pulled on her.'

He was equally exploitative in his relations with homosexuals. 'I was the man and they kept me, and I would do it to them up the anus. While I was having intercourse with them I would imagine some good-looking girl I had seen recently in a movie or on the street. I would treat these gay queens roughly while driving my penis into them. Then I'd take their money and get drunk on it. Sometimes I'd spend a few days with one of them, and then steal all that was worthwhile taking from the place, like radios and watches . . .'

This last example illustrates with unusual clarity the deadly progression common to most of these cases. Early rejection experiences engender ideas of worthlessness and doubts about masculinity. This produces an urge to prove oneself at all costs. Failure to do so results in increasing anger and resentment. An exploitative or violent approach to women, who are perceived as the main agents of frustration, relieves the anger temporarily, at the same time creating an illusion of masculinity regained.

* * * * *

Abbreviated and incomplete as they are, these case histories make one point abundantly plain. Although some were superficially withdrawn or subdued and others more extraverted and aggressive, if their own descriptions of their unhappiness are any guide, all twelve were chronically maladjusted individuals. They all complained of serious dissatisfaction with their sex lives, on the emotional plane if not in physical performance, which had been present long before their careers as sexual criminals began. Their troubles were quite serious enough to warrant an attempt at psychotherapy even if they had never gone so far as to commit a sexual crime.

CHAPTER IV

The Final Outburst

The few weeks or months prior to their final acts of sexual aggression proved the most fascinating part of these men's life histories. At this period the interplay between stressful situations and personality defects was particularly obvious. The descriptions vividly illustrate how inappropriate responses to difficulties create still more difficulties, increase frustration still further, until some catastrophic outburst occurs. In some cases there had been previous episodes of sexual violence, generally of a less serious nature, but the latest incidents, the ones that had brought the men into their present situation as penitentiary inmates, were the ones which forced them to admit to having lost control over themselves and made them acknowledge their need to change in order to prevent similar outbursts in the future. In half of the cases the incidents in question had taken place during states of intoxication resulting from increasingly serious abuse of alcohol or drugs, which was in turn a reflection of ever more frantic attempts to escape from mounting frustrations.

It will be seen that in this final phase of their stories the men reacted with extreme recklessness or extreme ferocity to stresses that others might well take in their stride. To appreciate why this happened, it is necessary to keep in mind the details given in previous sections. Each man had been sensitized to stress, first by the nature of his early upbringing, and second by life-long difficulties in heterosexual relationships and in the struggle to maintain his own conception of an appropriately masculine stance.

Example 1

'After several years of marriage my wife finally got pregnant and we had a baby boy. We were both happy about that. She was a perfect mother. I was doing well at my job and had had some promotion. I was now doing one of the best jobs at the plant, but it was also one of the hardest.' In an effort to cement his marriage and prove himself a good provider he borrowed heavily in order to be able to construct an ambitious new family home. The venture failed, owing to a series of unexpected misfortunes. First, he was sued for a debt from an old accident litigation that he thought was finished with. The court ordered him to make monthly payments and to stop building. At his work he had long been in dispute with his superiors about job assignments, but now some differences with his foreman led to him being demoted and taken off the job he particularly liked. Even after he ceased the building operations that he had set his heart on, he failed to keep up with payments on the loan he had borrowed to begin the construction. He became angry and discouraged.

His wife gave birth to a second child, but this time he was not so pleased, because it seemed to him she was becoming too engrossed in her maternal concerns. 'The attention I was used to from her was starting to decline. I realize now that my mother had spoiled me as a child and that in the first years of our marriage my wife had spoiled me as an adult. She used to wait on me hand and foot. Her mother was quite disgusted to see her do it. Now she started complaining when I asked for a cup of coffee, saying things like "Can't you get it yourself?" She started saying she was tired and resisted many of my love-making advances. I told myself it did not matter and tried to convince myself that I was not dependent upon her for anything.'

In recalling this period he realized he had been selfish and unrealistic. He would never help with the kids, because he thought it unmanly. If he heard the baby crying at night he would kick his wife out of bed, never thinking to see to it himself. She would stay out of bed for a long time, rocking the baby to quieten it, so he could sleep undisturbed. No doubt she resented his attitude inwardly, although she did not complain. When she began to rebuff his sexual advances sometimes, he was so unwilling to admit to any dependence upon her that he would actually push her away when she did try to put her arms round him. A vicious circle was set up which prevented him from showing his wife his real feelings for her. Although he hated the job he had been given at work, he was resolved to stick it out. Every time he passed the unfinished house he felt badly about it, because he could see no way he would ever get it finished.

'As I look back at this time, I can see a distinct pattern. The attitude of wanting to get away from it all, plus a deep despair and self-hatred that would at times make it impossible for me to stay around the house and relax in the evening. I needed only a few hours away from home to realize that I missed my wife and home. I would usually return within that period. I would always return home by ten or so as I did not like leaving her late by herself, but by that time she would be tired and not interested in talking about my low moods. At the time I never thought of these moods as a kind of danger signal, but my wife worried about them and did try to talk to me about them sometimes. She knew I was straining myself at the job, and many times she told me to quit and get a position that did not make such demands. I ignored her advice and worked all the harder, hating myself for not being able to bring home a bigger pay cheque and not being able to talk to anyone about my problems.'

It was during this period of strain, when he had got into the habit of driving round in the car in the evening to escape the tensions he felt at home, that he committed the sexual attacks that led to his imprisonment. It was a time when marital tension and failure to communicate was at its worst. Although she blamed herself for it afterwards, his wife felt at the time that refusing sex was her only weapon in the marital struggle. The situation in the home was complicated by the temporary presence of a problem foster child, daughter of one of his relatives, who was troublesomely lazy and undisciplined. 'She kept her room dirty, left the bathroom in a mess, and the wife was for ever picking up after her. Then she started coming in late. The wife began to resent her presence. It got to the point where either she had to go or the wife would have a nervous breakdown or our marriage would break up.' Although critical of his wife for failing to cope with the situation, he reluctantly arranged for the girl's removal, and after that the tension in the home lessened.

Feeling guilty about his sexual escapades, and especially about the fact that they involved cheating on his wife, who had no idea what was happening, he made a determined effort to curb himself. He paid more attention to his wife, took up a hobby that afforded a less dangerous distraction than driving around alone, and he secured a job that was more congenial. Nearly a year elapsed without any further offences, but then the cycle showed signs of repeating itself. Wanting, as always, to prove his powers as a male provider, he gave up his hobby and told his employer he was willing to work seven days a week to get more money. The more he took on, the more the old feeling of strain and discontent came back. One evening, when driving home, he had to brake suddenly to avoid a hitch-hiker. He stopped and gave her a lift. She happened to be one of his victims from a year before. She made no comment, but she recognized him, identified the vehicle, and reported him to the police. He was arrested and charged with the offences he had committed the previous year.

Following his admission to prison, he was tested by a psychologist who concluded: 'A tendency to pent-up emotions in a person with rigid but brittle defence mechanisms. Many people with this kind of defence, because they unrealistically avoid unpleasant conflicts, are customarily kind and considerate, but are liable to unexpected assaultative acts.'

Example 2

At the time when this man committed the sexual offences that led to his current imprisonment, he was still on parole from a previous sentence for similar behaviour. He was aged 22 when he was released. On his first night out he arranged to meet an old school friend called Leonard. He had always been a loner, a person who found it hard to make friends and especially hard to get on with girls, but with this particular friend, Leonard, he felt at ease. He did not approve about the way Leonard carried on sometimes, but he went along with it because he feared losing his chief source of companionship.

'We had a few drinks at a hotel, and then I walked with him to the bus stop. While we were in the hotel, two girls sat at a table close to us, but we never got together until Leonard and I were waiting for the bus. They had a car and offered us a ride, and we went with them. Doris drove the car. The other girl was her sister. She drove Leonard home first and then dropped her sister off, and drove me home last. We sat in the car for a while and arranged to go to a movie on the weekend; we went steady together for a few months. I explained to her my parole situation. I became jealous, and would keep buying her things to stop me from losing her, but it seemed to separate us rather than bring us together. An ex-boyfriend of hers turned up in the town. She told me he was only coming on a visit, so she wanted to spend some time alone with him to show him around. I met him, but never liked him. He looked to me like a lazy slob. I helped to get him a job, he couldn't stay sober and didn't want to work. I felt I was fighting a losing battle because Doris always seemed to be supporting him and spending time helping him. Finally, I told her to make up her mind to which of us she wanted. She said she wasn't sure and she wouldn't answer, so I got mad and walked out.'

At this point, he felt particularly miserable and inadequate at being unable to compete with Doris's boyfriend. He started associating with Leonard again, who seemed to be about the only friend he had. Together they went around drinking and picking up girl hitch-hikers. One of these girls complained to the police. This would be about two months after his release on parole. While this offence was under investigation, and before he was arrested, he met another woman. 'She was separated from her husband when I met her. Her three children were living with their father at the time. I liked her companionship and used to spend weekends at her apartment. I knew she was separated, but didn't find out that she had three children until after we moved in together and were living common-law. I liked her very much, but I would get upset when she would compare me to her husband. I told her that if she thought that much of him she should go back to him and try to straighten out their problems. I gradually got the impression that she was just using me to get back at her husband, or to justify leaving him. I walked out and left her a couple of times because of this feeling. She moved back in with her husband for a short time, but then a few weeks later she phoned and asked me to come to her place. She told me that her husband had come home drunk and beat her and the kids and then went out with another woman. She was still crying and shaking when I got to her place. This was the first time that I met her kids. After this incident she filed the divorce papers and asked me to move in with her and her kids. I loved her and the kids and probably would have married her then if it had been possible, but we decided on a common-law relationship until the divorce was finalized. I thought at the time that our relationship was good, but in reality it consisted of arguing, sex, and work. We never really spent much time together, at home or socializing, because our work and interests were different. We also had communication problems that were unresolved. I was working on shift from 11:00 P.M. to 7:00 A.M., and she worked from 8:00 A.M. to 4:00 P.M. She was also getting involved in extra overtime responsibilities. She was earning a better wage than I was, and in addition she was in a higher status position. Our daily routine began by my going to work at 11:00 P.M. to 7:00 A.M., then I would come home, pick her up and drive her to work, drive back home and take the kids to school. Then I would go back home and sleep until 3:00 P.M. before picking up the kids at school and then proceeding to her place of work to collect her. We spent supper and most of the evening together, and then I would go back to work. This got to be a monotonous routine, so on the weekends I would phone Leonard and we would go out for coffee or a couple of drinks together just to get out of the house for a change. I wasn't interested in dating or picking up other women for sex or companionship, because I loved the woman I was living with and our sexual relationship was more than adequate.

'At this time my feelings at work were mixed, some good some bad. I didn't like having supervisors watching over me, and I felt embarrassed when I was complimented. I felt inferior to most of the other workers. I got bored on some jobs, but I never dealt with my anger and resentment and I tended to act on impulse rather than common sense. I never dealt with any of my feelings. I usually rationalized all my problems, anxieties and frustrations and kept them inside, fearing to express them. I think this contributed a great deal to my behaviour.'

Such was his life at the time when once again he went out drinking with his friend, Leonard, and once again committed a sexual offence. The development was almost identical to that in the last example, with marked discouragement about personal performance at work and at home, inability to communicate his feelings to his wife and mounting resentment at his miserable predicament.

Example 3

The difficulties which pushed this man into a frenzy of frustration, and led him to commit several sexual attacks in quick succession, were little enough in themselves, but in his own super-sensitive, distorted viewpoint they amounted to intolerable burdens and insoluble problems. They rankled continually in his mind and he was furious with himself for failing to cope with them.

At the critical time in question he was planning to marry the woman he was living with and he was exceedingly anxious to do the right thing by her. He had a job that required him to pass examinations, and also to undergo medical fitness tests, in order to obtain the promotion and the increased pay that he considered essential if he were to be able to make adequate provision for a wife and a prospective family. He was hurt by the fact that his fiancée felt she would need to continue working, even though she did not seem to mind very much. Unfortunately, he was not the sort of person to confide his anxieties to her or to lower his self-imposed masculine ideals to suit the limitations of reality.

What did concern his fiancée was his moodiness, irritability and uncommunicativeness. As he himself admitted later, 'I was very difficult to get along with at this time. I was a great worrier about everything, and there were several things on my mind.' He had recently sustained a heavy blow on the head in an accident at work, which was never reported. Ever since he suffered from recurrent headaches and occasional blurred vision. He worried a great deal about these symptoms, but kept them secret from everyone for fear he might be found to suffer from some condition that would ruin his chances of promotion. Meantime, he was anxiously awaiting confirmation that the successful results of a recent examination would lead to the anticipated promotion. He had agreed to a date for the wedding, and preparations were going on for a celebration on a scale too large for his taste. He hated the prospect of enforced sociability and disliked having so many people necessarily involved in arranging things for him. He could not reveal how badly he felt about it, because he did not want to do anything to spoil what might be for his fiancée the most important day in her life. He resolved to sacrifice his own feelings and suffer in silence, but inwardly he was anything but calm and happy about the situation.

One evening he was in a particularly bad mood. His fiancée did not want him to go out, but he had a repair job that needed doing and he went out to call on a friend who had promised to loan him some tools for the purpose. He found that his friend had gone out forgetting to leave the tools, so he decided to drive on to his place of work to get them from there. On arrival, 'I felt pissed off, so I just turned around and parked the car and sat there thinking.' He sat in the car a long time, brooding over his troubles. When finally he drove off, he noticed a woman walking along. He stopped, got out, and assaulted her.

After his release from prison, his fiancée stuck by him, but everything else went wrong. He had expected to be reinstated at work, but when he turned up he found to his fury and consternation that his job was gone. All he could find was a very low-paid caretaker job arranged in a humiliating way through a friend. When he asked for a rise he got it, but was put on half-time, so that in effect he was poorer than ever. He started fretting about debts, and every expense that came along was a cause for anguish. 'Things were very unstable at this time. I was hardly talking to my fiancée. I had a lot of time on my hands that I did not know what to do with. I felt pressured by the second wedding date that had been fixed for a month ahead. I was very down. I felt angry inside all the time, and I was intolerant and demanding with my fiancée.' She continued working while he kept trying for a better-paid job, but with no success, and becoming increasingly depressed. He knew he needed psychiatric help, but he could not pay for it and a referral he had expected through the penal services had not materialized. His fiancée was aware he was in a dangerous state, and anxious about his using her car. There were times when he would shut himself up alone in a room and become so self-absorbed, 'spaced-out', that he did not seem to hear when spoken to. She tried without success to obtain a psychiatric referral for him through her own doctor. One evening a small thing went wrong with the electricity. He tried to fix it, but failed to do so, and was forced to call an electrician. The thought of this petty failure and the extra expense involved in calling in outside help proved the last straw. After the repairman had gone his fiancée found him literally shaking with impotent rage, but quite unable to explain why he was so upset.

Next day, less than a month after his release from his previous prison sentence, he committed the first of three further sexual attacks, spread over a period of two weeks. After his arrest his fiancée realized, from the enormous quantity of petrol he had charged up to her account, that during this period he must have been driving around on his own for hours at a time every day in a vain attempt to calm himself down. Had he been given some psychiatric help or more effective after-care during this critical period, the dangerous build-up of tension might have been interrupted and the sexual attacks prevented.

Example 4

This man's engagement and marriage were his first serious commitments to a lasting heterosexual relationship. Unfortunately, his image of the dominant, masculine role in the ideal marriage was hard to reconcile either with his own inferiority feelings or with his wife's temperament.

'Brenda's parents had told her to stay away from me, but it worked the opposite way, for she was curious to see what I was like . . . At first I tried to have sex with her on a few occasions, but never got very far. I still kept going out with her because I liked her as a person, not purely for sex reasons as was the case with most of my previous girlfriends.' After a time, she took a secretarial course and obtained an office job. Following various attempts at different jobs he swallowed his pride and took a cleaning job in the same organization as his fiancée. 'It bothered me that I was a cleaner when she was working in the office, but then I got a job advancement to the maintenance department, taking care of the machines. I was really happy with that.

'Her parents had changed their minds since I had settled down and did not object when we got engaged. It was my mother who got worked up and kept telling us we were too young. She thought Brenda was too outspoken for me. She was 18 and I was 19 at the time. She was bugging me for a year for the engagement ring, so I was pressured into getting her one a little bit sooner than I had wanted to. Brenda liked drinking and going to parties, so we got along in that area, but we were complete opposites in lots of ways. She would be the life and soul of the party and not shy to talk to anybody, while I would usually sit back and talk to just one or two of the friends I knew. She never had any trouble meeting people or making new friends, although her outgoing nature did get her into some bad arguments. I've always wanted to be that way, but with my personality I couldn't, so I think I looked to her for what I didn't have myself. . . . She embarrassed me sometimes by saying silly things before really thinking them out. I had told her about it, but she seemed just to brush it off. When that happened, I would go on drinking until I couldn't care less.'

From the outset, Brenda disliked his close tie with his family and resented the time and money he would spend on his mother's concerns after they were married. 'With both of us working we managed to get the house into some sort of shape, financially and otherwise. But because of all the work needed on the house, and our shift hours, we never went out too much. If I did go out it would be to help my mother get her place fixed up. I didn't like my hours of work because of the lack of time I could spend with my wife, and she didn't care for it either and told me so quite often. . . . There wasn't much going to parties now. I started going out drinking quite a lot at weekends. I think at this point Brenda and I started to grow apart. She had her own girlfriends she visited sometimes during the week and at weekends while I would go out with my boyfriends to beer parlours and night clubs. She had cut her drinking almost completely, but I had continued on as before. She rarely came out to the beer parlour with me because she did not like the atmosphere there, or all the drinking involved. We didn't have many interests in common that we could do together. We went to a show the odd time at weekends, but I would always want to go to the beer parlour afterwards, and that caused some bad feelings between us. My friends would be there with their girlfriends and I wanted to join them. I always felt there was something missing if we didn't go. This was a consistent clash between us, and most of the time it would turn out that she stayed at home. I couldn't stay home on my days off, I was too bored. I thought that going to the beer parlour was the only thing to do. We never had any recreational things we could do together.

'We had many arguments about my going to the beer parlour with my friends and coming home drunk, but I kept going anyway. Brenda could be quite domineering and had a bad temper, which would come out over any little thing. It really got to me, but I rarely said anything for fear it would make things worse. I would rather sit back and try to forget it than sit down and talk things over . . . I got into the way of holding things inside. We were both lacking communication between each other.'

Very reluctantly he gave up the job he enjoyed because she objected to the hours. 'I held off as long as I could and hated to leave, but I didn't have much choice.' The change failed to improve his feelings about the marriage. 'There was no talk between us about why I was going out drinking all the time or what we could do together instead. I wasn't all that happy sexually either. She would come up with the usual saying that she was tired and didn't feel like it at the moment. She said she felt that every time I touched her I had only one thing on my mind, she knew exactly what would take place next, and I was just using her. I had never thought of it that way.' On one occasion there was a jealous scene when they did go out together. Annoyed that she had got into conversation with some people, he went off to speak with his own friends, leaving her to look after herself. Then he more or less challenged her to go off with the man she was talking to if she wanted to. She did so, and did not return until very late. That episode hurt him more than anything. In addition to these domestic troubles he was worried about his work. He was made redundant and forced to look for another job. He resented the fact that his wife was able to earn so easily and readily, and he brooded over her silence about what went on at her work.

'I started having fantasies of following girls in the street and having sex with them. These thoughts would come to me after I had been drinking, I can't recall really thinking about it when I was sober.' It was one evening, when he was sitting alone drinking in the beer parlour, his friends having all departed and left him mulling over his problems and reluctant to go home, that his thoughts turned to rape. He walked out into the night with the intention of looking for a woman, any woman, and so he committed his first offence. According to a police report his blood alcohol level, which was assessed shortly after he had attacked a woman, was extremely high. It was surprising that he was still capable of coordinated action, and certainly his judgment must have been seriously impaired.

Example 5

Abuse of intoxicants, an unstable marriage, and a continuing desire to try to prove his masculinity were the most obvious factors in precipitating this man's crime. As with several others in the group, his final outburst was preceded by a number of danger signals that might have served to prevent what happened had action been taken in time.

Very soon after his marriage to an already pregnant girl, he began to find the domestic ties of a young wife and baby extremely irksome. He had long been a heavy drinker and until he married he had been accustomed to an unfettered way of life, cruising bars, accepting invitations to parties, and meeting many different girls. 'After work the other guys would go to the bar, and I really wanted to stop with them. I didn't do so, but there were times when I wished I could do away with all my responsibilities if only I could do so without hurting my wife.

'We had been together for about three months when one of the guys asked me if I would like to go into town with him. I said yes. I told the wife, and she was kind of angry, but she said I could go.' He went off with his friends and, of course, they were drinking heavily. 'After we left that night club, Bill gave me the keys of his car and asked me to get lost for a few hours while he tried to make it with the broad he was with. I drove around not knowing what to do with myself. I gave a couple of girls a ride who were hitch-hiking. The thought came to me that I would like to reach over and hold their breasts or pussy, but I made no move. Then I picked up another girl. She was going quite a distance. We started talking and she told me she was 19 years old. I thought of making a pass at her, but did not do so. When I stopped to let her out, I grabbed her by the shoulder. She screamed and I let her go. We sat and talked for a few minutes and I tried to make excuses for grabbing her. She said she had been grabbed by some guys once before. I then drove her the rest of the way down the road to her home and she got out. I drove around for about an hour after that but did not try to pick up any more hitch-hikers.'

His own reactions on that occasion surprised and worried him, but worse was soon to come. He was feeling particularly tired of both his domestic and his work routine. 'I became fed up and one evening I told the manager I needed some time off.' He took a week off from work and went into town where a friend was getting married. 'I talked the wife into not going because I wanted to get away from her for a while.' On one of the evenings during this stay in town 'I met some friends and went with them and took some LSD. On the way home I met another friend of mine with his girl. They saw that I was stoned. I gave them a ride home. Then the idea came that I would like to go looking for a woman to rape her.' He became very disturbed by these thoughts and went home and started talking to his wife, telling her that he needed to see a psychiatrist. He did in fact try to be seen at a clinic as an emergency, but was sent from one place to another. In the end he was told he would need to obtain a doctor's referral and that it would be several months before he would have an interview. 'I hung up the phone and decided to run away.' He withdrew some money and drove off. 'On the way I started to calm down a bit because I was away from it all and free . . .' He turned back and went home. He told his wife he had done it because he had been stoned on LSD. He did not tell her that he had long felt like rushing off to escape from work and responsibilities.

He continued to have fantasies about rape. Soon after, he found himself fascinated by a television play in which a man used ether to put girls to sleep before raping them. He thought a lot about this, because it seemed to him that he could never get what he wanted from certain girls unless they were overpowered. He noticed a can of industrial ether at work, but it was labelled poisonous, so he tried to put the idea out of his mind because he did not want to hurt anyone.

For some months longer he continued his routine married life. His wife became pregnant again. He was always yearning to go out and have a good time, and she was beginning to nag him. One evening he went out with a friend and got drunk. She came to the bar to take him home. 'I got mad and drove her home and told her to go to hell and went out again.' He began imagining having sex with other women while he was having intercourse with his wife. Sometimes when she was out of the house he would masturbate to fantasies of other women.

One night it was arranged that his wife should go and stay at her sister's because her sister's husband was away, and this would give him a chance to have a late night at the bar. 'I told her that, but truthfully I wanted the chance to be with another woman. I drove up to town and met a friend of mine, who was with some girls. I picked them up and drove around for a while. The girl who was sitting beside me suggested we buy some booze. I told her that I wasn't spending money unless she planned on sticking around the whole evening. She said sure, so I went and bought a couple of cases of beer and some wine. We went to my friend's place and started drinking. After a while she said she would just run across the road to fetch something from where her girlfriend lived. She did not come back. I was really angry inside. I should have known better than to trust the bitch.'

In this mood of anger and frustration he remained drinking on his own for a couple of hours. 'Then I decided to go downtown for a while. I went driving around and I had definite thoughts of raping a woman.' He saw a young woman walking down the street and got out intending to waylay her. He had thoughts of knocking her to the ground and raping her. Had she not unexpectedly crossed the road, thus avoiding the confrontation, he would certainly have attacked her. When the enormity of what he had nearly done came to him, he was quite frightened. 'I drove around in a sort of daze for half an hour. Then I saw the girl that had been with me earlier hitch-hiking. I picked her up, drove out into the bush and parked. We started necking for a while. I wasn't angry at her any more. All my frustration was out of me by this time. She wanted to go home because it was late, so I just took her home.'

For some weeks after that he tried to keep a tighter rein on himself and did not go out so much. However, as the wife was expecting her baby soon, he had fantasies of bringing women to his home during the week she would be away. On the evening of her first day's confinement in hospital, he visited her and then went to the bar to do some drinking. He met an old friend who had some marijuana. 'I remember him saying he had one joint of super weed left. We smoked it and I was nearly stoned almost instantly. We then drove to the bar and started to drink beer.' From then on his recollection becomes uncertain. He was playing pool and trying to pick a fight with some other men who wanted the table. There was so much disturbance that the barman refused to serve anyone in the place until he left. He refused to go and said they would have to throw him out. He must have seemed very wild for nobody made a move to force him. He walked out of his own accord in the end, shouting that he was going to get a gun to shoot the bartender.

'The next thing I knew, I was driving along the street with the idea of rape on my mind.'

Example 6

This man's final outburst of crimes took place soon after his release from prison where he had been serving a sentence for previous similar sexual offences. He had lost his wife and family and lost all respect. He felt there was nothing more to lose, so he lived only for sexual gratification. 'I was feeling bitter against the law, but even more bitter against myself. I wasn't long out of jail before I was assaulting again.' He mixed with prostitutes and the like, and found a woman to live with, but he was also going out with lots of other girls at the same time. Even so, he was restless and dissatisfied. When a friend lost his job and moved away to look for another, he went along too, telling the woman he had been living with that he had to go to see his sick mother. 'By this time I had reached my deepest degradation. I would do almost anything to satisfy the sex urge, but I was never violent just for the sake of being violent.'

He moved back temporarily to a town where he was known. Unfortunately, 'everyone knew my record, and I got into many fights . . .' He had found another woman, but she started to drink, so it was time to move on again. It was late at night and he had been the round of the drinking bars when 'the urge to prowl came over me again. I parked the car and started walking, checking windows.' He was looking for a woman on her own. Before long, he found one and forced his way in . . . 'I knew I could not go on without being caught, but I could not stop either. I didn't think too much at that time. I don't think I really cared what happened to me.'

Example 7

As with so many examples in this group, this man's marriage proved only a temporary solution to his sexual problems. 'Before and after our marriage we got on really well. We did everything together, and I helped her with the house and washing the dishes whenever I had any spare time. We would sit and talk for hours at a time, we were never at a loss for something to talk about. We went everywhere together. We waited on each other as if we belonged to each other. I have never known a friendship such as this. We shared our time, knowledge, our bodies, and our lives. . . . We went to a few drinking parties with the same bunch of kids that we had grown up with. We knew all the same people and didn't have the hassle of getting to know and like each other's friends. We didn't drink very often or very much, only to be sociable. When I got married, I decided that there would be no alcohol problems in my marriage. Alcohol had played an important part in my parents' troubles and I wasn't going to let it destroy my marriage . . . I was an avid sportsman, and she was very understanding when I wanted to partake in my sports. She would come with me sometimes, although she didn't care for sports.

'Our problems started when we moved into the upstairs suite of her parents' house so that we might be able to save enough money to put a down payment on a home of our own. After about three or four months of living there, I got laid off from my job. I was without work for three months. My wife went out and got a job. I didn't want her to work, but I had no choice. We needed the money, but it hurt that my wife had to go out to support me. I felt guilty about it, and went into a depression. I couldn't find a job no matter how hard I looked, I had guilty feelings about that. Some days I didn't even bother looking for a job, I just gave up and felt sorry for myself and lied to the wife about how hard I had been looking.

'At this point I started feeling that I couldn't talk to her, I really felt inadequate and sorry for myself. I started thinking about taking out other girls, and I started masturbating, which I hadn't done since before we were married. Nothing was going right any more and I didn't know whether I was coming or going. Some days I would go uptown and fantasize about taking out other girls. I wanted to talk to someone and prove that I wasn't all that bad. All this time my wife was working and I was jealous of her. She would come home and tell me about this guy and that with whom she worked. She made it seem that she thought the world of them, and I would get all choked up inside and try to get her to quit the job, but she refused. All this time that she was working, I was running her to the hilt with sex. Whenever she was in my sight I had to have sex with her, sometimes three to five times a day. Even then, I had thoughts that maybe the child wasn't mine.

'Then my father died and I was really broken up about it. She sympathized and did everything she could, but I found it hard to accept that Dad could be dead. I took out a couple of girls and had sex with them without my wife knowing but nothing seemed to make me any happier. I drove around the streets looking for girls to pick up and started thinking seriously about raping someone.

'I was still striving to have sex with my wife whenever she would allow it, forcing myself upon her all the time. I felt really inadequate and unloved and I was determined to get some sex outside. Picking up strange women and never seeing them again was a way of doing this without losing my wife. If a girl said no to sex, I would have it anyway. I could not talk to my wife and I longed to talk to someone. I had got so that I couldn't open up at this time. I think that if I had been able to talk to some of the girls, I would not have raped them.'

When his baby was born, 'My wife wanted me to buy some flowers to take to the hospital, but I didn't have any money and I was unable to get her anything. I really felt like an inconsiderate cheapskate. Well, when she came home with the baby things went pretty good for the next few months. Then we moved into the basement of what had been my father's house in order to save money, but we were not happy living there. We argued a lot about it. I went out then and committed the sexual attacks that first brought me to prison. These offences were all in the space of a month. I was bailed out of prison, but when I got home, I found the police and a social worker had talked to my wife and had convinced her that I was no good for her and she was going to leave me. I talked to her and told her that I was not guilty of the charges, and I finally convinced her to come back to me and keep trying. We stayed living together, but our marriage went very cold. We were both very unhappy and I was pretty sure I would be going to jail for a long time. We didn't talk about it much, but I think she had the same idea. When I was sentenced, I appealed and was out again on appeal bail. . . . When I got out I learned that during my stay at prison, my wife had been to bed with a friend of mine. I discussed it with her, but she denied it. I didn't believe that. I told her that I understood why she did it, and that I forgave her. But I never did forgive her. That happened only two or three days after I got home on bail. It set me off on another depression and raping spree. I was caught and given a much longer sentence.'

This was a particularly clear example of a man angry at his inability to control and dominate his wife and taking out his anger on victims whose only fault lay in belonging to the female sex.

Example 8

This was another example of a man whose final outburst of serious sexual aggression occurred shortly after his release, without psychiatric treatment, from a prison sentence for previous sexual offences. During the sentence he had been under considerable stress. He feared that some inmates were going to kill him. 'I became a little paranoid, and constantly seemed to be on edge and tense. I half wanted to go back to the high security prison where conditions were less open, and even requested it once. Towards the end of my sentence, an unknown inmate punched me in the head. I had been feeling nervous and afraid prior to this. Now I simply gave up and asked for protective custody. I was sent to a solitary confinement area where I spent the rest of my sentence. It is more commonly known as the hole, with twenty-three and a half hours daily locked up in bare single cells . . .' He emerged more bitter than before.

A relative who had visited him in prison met him on his release, bought him clothes and gave him the use of her apartment. 'Looking back, I felt guilty over her concern for my welfare. I tried to find a job, half-heartedly I think, for I had tentatively decided to do some chain-store robberies. I had had fantasies about this while I was in solitary confinement, along with aggressive sexual fantasies of rape. Just ten days after release, I decided to go to a distant town where I knew someone whom I could stay with for a few days.' He set off hitch-hiking, but turned back because the weather was too cold. He resumed the journey a day or so later, taking a gun with him. He had no settled plan, except for the fantasies of robbery. He felt somehow confused and desperate, and so preoccupied with his thoughts that he could not make conversation with the drivers who gave him a lift. Before reaching his destination, he had committed rape.

Example 9

This was yet another example in which masculine insecurity in the husband, through unrealistic aspirations and anxious over-striving, caused a potentially happy marriage to end in disaster. The couple met when they were both fellow students on the same course. He had had a number of previous affairs that had turned out unhappily, but this was 'the only time that I had thoroughly enjoyed sex, and that it had had the deepest meaningful value for me. Things went very well for two or three months. I was able to talk considerably more with her than I ever had with any girl before.'

Because he was not doing so well, he quit the course and persuaded her to do so as well. Then, because he could not find work locally, he persuaded her, this time with more reluctance on her part, to move with him to his home town. On arrival there, through the good offices of an old employer, he obtained a well-paid job working on commissions for a sub-contractor who arranged the cleaning and maintenance of office buildings. It seemed almost too good to be true, and he plunged into the job enthusiastically. 'Within no time at all, I was on my own and doing well. I had big fortunes at my finger tips, in the shape of bunches of keys, and I was proud of keeping the whole thing clean and straight, as if each place where I worked was my own pride and possession.' On the strength of this job he secured a good house, but 'my hours had to be haywire and long, at times impossibly difficult to maintain.' He worried about what the owner of the firm would do if his past delinquency record were to be discovered. In fact, unknown to him, the owner already had that information.

The strain of the responsibility, the long hours, and a recrudescence of deviant sexual fantasies grew worse and worse. 'I saw myself gradually losing control of everything, going on endlessly at ever-quickening pace, getting more nervous, bitchy and bad-tempered, driving like a maniac and losing patience with everyone around me. The wife and I were spending less and less time together and having less sex as well. I was treating her rougher and more distantly, and she was showing signs of unhappiness. Then the car broke down. Shortly after I bought a new one, and in that month we had five hundred and fifty dollars in payments going out for one thing or another. It was a definite landslide downhill. By now, the wife and I were barely on speaking terms. Bit by bit I made our relationship deteriorate. I was caught up to the hilt in sexual preoccupations, and becoming less satisfied with everything. The demands of the job day in and day out, and the responsibility of the wife and baby, both wanting time and love which I couldn't give, were too much. I couldn't handle it any more. I was unable to relax, to slow down, I couldn't cope with the time and patience of giving myself to them. I had made a dream world in a way come true, only to watch it all blow away.'

The final straw was a tumultuous extramarital love affair with a waitress aged 18. She was supposed to be trying to get away from an older man who was pursuing her. She led him to believe that the other man was jealous and threatening to kill him. 'I started taking a gun around with me that I had stolen. She had a hell of a lot of control over me, more than I knew at the time. Everyone warned me against her. My wife found out, but she didn't squabble too much. The work was getting on top of me and I was becoming more and more negligent. One day I said, "To hell with it" and didn't go in at all.' Meantime, his wife had left and gone to live in another apartment. 'I moved the rest of the stuff from our house and she let me stay with her, sleeping apart on the couch. I was still glad to be with her, and to a point I think it was the same with her.'

His love affair lasted in all some four months, during which his situation became more and more stressful. Unknown to him, the girl was sharing half her time with the other man friend. All he knew was she kept coming and going, blowing hot and cold. Eventually, when he met the man in question, he found out how much he had been deceived. Far from wanting to pursue a jealous vendetta, the man wanted to let him know that the girl was unstable, an ex-mental patient, and had played similar games with a series of men. 'I walked away in a shocked state, hell-bent to my drug cache, trying to obliterate reality.' He was working during the day at this time, struggling to pay off debts, 'but in the evenings and at night I got out of reality as much as I could.' It was while walking the streets in an intoxicated state, ruminating over his deception, and intermittently hallucinating, that he committed the sexual attacks that led to his present imprisonment.

As in several of the cases already quoted, this history shows the tendency diffident males have to overvalue material success. This man's financial troubles, brought on by overstretching himself in his eagerness to succeed, precipitated a crisis of confidence in the home as well as at work. Seeking comfort in sexual escapades only heightened his feelings of inadequacy. The experience of being jilted was a last straw. The subsequent flight into drug intoxication, far from reducing his anger and tension, served only to render him still more reckless and violent.

Example 10

Soon after his release from prison for previous sexual offences, this man met a woman who had a small child. After six weeks of whirl-wind courtship he married her and took on responsibility for the child. 'I learned her full names for the first time at the altar.' Unlike his previous affairs, which had been marred by sexual inhibitions and guilt feelings, his relations with this woman were very happy. She was experienced and uninhibited, happy to go along with any variants of intercourse he wanted. 'She educated me sexually, she was crazy over sex, I couldn't keep up with her.

'Two weeks after we were married we were sitting in the basement of her folks' place where we lived. I wanted to tell her what I was all about. I told her about my sex offences. She immediately left the house and went for a drive. When she returned, she told me of her own past. She had been a prostitute for the last three years or more. I was shocked now, but we decided that the past would be forgotten and we would live from this day forth.' For a time all went well, and there was a notable lull in the sex fantasies and peeping habits that had been a problem previously. They both liked parties and drinking and smoking pot. During their association, his use of intoxicants increased greatly. He enjoyed the weekend parties with lots of drink and couples enjoying sex, although they drew the line at wife swapping.

His wife became pregnant. He had a long-distance driving job. In order to make more money, he took on more and more journeys, so that he had little time for rest and little leisure to spend with his wife. 'After our baby was born, I began feeling the job creeping up on me. I missed the wife so much that sometimes she would get a baby-sitter and come on the driving trips with me.' After a time, the new life with his wife came to seem more 'routine'. Fantasies of deviant, extramarital sex took hold of him. The happiness with his wife had not quelled the hostile feelings towards women that came to him sometimes. He blamed them for being seductive and for arousing his sexual guilt feelings. At the same time, he envied them the power of their female sexuality, which could seemingly get them anything they wanted without the trouble of working for it.

One time he returned home in the early hours of the morning from a heavy drinking party. He was quite far gone himself, but his wife 'was completely plastered. I carried her into the apartment. I drove the baby-sitter home and then returned. The wife was passed out, and I undressed her and put her into bed. I was sexually aroused, but there was nothing doing with her, so I went out.' He had gone only a few blocks when he spotted a woman, followed her and attacked her. 'In the three months after that I had a miserable time. My conscience let me have no peace. Everything seemed to fall apart.' He thought of going to get psychiatric help to prevent further outbursts, but believed that would mean hospitalization and removal from his wife and family, which he could not face. So he continued as before, hoping the problem would go away. He tried to put on an act that everything was fine, but he became more and more irritable. Then he committed another assault, was caught red-handed and put away for a long time, losing his wife and family in the process.

Example 11

On the surface, this man's marriage was a great success. To their many acquaintances, the couple were an ideal match, and the well-controlled sociable husband was the last person to be suspected of being a potential rapist. All his inner doubts and resentments he kept bottled up in himself. The only obvious external sign of a gradual and dangerous build-up of tension was an increase in his drinking, until it exceeded the bounds of any reasonable social habit. He found himself all the time looking for excuses to take a drink, and becoming intoxicated regularly every day. He was also experiencing memory black-outs, so that he worried whether he had made a fool of himself the previous evening.

'At the start, I was extremely happy with both my married life and my job. My drinking had tapered off, but was far from stopped. When our first child was born, it seemed that life could not be better. . . . The feeling of inferiority I used to have, which kept me from having sexual encounters as freely as my friends did, died down inside me, but it remained very much a part of me. I really never knew if I was as satisfying to a woman as the next guy.'

So long as external circumstances ran smoothly, his emotions remained under control, but his latent insecurity made him dread the prospect of failing in any way as a perfect family man. 'I felt I had really to strive to get ahead on the job so as to make money for us. This was a continual worry for me, right up to the time I was arrested.' Any doubts about his capacities in this direction he kept to himself. He feared to expose any personal shortcomings to his wife. He had the idea she did not hold him in too great esteem, and he did not want any unfavourable views to be confirmed. He loved and admired her, but feared she might reject him if she guessed his weaknesses. Rejection by his wife was his greatest dread.

He and his wife took a very active part in community activities and voluntary social service. He was always serving on committees and continually being called upon to do this and that for friends and neighbours. 'I felt I had to keep up the front of a knight in shining armour to win acceptance by the community. I was at everyone's beck and call to help with tools or fix machines. I was the town handyman. I couldn't refuse, because I wasn't man enough to say no, however much I felt fed up and wanted to tell them where to get off.' He used to receive presents of drink in return for these favours. On occasions when he was busy elsewhere, his wife would do things at home to help out, such as mowing the lawn. He appreciated her good intentions, but it upset and angered him to think how the neighbours would criticize him if they saw her doing things he ought to be doing himself.

His discontent was well concealed. He was of superior intelligence, but relatively restricted in formal education. Verbally fluent, with a gift of quick repartee, he would appear optimistic and jovial most times, but in more sullen moods he was capable of a biting sarcasm. This facility he put to dramatically effective use on occasions after he joined the therapeutic group. It was one way in which he betrayed the hostilities lurking behind an equable social facade.

Tension mounted when incidents took place at work that wounded his self-esteem. A new man hired by the firm as his superior seemed to take pleasure in giving him a hard time, reminding him of his subordinate status. It was a sore point with him that he was several times passed over for promotion by men less able and experienced than himself. 'By this time I was again getting drunk as often as I could.' One result of his drinking was a car accident in which his wife and child were involved.

The fact that his employment was intermittent was a particular aggravation. 'It finally got to the stage where I could hardly tolerate the guys I was working with. This caused me to start drinking again to drown out the bitter memories of the working week that had gone by. This drinking carried over into the lay-off periods, as I could not stand the thought of having to fall behind in the bills again.' He had undertaken some house construction, which he could not complete on account of shortage of money, and this caused him a special bitterness.

'The inferiority feeling I have mentioned, plus the frustrations on the job and around the home, reinforced my ideas of being something less than the next guy. I could not get ahead on the job as I felt I should be able to. I knew I could do the job, but I couldn't seem to get a chance to prove it. At home the largest frustration was that of economics. I was trying to add a very much needed extension to our house, but I simply could not see how I could afford it. The frustration of looking at an unfinished addition day after day for a couple of years really got at me.

'All these feelings led me into what was for me a very real world of inadequacy. I simply could neither perform sexually nor provide adequately for my wife and family. I felt I was a total failure in most all respects. It was at this time I stopped communicating with my wife. I felt I could not tell her how useless I thought I was . . . I began to think she must feel that I was as much a sissy as I feared I was. This was about the state of mind I was in when I began to live out of the bottle. I drank for the effect on me rather than for the enjoyment. I could not deal with what I thought was reality, therefore I created a drunken fantasy world for myself as often as I could. When I was drunk, I could fool myself into thinking I had no problems, but my drinking led me into deeper feelings of frustration and consequently into a deeper feeling of depression. I finally arrived at the point where I didn't think there was anything I could do right, and also I didn't care to try to do anything at this point. I had to have a drink as soon as I could get one and as often. It was at this time that I found any excuse to start drinking. Almost anything would do from "I'm thirsty" to "I've got to drown this headache".

'My feelings of sexual inadequacy also had reached a climax in the last few weeks prior to my first offence, for my sex drive had really tapered off due to the drink. It was at this point that I began to get ideas of attacking a girl . . .'

A brief period of calm followed his first and as yet undetected offence. He had a short holiday with his wife. 'We had a good time, except for the worry over having no spare money.' Once back to work, the fretting and the drinking started up again. One evening he got drunk with his friends, came home late, and for the first time expressed his frustrations by becoming violently abusive to his wife. 'My wife related to me later that I had come home in a very surly mood, that I was very vulgar in my language, and that for the first time in our life together, I had actually scared her. I became violent and disoriented when I got home. I could not find either the bathroom or the bedroom, and wandered about the house looking for them. I expressed verbally my feelings of hate and bitterness towards the world by becoming vulgar and bitter towards my wife. This I believe is the only time it ever happened, for usually I was known as a happy-go-lucky drunk.' It was just a week after this outburst, when he was out drinking on his own, that he again assaulted a female and was subsequently arrested.

In this case the part played by alcohol is of particular interest. The root problem of masculine inferiority was evident in chronic anxiety about performance as a husband and provider, in the oversensitivity to financial set-backs and in the fear of communicating frankly with the wife. Alcohol was used increasingly to gain temporary relief from the tension of the situation, but of course it was no solution, and in the long run probably aggravated the strained domestic relations. Moreover, it was only after a bout of heavy drinking, with resultant loss of judgment and restraint, that thoughts of rape could be translated into action.

Example 12

At the age of 25, following his release from prison for a non-sexual crime, this man tried hard to settle down to an orderly, non-criminal way of life. He obtained a regular job, joined a church group, made some new friends there, and for a time really believed he had 'changed'. His attempts at heterosexual relationships were less successful. Among the people he met at church, he felt something of a fraud, partly on account of the nature of his sexual thoughts. 'I masturbated by all sorts of means. I imagined the girl from the church, violating her body, and in my fantasy she would scream out for more. On my first day out I was attracted by a young waitress. I ended up getting drunk and tipping her like crazy. I got up enough courage to pass a note to her asking if she would join me for a drink after she had finished work. I waited around while the place was closing, but she must have gone out by another entrance. I felt angry, hurt, rejected and like a fool standing there.'

At this point he had to go and give evidence at the trial of some men he had known in the past as fellow prisoners. The experience, and the anticipatory worry of it, upset him enormously. 'I was having bad dreams of dying or getting killed. . . . At the trial, there I was, the quiet con, ratting and singing on the stand like a bird. The mental pressure was awful.'

After this he began to slip back into old habits. He stopped going to the church so much. He left his job. He started drinking again. His attempts to succeed in heterosexual relationships became wilder and wilder, motivated at least as much by a desperate attempt to prove his masculinity as by a need for sexual gratification. 'I picked up a couple of Indian girls on different occasions and took them back to my room to satisfy myself. I treated them roughly, then kicked them out afterwards. I knew by that time I was a sex criminal . . .

'I was out drinking with this new friend of mine. I met a girl called Margery. We started drinking together, and then I went to her place, buying some more cans of beer on the way. I remember her saying earlier that I could sleep on the couch. I told her I would. Back at her place I opened another beer and asked if she wanted one. She said no, because I was drunk. I made advances to her and tried to rape her, but I couldn't get an erection and she put up one hell of a struggle. I woke up in another room, then I went into the room where she was sleeping and woke her up, wanting to satisfy myself. This time she didn't resist. I attempted intercourse, but again couldn't get an erection. I made her go down on me, but still no erection. How I hated her! What a fool she must have thought I was, or a queer. I looked in the mirror. My face was still terribly scratched from the struggle with her the night before, but I had been so drunk I had felt no pain. I felt like a complete failure, an animal, and I thought that perhaps I really was a queer, but just didn't want to accept it. I'd asked myself that question before.'

After this he 'started drinking every day.' Before long he committed another, more serious, sexual attack upon a stranger and was arrested.

As these histories show, discontent and conflict about sexual outlets and sexual performance afflicted every man in the group. One day, when someone was trying to argue that he had no sexual problem, since he had no difficulty about normal sexual intercourse, another retorted 'No, but you have got the sex offender personality.' He was referring to what psychiatrists sometimes call the passive-aggressive personality, the man who tries to suppress or bottle up his feelings, appearing outwardly subdued and acquiescent, but inwardly seething with anger and resentment. When insults to his over-sensitive masculinity reach a critical point, he suddenly erupts with a wildly aggressive sexual assault that strikes observers as altogether unexpected and out of character.

This interpretation obviously fitted well those members of the group who were socially unassertive and sexually repressed. That it applied also to those whose sexual lives appeared to be superficially less restrained became evident only gradually. Some of the men described a variety of sexual outlets which they pursued with compulsive dedication. One or two were aware of a pressing need to seek out extramarital adventures in spite of having a good sexual relationship with their wives. Others reported a predilection for encounters with prostitutes or hitch-hikers, since these strangers posed no threat of social or emotional entanglements. Others again, indulged in various sexual pleasures regarded as deviant, notably, peeping and exhibitionism. They were not, however, simple hedonists. They pursued their sexual habits at the cost of considerable guilt and self-blame. The strong puritanical element showed through in the shame with which they spoke of sexual irregularities that were of minor significance in comparison with their sexual crimes. For instance, some men expressed as much remorse for acts of infidelity to their wives as they did for acts of rape. One man found the recital of sexual acts with his victim more harrowing than the description of the homicidal violence that he had used against her. Another man, who had treated his victims with frightening brutality, found less difficulty in admitting to that than in confessing that he had once achieved orgasm by allowing a dog to lick his penis. In another case, a man who had fought with women to obtain sexual gratification was terrified when an older man made a homosexual proposition. 'If he would have tried anything I think I would have died. I quit the job the next day and I would never go back as long as he was there. I couldn't care whether I got paid. I had to leave at once.'

Whether in reality his behaviour was inhibited or restrained, none of these men was free from sexual guilt, none of them felt he had attained a satisfying balance between his masculine needs and his social and sexual outlets. They all felt constrained and eventually, after periods of increasing tension, all of them broke out of their constraints and committed serious assaults.

Recognition of the problem of insecure masculinity, aggravated by the passive-aggressive temperament that is apt to swing to extremes, helps towards an understanding of the genesis of these sexual attacks. Of course no such simple formulation provides a complete explanation. Even within this unusually homogeneous group considerable variations were evident. Each man's personality development and life circumstances present a unique pattern, and not all hen-pecked husbands or men who feel cheated of their dominant masculine status end up as rapists. But the insecure masculinity theme seems to be a big factor, and if this can be changed through psychotherapy there is a prospect of helping these men to control themselves better in the future.

CHAPTER V

The Crimes

All members of the group had offence records that could be described as serious; some were extremely serious. Most of the men had multiple convictions for sexual crime, indicating considerable persistence, if not an actual compulsive element, in committing the offences. Some of the men had resorted on one or more occasions to extreme violence or to intimidation with a gun or a knife. When their admissions to matters not brought to official notice were taken into account, it was evident that some of the men had been liable to aggressive sexual outbursts for much longer than their recorded convictions might have suggested. The examples given in this section are taken from the offenders' own descriptions, with no distinction made between crimes which led to a charge and those that did not, and no attempt has been made to associate particular crime incidents with the individual histories and life circumstances described earlier.

The anti-social sexual behaviour described varied from peeping through windows at women undressing to murder in the furtherance of sexual assault. As far as actual physical attacks upon women were concerned, they ranged from mild intimidation of moderately reluctant girls who had accepted lifts in the offender's car, through house-breaking by night with the intention of gaining access to an unprotected female, to suddenly pouncing on an unsuspecting woman innocently going about her business on the street. Except for the offences against hitch-hiking girls, the attacks came almost always out of the blue, and were not preceded by any kind of meeting or social interaction between the offender and victim. Almost without exception, the occasion of the assault or the rape was the victim's first encounter with her assailant. None of the attacks described by members of the group were against their current girlfriends, and hardly any were against females with whom they had any kind of social relationship. The rapes that had led to the men's present imprisonment were all of a kind that would be defined as first degree by the U.S. Model Penal Code, Section 213.1, namely: '. . . the actor inflicts serious bodily injury upon anyone, or (ii) the victim was not a voluntary social companion of the actor upon the occasion of the crime and had not previously permitted him sexual liberties . . .'

Examples of assaults during car rides will be considered first, since hitch-hiking was one of the commonest settings for a sexual attack. It was a situation in which an offender could sometimes claim that the victim was an apparently inviting and permissive female who at the time made no indication of unwillingness to participate in sexual activity. More typically, however, the offender admitted frankly that he had deliberately coerced an unwilling woman and felt guilty about it afterwards.

1. 'The first time I made an effort to rape a hitch-hiker, it didn't work out. As soon as I told her what my intentions were, she slammed my gear shift into reverse, and opened the passenger door and jumped while the car was coasting at about fifty miles per hour. I didn't stick around to see what happened to her. I was really afraid, so I took a country road and went back home . . .'

2. 'Sometime after that I picked up another woman who had been hitch-hiking. She was about 35 and she didn't know the area very well. She explained where she was going and I dropped her off at a restaurant, telling her that when I had finished my errand I would come back and pick her up and take her to a place where she would be able to catch a ride easily to where she wanted to go. I did go back and pick her up. Then I drove her out into the country and raped her. There was no physical violence whatsoever. I told her that she was going to get hurt if she didn't make love to me. She was really afraid, so she gave in. I drove her back to the highway after I had used her. I felt really dirty and sorry for her. I felt ashamed of myself for doing it and for cheating on my wife. When I got home I had a bath and I still felt dirty.'

In a few cases the offenders grabbed women against their will and bundled them into their cars.

3. 'I got off work and instead of going home, I went driving around looking for a girl that I could rape. I saw one walking down the sidewalk towards me. I stopped the car and waited for her. When she got up to the car, I got out and asked her for directions. When she turned around to leave, I grabbed her and forced her into my car. I said that I had a knife, and if she didn't do what I told her, I would kill her. I didn't have a knife, but I thought that if I threatened her she would not resist. I drove her out into the country and told her to take off her clothes. She took them off and got into the back seat and that is when I had sex with her. After I had done, I drove her back to where I had picked her up. She asked me if I would have hurt her had she resisted. I told her that I didn't even have a knife, and that if she had resisted I would have let her go.'

In other cases the victims were terrorized with the aid of a weapon or threats.

4. 'I was driving along one morning and saw a young girl (aged 13) walking along the road and I offered her a lift. As we were approaching the point where she was to stop off, I drew a knife and told her to lock the door on her side and we were going to carry on driving.' She appeared calm and they had some ordinary conversation. He drove her about fifteen miles out to a quiet spot where he raped her. She undressed and cooperated fully as if she had just accepted the situation. He believed she was not a virgin. Afterwards, he drove her back to the town and let her off at the place she wanted. He did not think it likely she would scream for help when she alighted, but he expected that she might report him to the police.

5. 'The day of my first offence, I had been drinking earlier on, and then I took my wife out for supper. We went back home at her request. I told her I was going out for a few drinks with the guys. I then went out for the remainder of the evening. I don't recall having any sexual thoughts at all at this point. I was unable to find any of my usual drinking partners in any of my usual bars, so I went off to another part of town to see if I could locate any of the guys that I worked with. I was drinking beer at this time. I was unable to locate anyone that I knew in the bars that I called in, so I ended up drinking alone for about the first time that I can ever recall. While I was drinking I started to get angry. I was angry at my financial situation, at myself, at anyone and everyone. It was at this time that I thought about going to find a girl. I thought to myself, "What the hell!" I left the bar and started to drive, looking for girls that were hitch-hiking. I eventually arrived into the city. I felt sure there would be some girls there looking for a ride.

'I spotted two girls on the side of the road and experienced a great deal of sexual anticipation over what I knew that I was going to try. After the girls got into the car this feeling of anticipation was mixed with a feeling of hate directed towards these girls. I showed them one of the threatening notes that I had prepared. Their first response was to start to laugh, at which I told them I was serious about it. They then started to argue about it, at which time I told them they had better do what I said, otherwise they would not get to where they were going. They then undressed as we were driving off the highway onto a side road. This all took place close to midnight. After I had pulled off the road I started to fondle the girl next to me. She soon asked me if I would like her to switch with her friend. I said that I didn't care, and so she did. Her girlfriend sat next to me and I started to fondle her and she seemed to respond to a very high degree. This soon resulted in a necking session at which time I said, "Let's get into the back of the station wagon." All three of us got into the back, and I had sexual intercourse with the last girl that I was fondling in the front seat. The three of us then dressed and I started to drive them home. All the time that I was involved in carrying on with these girls, I cannot recall my feelings as any other than straight sexual feelings. I wanted to get it over with as quickly as possible and with as much pleasure as I could get out of it. I was totally unconcerned about the feelings of the girls. It was as though we, the people in the car, were the only ones in the world. The thought of being caught or punished or even the thought of my wife and family never even entered my mind. I was simply concentrating on sex with either of these two girls. Driving them back on the way home, I began to think beyond the present and became quite scared and remorseful. I felt even less like a man than I had done earlier in the evening. I looked upon myself as having gone as low as anyone possibly could. I started to apologize to the girls over and over again. One of the girls was scared and didn't talk very much, but the one that I had raped sat very close beside me and carried on what seemed to be a pleasant conversation. She kept telling me not to worry, trying to reassure me. It was during this conversation that she not only told me her name but her phone number. Later I felt really bad about what I had done. I felt so bad that I started to cry. I suppose it would be more like sobbing.'

In the worst example of a rape at gunpoint the offender actually killed a fellow hitch-hiker, before turning his attention to the woman driver who had given them both a lift.

6. 'I was picked up, along with a young couple, by a woman in a small truck. I sat in the back portion while the others were in the cab. While riding in the back I began to have thoughts of rape and assault on all three. I was cold in the back while the front must surely have been warm. When the couple got out I moved into the front. A few minutes later she picked up a man in his early twenties. He was about six feet tall and heavily built. He asked the girl to pick up a companion of his a short distance ahead, which she did. This fellow went into the back and was soon dropped off. The fellow in the front was sitting between me and the girl who was driving. I had taken an immediate dislike to him on account of his loud voice and air of commanding or taking over. This was intensified when, after asking if my window was closed because there was a draught, he did not accept my answer that it was, but rudely stretched his arm out to feel around the window frame, sticking his elbow in my face while doing so. I said nothing, instead, I reached for my bag, took out the gun I had brought, and told him to stick his head between his knees. I told the girl to turn off the highway onto a dirt road, where we stopped. I then made the fellow kneel on the floor while I searched his pockets.

'Before taking the gun out I was frightened, partly over what might happen with the gun, and partly because of the fellow himself. I knew he could beat me if it came to an even fight. Thus, whether I shot him because he suddenly made to turn around, or whether I had meant to shoot him anyway, I can't really say. I recall feeling shocked yet calm, my thoughts seeming to be slowed down considerably. This lasted for a minute or two. Only then did I look at the girl, who thought I was going to shoot her too . . .

'She spent sixteen hours with me, during which I raped her once. At one point I briefly tied her hands in a painful manner, because her insistent questioning about when I would let her go made me angry. This was only for a few minutes, however, and was the only time I hurt her, if rape could be called not hurting a woman. My state of mind was lucid, yet I was not thinking of the consequences. I was depressed for the last few hours and broke down and cried for some time. At one point, I thought of killing her also, for that would ensure my not being caught, but eventually I asked her to drive back onto the highway, where I was soon arrested at a road block. Being arrested was a relief . . .'

While some offenders expressed an immediate revulsion for what they had done as soon as the act was completed, others tried for a long time to deny guilt feelings, maintaining that they had not really hurt their victims. They seemed incapable of thinking realistically about how their victims must have felt, or perhaps afraid to do so. They were not necessarily deliberately callous or brutal in their assaults, but being so absorbed with their own feelings they were insensitive to what was going on in the minds of the victims and oblivious of how offensive their behaviour actually was. One indication of this insensitivity was the occasional attempt, following an assault, to get to know the girl, to exchange telephone numbers, and to behave as if nothing untoward had occurred. In spite of the obvious increase in the risk of detection they incurred, driving the girl home after a hitch-hiking rape, like escorting a girl home after a date, was almost routine. This is not as extraordinary as it seems. As Barbara Cohn explains (Schultz, 1975), terrified rape victims may readily agree to future meetings if, by so doing, they think they can extricate themselves more quickly.

A delayed realization of how the victim must have felt dawned upon some of the offenders when they found, to their surprise, that a complaint had been laid. Others realized it only when they perceived the victim's distress as she recounted her ordeal to the court. In the following example, the offender had been accustomed, as a young man, to picking up teenage girls in his car and seducing them with ease and without complaint. Many years later, when he reverted to similar behaviour, he probably failed to appreciate that girls of that age were no longer so likely to welcome his advances.

7. 'I was about to drive onto a ferry when I noticed a girl of about 16 hitch-hiking. She got in and I dropped her off where she wanted. After a few miles I turned around, passed her again, and picked her up once more. I asked her if she would like to go for a drive. She said she would for a little while. When I parked the car I told her that if she did not take her jeans off she would have to walk home. She asked me whether, if she did what I wanted, I would drive her home. I told her I would. She was easy to seduce and was well experienced. I took her home afterwards, dropping her off in front of her house. We said good-bye to each other, and I never expected her to complain to the police. If I knew then what I know now, I would have expected her to do so.'

In this and other similar incidents in which he had been involved, the offender felt he had done wrong, but there had been no actual violence, and he did not regard what he had done as real rape. He thought the victims were all girls who were free and easy sexually, but looking back on it, in the light of what they said when they gave evidence against him, he realized that they all had troubles and problems of their own, and that he had taken an unfair advantage of them.

The following instance is another example of an offender developing guilt only after seeing the victim in court.

8. 'One evening I met Don after work at a beer parlour, and then we went roller-skating. We left the rink about nine-thirty P.M. and drove around the city for a while. We had stopped off for a coffee and were driving along again, on a main street, when Don asked me to stop at a bus stop to pick up two girls and give them a ride as it was raining. They were both foreign girls who were working as housekeepers. They said they had been looking for an apartment as they were going to live together. One of them asked us to take her home first because she was late. We talked briefly during the drive and took her straight to her place. Her friend then said that she would like to drive around with us for a while as she did not have to be home until midnight. We drove along and just about everything was closed up, so I had to park the car near a warehouse to find a spot to relieve myself of the beer and coffee I had been drinking. The girl had been sitting in the back seat alone, so when I parked Don got out and sat in the back beside her. He tried to force himself on her, but she seemed frightened. She told Don she was not interested in him and that she wanted me to sit with her. So we exchanged places. I talked with her for a while about what she had been doing that day. She gave me her name and phone number, but they turned

out to be phoney, and we listened to the radio. She told me that she was afraid Don was going to hurt her because she had rejected him, and then she started crying on my shoulder.

'I held her and kissed her for a while, then I fondled her breasts. We both undressed and had intercourse. I was nervous, knowing that Don was in the front seat, and she seemed anxious and was in such a hurry she helped to insert my penis. After we finished, I got dressed. She said she wanted a cigarette and then she would let Don have intercourse with her. Don gave her a cigarette and they had intercourse. They got dressed and I drove her home. During the drive back Don made a comment to the effect that she was a no good slut and that he felt like kicking her out of the car and making her walk home. When we got to her home, we walked her to the front door.

'I pleaded not guilty because I didn't consider it to be a rape. I felt that she was willing and seemed to give consent to intercourse. I had never thought of her feelings and the fears she must have had. I felt ashamed of myself and compassion and sympathy for her when she described the incident and her feelings in court. I didn't like the way the lawyers and the judge degraded her by probing each detail over and over again. This was the first time that I experienced any feelings for her. I felt like changing my plea to guilty so that they wouldn't keep nagging and pressuring her. I felt that they were sort of torturing her mentally.'

There were very few instances in which the men in the group gave accounts exonerating them from moral, if not legal, responsibility for their crimes. The following was a striking exception, in so far as the convicted offender attributed all the culpable action to an accomplice.

9. 'One evening I went to a hotel in the town with Jim. We had a few drinks. I had about two glasses of beer. I never drank much because I usually had to drive. We left the hotel about 11:00 P.M. and drove back to the city to take Jim home, but it began to rain so we stopped at a cafe for some coffee. It was raining when we left the cafe and drove towards where Jim was staying. As we were driving along a female hitch-hiker who had been at a bus stop suddenly jumped out in front of us, so I had to stop. She was about 26 years old, dressed like a hippie. She was dirty and stoned. She told us that she had missed her bus and wanted a ride home. She told us what direction she wanted, and as we were going the same way we gave her a lift. Jim got out of the car and the girl got in and sat between the two of us. We talked briefly and she asked where we were going. When I stopped to let her out, she asked if we could take her a little further as she did not have enough money for the bus fare to get

where she lived. I told her it was a little out of our way, but then we agreed, since we could go that way by taking another route. As we were driving along, we had to make a detour because the road was blocked. We stopped at a traffic light about a block away from her destination. She and Jim had been talking quite a bit during the drive and they began necking and petting while I was stationary at the traffic light. They said they wanted to talk a little while longer and asked me to drive to the museum. I agreed and parked the car nearby. Jim got into the back seat and pulled the girl with him. She never resisted him at first, but she began fighting and screaming when he began to remove her clothes. She told him to stop because she was shacked up with a guy and didn't want to have intercourse with Jim. Jim hit her a couple of times and she became hysterical, screaming and fighting with him. I told Jim to leave her alone, but he continued taking her clothes off. I hit Jim in the face and got him off of her. He swore at me, and told her to get out and walk home. I told him to cool off and get back in the front with me, and then I got in the back seat to try and calm the girl to reassure her that I would take her right home. She began getting dressed, and then someone banged on the car window, asking what all the screaming was about. She began screaming again, and Jim was scared, as I was, so he got behind the wheel and started the car. He drove part way out of the parking lot, but he didn't know how to drive and almost smashed into a light pole. I hollered at him to stop and let me drive, so he slammed on the brake. I got back into the front seat to drive and Jim moved over to the passenger side of the car. I noticed a car with high beam lights coming up behind us as I exchanged places with Jim. During this time the girl opened the door and threw herself out of the car and jumped out onto the road. She got into the car behind us. It was the same guy who had banged on the window. The car then followed close behind trying to run us off the road. I could hardly see where I was going because of his beam lights blinding my vision. We managed to lose them, but then an unmarked police car with his highbeam headlights on began chasing us. They pulled us over to the side of the road. Jim and I explained to the police what had happened and we were taken to the city jail and held for investigation. The police said the only reason they had been chasing us was that we had been speeding through a stop sign.'

There was only one instance in which a man claimed he had been accused completely falsely. His statement was made the more convincing by the fact that he readily admitted to some other offences that had not led to a conviction.

10. He was standing by his car, which was stationary, when a **teenage** girl passing by asked if he was having trouble. They started

talking and she sat down in the car. They went on chatting about horses and other things that interested her, until he felt he must get rid of her without hurting her feelings. He told her he had to go in order to get to work. He said he would drop her off at the corner, near where she lived, and began to pull out. 'As I was starting up the next thing I knew she was opening the door and appeared to be about to jump out. I grabbed her wrist and asked her why she had scared me like that. She said she had just remembered she wasn't supposed to ride in a stranger's car. I stopped and let her off. We waved to each other as I turned the car and passed her again.' The next day he was questioned by the police. She had taken his licence number and told her parents that he had forced her into his car, driven her to the city and tried to get her drunk. The police appeared to believe his story, but because the parents were making such a fuss they wanted him to plead guilty to a common assault. He did so, because he did not want to be kept in jail and because, above all, he did not want his wife to hear about the incident.

Some of the reported crimes were of such a nature that no amount of rationalization could convert them into anything other than hostile acts of the cruellest kind. In view of the mixture of hate and attraction towards women revealed in these men's histories, it was not unexpected to find that some of their crimes appeared to be primarily directed towards venting animosity, humiliating the victim, or demonstrating their power and dominance. If the mere satisfaction of sexual lust had been the motive, it is hard to see why rape should have been necessary, considering the fact that most of the men had wives or girlfriends available for intercourse. The desire to gloat over the victim's humiliation was sometimes stronger than the urge to consummate the sexual act. Several offenders reported that they had been impotent or nearly so when it came to the rape itself. Here is a case in point:

11. 'We went out intentionally looking for girls. Each time we were drunk. It was towards the end of the month, I believe, that we grabbed our first victim. She was walking along the street with a carrier bag. We drove slowly by and asked if she wanted a lift. She said "No." I told Derek to slow up and that I was going to grab the bitch. When she was about even with the car, I rushed her, grabbing her by the throat and telling her to shut up or I would kill her. At that moment I felt like an animal, strong and sure of myself. I dragged her onto the front seat, while she let out a few screams. I remember her dropping her purse and the carrier bag before I got her into the car. She was wearing a sweater and ordinary socks and high boots and she kept repeating "You won't kill me will you?" After a few minutes she quietened down and we drove out. On the

way, I kept telling her to be quiet or else my buddy, who had a gun, would kill her.

'I then told her I would help her to escape. As soon as the car stopped I would open the door for her to run for her life, while I fought to hold Derek back. I had no intention of letting her go, and I got a laugh, deep down, that she believed me. When we finally did stop on a farm road she began to run a few yards. I let out a laugh and went running after her. When I finally did catch her, I dragged her roughly back to the car, asking her if she really thought I was such a fool as to let her get away. We made her get into the back seat, and I was already sexually aroused for the degrading raping of her. I wanted her to take everything off by herself, making her feel ashamed and abused. We were on each side of her in the back seat, and Derek started telling her to strip, giving her a few slaps, but she didn't move. Suddenly I grabbed her by the throat and started shaking her, feeling powerful and not wanting to stop. I said to her something like "Listen you bitch, you start stripping now or I'll kill you. Who do you think you are?" I felt so strong, and in a way maybe I would have killed her, but she kept croaking "All right, all right," and Derek kept calling my name to make me let up. After I let her go, I told her to get into the front seat to let me have first shot at her.

'She slowly disrobed and I attempted to have intercourse, but due to the cramped space and my state of drunkenness, I kept getting an erection and then losing it. Finally, in rage and frustration, I got out and let Derek have a go. I waited only a few minutes and became insanely jealous and selfish and told him now it was my time again. This time I dragged her out of the car, both of us naked, and attempted intercourse on the cold ground, but it was just like in the car. Finally, she got on top of me and got the head of my penis into her. She kept rocking back and forth as my penis got stronger. I didn't like her on top of me, so I slowly rolled her over onto her back, trying to keep my erection hard inside her. She was very tight and finally I started to pump away. She kept repeating, "You won't come inside me, will you?" I kept telling her I wouldn't, but the sexual feeling, the tightness of her, and her pleading words, drove me wild and I let myself go inside her, knowing all the time I would. We made her get dressed, drove her back, let her out, and made off.'

12. Another offender described an even more aggressive incident. It took place after an all-night drinking session. He saw a woman walking along the street early in the morning on her way to work, and he got out of his car to follow her. He overtook her as she was crossing a yard and pounced on her with great violence. He pushed one hand into her mouth to stop her screams, causing her to choke

helplessly, and pulling several teeth out in the process. With the other hand he tore at her genitals, ramming several fingers into her vagina. He wanted to get his whole hand up to claw at her. Had he succeeded in doing so, he might have caused even worse damage, as it was, she sustained internal injuries and was in hospital for three days. At one point during the attack, when he was in the 'sixty-nine' position, he bit savagely into her labia. The accompanying fantasy, which flashed back into his mind again and again in the months that followed, was of the satisfaction of destroying the victim's femininity. It was the attack on her genitals that mattered, the remembrance of nearly choking her to death gave him no satisfaction. After this incident happened, there were times when he felt utterly crushed by the horror of his own thoughts and actions. When finally he was caught, he did not care what happened to him, he wanted to see nobody, he wanted no legal defence, he just felt like being shut away, forever if need be.

Many of the crimes occurred after heavy drinking, and some of the worst acts of physical violence were committed while the offenders were thoroughly intoxicated from alcohol or other drugs. The intoxicants were not to blame for the offenders' unhealthy sexual attitudes, but in the state of chemically induced disinhibition and emotional excitement, their normal restraints dissolved and their hostile, aggressive fantasies, intimately intermingled with sexual lust, were converted into action.

13. 'I was quite stoned and hallucinating somewhat, but I was aware of my purpose and that the woman I was following was not Nancy (the girl who had deceived him). But I recall some flashes that left me wondering about that a few times. I used the gun that I had stolen. I had her take her clothes off and I made her walk ahead of me on the street for a few minutes. In one of the more severe hallucinatory periods, when I had a flash for two or three seconds and suddenly saw the face of Nancy, I took a shot at her. The girl thought it was intentional and almost became hysterical. I got her onto a lawn beside a house and my clothes came off. I made her do a number of sexual acts and then I committed the rape. I ran off as soon as I had my clothes on again. I had distinct feelings of satisfaction at her reactions to being made to walk naked in the street and to carrying out the sex acts, all obviously embarrassing and humiliating for her, to the point of being aghast by it all. That was the primary concern of mine, the purpose it was to serve. The rape was secondary. In fact, it took me some time and a lot of trying to maintain an erection and reach a climax.'

The following crime took place after the offender had been smoking hashish and drinking heavily for some hours and was in a wildly excited and belligerent state of mind, scarcely knowing, and certainly not fully appreciating, the consequences of his actions:

14. The victim in this case was a girl who had been flirting with and sexually teasing the offender without permitting him any satisfaction. That may be why he chose this particular woman, but as he himself said, on looking back on it, the important fact was that the idea of violence was in his mind at the time. 'I drove past the place where she lived and stopped under some trees. By now I had it in my mind that I would like to rape her. I shut the car off and walked up to her door and knocked. She came to the door and let me in. She was wearing pyjamas. I told her my car wouldn't start. There was something said then about me being so drunk. I asked her if she would give me a hand. She said sure, and went into the bathroom and changed. We walked down to the car. There was a tyre lever in the car and I got this out, telling her I was going to use it to tighten up the battery posts. I asked her to look for a flashlight which was somewhere under the front seat. She bent over and started looking around. I lifted the lever and stopped. My mind was racing away on me. I could see part of her backside above her low cut hipsters. It was like being on a high diving board and afraid to dive, but there's no stopping once you start. As she went to stand up, I hit her. She slumped down without making a sound. I bundled her into the car and drove off.

'I thought to myself that I would have intercourse with her and I parked the car. I had started to masturbate as we drove along. I had some trouble with an erection, but when I got into position it only took a few seconds. I don't know if I realized that I was having intercourse with an unconscious woman or not. Then she started to move her arms. At this point my mind started racing again. I thought that she would tell what happened and I would be caught. I thought to myself what would a man do who was raping and killing a woman. I pretended to myself I was angry and I hit her on the head a few times. I think I even swore at her, and I beat her on the stomach and breasts with my fists. I listened to her heart and she was dead . . .'

He drove on and dumped the body over the side of a wharf into the water. 'I was exhausted and started to come down. I prayed, hoping there was a heaven and that she would go there. I then drove home. I set the alarm for early in the morning. I fell asleep and started to dream I was in a coffin and the boards were rotten and water was dripping in and I couldn't move. I woke up. It was only an hour since I had gone to bed. I went into the bathroom and began to throw up. I was so sick I couldn't breathe and I thought I was going to die. I went back to bed and woke up again at 7:30. I had to go and look at my car. I was sort of hoping it had all been a nightmare. There was blood in the car, and then I was sure it was all real.'

The examples which follow illustrate the reckless disregard of time, place and circumstance, which was a feature of many of the alcohol-related sex crimes:

15. 'After I had been drinking in the beer parlour for some hours, I got on a bus to go home. I saw this young girl sitting by herself across from me. She was ordinarily dressed with jeans on, and a dark jacket affair. There wasn't anything special about her at all, but the urge to rape her became real. When she got off the bus I decided to follow her home. I followed her down the street till she came to a fairly dark section where nobody was around. I came up behind her and put my hand over her mouth, so that she didn't scream out. I told her to keep quiet and come with me, meaning beside the house where we were standing. We fell to the ground while I was taking her there. She told me she didn't want to get hurt, and I told her that she wouldn't if she kept quiet and did what I said. We both got up again and walked to the side of the house. She then asked me if I would let her go afterwards, and I said that I would. I was pretty drunk, and was only just able to get an erection and have sex with her. There was no physical violence in this case, probably because of her being scared. I left and went home feeling pretty scared. I did not really realize what I had done. The whole episode seemed like a dream, though I knew full well that I had done it. When I was sober and looked back on the whole thing, I couldn't actually picture myself doing it.'

16. 'It was a late hour and I was drunk. I grabbed one girl right on the main street, but she screamed and ran away. This was about 1:30 A.M. I caught a bus with the intention of going home. After I got off the bus, I still didn't have any intentions of getting a girl. As I was on my way home, right on the main road, I noticed a young girl in a phone booth. At that point the urge came to me to rape her. It didn't matter to me what she looked like or what she was wearing, the uncontrollable urge to rape her was there, and I didn't think about where I was or what would end up happening to me. I crossed the street and walked by her once, and then came back to the phone booth. I told her that I had a gun and that she was to come with me. She then hung up the phone and told me I was bluffing, so I grabbed her and tried to pull her out of the booth. She started screaming and scratched me on the face. Then I hit her a couple of times. Then, at that point, she said okay. We walked over to a large truck in a parking lot and got into the back of it. I then had intercourse with her. When I had done and got dressed we sat and talked for ten to fifteen minutes. Then I decided to drive her home. I am not sure why I wanted to drive her home instead of just running off. I told her I

was sorry for doing it, and maybe I wanted to try to make it up to her in some way. She had her car parked across the street, so I went and brought it over to the truck. I told her to get into the back seat and asked her again where she lived. She told me, and as we were pulling out, a police car drove up and started to follow us.'

17. 'It was about midnight and I had sobered up just a little. While parking the car outside a restaurant I saw this good-looking blonde parking her car and I gave up my spot to let her in. Inside the restaurant she was sitting alone, so I asked if I could join her and she said sure. She was wearing a vivid coloured mini-skirt and was very good looking. When she left I suddenly had the urge to molest and rape her. I followed her in the car. I pulled up behind when she stopped outside her place and made a mad dash. Just as she opened her driver's door, I was there and told her I wanted to talk to her. She didn't want to come into my car, I had to choke her and drag her and threaten her to get her in. Even then I had to slam the door on her legs and feet several times, till she couldn't stand the pain, to make her bring her legs inside so that I could close the door. I drove off out of town, knowing the cops would soon be following, but I wanted to satisfy my craving . . .

'I got her into the back seat and made her have a drink of the whisky I still had with me. I got her laying across the seat completely naked and I entered her with no trouble at all. Just as I started to feel good I noticed some headlights approaching. I felt it was the police, but I didn't care. I was still going to get my sex release, so I went at it again and she started to moan as if she were enjoying it. I kept on and finally ejaculated while the cops were banging on the windows. I was pulled out by the hair with my jeans round my knees. I knew I would be in for a rough time.'

After the arrest his mood was very different. 'I had terrible headaches and nightmares of dying. I thought of hanging, but didn't have the courage. Finally, I swallowed a dose of lavatory cleanser . . .'

18. 'One night after I had been drinking I met a girl in town aged about 16. I asked to walk her home. As we were walking along I felt I had to have this girl. We got to a place where there was not too much street lighting and I grabbed her and went to the ground with her. She started to yell and I told her to shut up or I would smash her with a rock. After we had had sexual intercourse, we got up and I helped her to brush the dirt off her clothes. We kept on walking towards her place. When we got to her home I said, "I guess you don't want to see me again." She told me she did not. I left and expected to have the police pick me up soon. I saw her in the street about two weeks later and I turned away. I felt quite ashamed to face her.'

19. 'I was drinking with a friend one evening. After we had a few rounds he left to go elsewhere and I sat there for a few more rounds, as I was really beginning to enjoy myself. Not long after he left, I began to feel angry and bitter as I had done before. I then decided to try my car out to see if the garage had fixed it properly as I felt that they had not done it in the way that they should have. Once I started driving again I thought of picking up girls. I stopped and picked up three girls who were thumbing a ride. There was very little conversation between us. I think perhaps that they were scared of my driving. I let them off without any sort of incident happening. I then saw three more girls hitch-hiking. I stopped and gave them a ride out of town. When at first I began to threaten, they refused to do anything, but after I drove past the point where they wanted to get off, they started to undress. I suppose they felt at this time they had no choice. I should say that the two of them got undressed, the third one became hysterical and started to cry. The others asked me to leave her alone, if they would do what I wanted to do. I agreed to this and never bothered this one girl at all.

'The other two disrobed, while I drove the car. When we were parked off on a side road, I began to fondle one girl, and then said to get into the back of the car. When we got into the back, I started to fondle the second girl. I got her to lay back and was now in the process of starting to have sexual contact with her, when she began to cry. This caused me to think of things other than sexual pleasure, and I immediately stopped my actions. It was then that my conscience took over and I realized just what I was attempting to do and how wrong it was. I proceeded to drive the girls home. I felt really scared, not only for what I had done or tried to do, but for what I had become, an animal in my own eyes. I dropped the girls off and went home. By the time I got home the fears inside me had really sobered me up to the point of being almost completely sober.'

Apart from their sexual crimes, the majority of the group had not been living a life of crime, at any rate not since becoming adults. However, among the minority who had a record of repeated crimes against property, or who had lived in a criminal milieu, it was sometimes hard to distinguish between ordinary crimes and sexually oriented crimes. The two sets of motives intermingled and were not always separable even by the offender himself. One man who had a string of convictions for house-breaking admitted that his sexual and his thieving motives were 'all mixed up'. His break-ins often began by peeping through windows, which he did primarily for voyeuristic reasons, hoping to catch women undressing. His peeping habits would sometimes be so compulsive that he would excuse himself from the company he was with to visit the lavatory in order to spy into the female section. This is how he described one of his sexual crimes:

20. 'I saw the back door of one house was open a little, so I pushed my way in. In the large bedroom there were two girls together in bed. I started feeling one of them. She woke up and asked me if I was some guy, her boyfriend I guess. There were a bunch of bottles on the dresser, so I told her not to make a noise or I would hit her with a bottle. I got into bed, but I had had too much to drink and could not get an erection. The other girl got out of bed and went out of the room. I followed, but she was only going into another bedroom. She must have thought I was the other girl's boyfriend. I went into the room with her and got into bed. Then the other girl came in and said "You just want my sister anyway" and then left the house. I knew that she would go to the police, so I left right behind her. These girls were 17 and 14 years old.'

Another offender described his mixed motives for house-breaking in similar terms: sometimes he did it for straight theft, sometimes to steal female clothes to meet his fetishistic urges, and sometimes it was for the purpose of rape.

21. 'I also got into extensive peeping activities, though this was also tied in with my breaking and entering activities, which had been heavy since first I came to the town. Most times I broke in for the sole purpose of stealing women's wear, but a small percentage of the things I took were for my personal use, radios, stereos and so on, although all too often, these would end up in the pawn shop for money. As the peeping through windows into girls' bedrooms progressed, the satisfaction of merely looking at nudity was less and the obsession to feel and to touch took over and the idea of rape grew stronger . . .

'On one occasion, a rape attempt was the direct consequence of peeping. I happened across an open, lighted window and saw a girl of 14 or 15 in bed, playing with herself under the blankets. When the light went out I got through the house door and into her room. I squeezed her windpipe and made her come outside with me, threatening to choke her if she gave me any problems. I took her nightgown off in a carport on the property. While standing behind her, I felt her and played with her. This went on until we were startled by a car turning into the laneway. . . . It was more looking and feeling than anything else, for during the whole time I hadn't been able to get an erection of any sort . . .'

The question is often asked whether the women or girls involved in such crimes could have done anything to avoid becoming victims of rape. One obvious answer, arising out of the descriptions of some of the crimes, is that some of the victims might have exercised greater discretion. Women's organizations are naturally irritated by suggestions that involve curtailment of the freedom of the innocent. Ideally, women should be as free as men to go about as they please and to walk home alone late at night without fear of molestation. On the other hand, like the man who goes off leaving the ignition key in his car, thereby inciting some young delinquent to drive it away, some girls are incautious to the point of culpability. Seeking car lifts from strange men, especially at night, may sometimes seem a social necessity, but it invites trouble. Offenders are not always without justification when they describe a hitch-hiker's conduct as provocative. One lady who drives a great deal about British Columbia commented to the author how frequently she noticed girl hitch-hikers turn away on seeing a female driver approaching and then immediately signal the next car if it happened to be driven by a man.

The sources of misunderstanding between couples that sometimes result in male sexual aggression have received increasing attention in recent years. A man who spends all his money on a girl, because she has given him reason to anticipate sexual gratification, may simply not accept a refusal at the end of the day. A woman whose dress, manner and sexually teasing behaviour lead her partner to regard her as sexually available has little moral justification for declining to cooperate. It seems that prospective sex partners from different social groups are particularly liable to misunderstand and offend each other, especially in the early phases of acquaintanceship (Kanin, 1969). In a survey of sexually violated females on a college campus Schultz and DeSavage (Schultz, 1975) suggest that lack of realistic instruction in sex crime definitions and sex communication methods, and too much reliance on non-verbal hints during courtship, contribute to the high incidence of sexual aggression.

Stanley Brodsky has analysed the reported methods of deterrence used by women threatened with rape (Walker and Brodsky, 1976). These range from fighting back, verbal attack, loud screaming, appeals for sympathy, attempts at distraction and pleas of illness to simple compliance to avoid injury. With the aid of professional actors and actresses he produced videotapes of rape scenes depicting women attempting a variety of ways to avoid the unwanted sexual act. These scenes were subsequently shown to convicted rapists who were in custody in a forensic unit. The men were asked to assess how effective the reactions depicted would have been in their own cases. The number of rapists who reported that signs of weakness or distress would have turned them off the act and of those in whom such signs would have served to increase sexual excitement were almost equal. Some men felt that they would have been deterred by determined resistance or angry verbal attack, whereas others admitted that this would have only excited them further. The tentative conclusion was that verbal discouragement, success in communicating with the attacker and arousing his sympathy were the most effective deterrents, but that they only worked in certain cases. Some men were made all the more hostile by what they considered phoney protestations of distress or all the more aroused by struggles or screams.

Planned strategies for defending themselves against rape would have been of little use to the victims in many of the crimes in which the men in the group were involved. Very often the circumstances were such that the victims could not, by any stretch of the imagination, have been held to have actively contributed to the incident or to have given the assailant any scope for misunderstanding. Some victims were attacked in their own homes by an unknown intruder, others jumped on in the street and dragged into a car, or waylaid by a stranger who had been waiting his chance to pounce. Having been so taken by surprise there was usually little they could do to prevent events taking their course.

From this group's reminiscences, and from perusal of the literature, no clear guidance emerges on what a woman threatened with rape ought to do to save herself. In some of the incidents described the assailants were so overwrought and so determined in thought and deed that screams, protests or physical resistance might merely have incited more serious violence. On the other hand, in some cases, as the offenders explained quite clearly, they were still capable of being deterred by firm resistance or touched by frantic tears and pleadings. One potential victim successfully diverted her assailant by talking to him kindly and showing an interest in his problems. In short, there is no simple rule. Confronted by an armed stranger who is himself in a desperate state of tension and hostility a woman would be foolhardy to do anything to provoke him further. In such a case, self-defending moves sufficient to dampen the ardour of an importunate boyfriend might only aggravate the situation. Efforts to reason with the aggressor can also backfire if the man perceives his victim's apparent calm as one more outrage to his masculinity. An example of the difference a victim's reaction can sometimes make was quoted by Gibbens et al. (1977). The offender, a neurotic and frustrated young man, demanded sexual intercourse with a married psychiatric social worker, while threatening her with a knife. She remained calm and used her therapeutic skill to turn away his aggression by flattering his masculinity and assuring her how good he would be as a lover. He subsequently attempted to rape a foreign au pair girl. She panicked, screamed and was cut by the knife.

CHAPTER VI

Some Tentative Interpretations

The selection and ordering of the content of case histories inevitably imposes in some degree a preconceived pattern. Patients volunteer the themes which they think are required, therapists listen to what they consider most significant and the theorist highlights those points relevant to his particular hypothesis. The material here has been chosen and presented to illustrate the point of view that rapists, or at least these rapists, suffer from an inferiority complex centred upon insecurity about masculinity. The origins of this complex, it is suggested, are traceable to inappropriate upbringing, hindrances to childhood social development, especially in the sphere of sexual relationships, and unfortunate incidents later in life that serve to aggravate rather than to ameliorate the tendency to irrational anxieties and unrealistic attitudes towards women. This approach provides a useful counterweight to the notion that all rapists are just oversexed and uninhibited hedonists. It directs attention away from the aggressive sex act itself to the psychological meaning of the use of sexual force to gain advantage over women. The man who has an urge to rape is often the man who feels at a disadvantage with women. He doubts his attractiveness as a mate, he fears exploitation, he doubts his sexual proficiency or he is afraid of being cheated and so becomes demanding and jealous. To make up for this suspected inferiority, he has to resort to desperate measures to reverse the position, to prove himself capable and dominant, or to obtain revenge for past humiliations.

This interpretation, formulated through experience with the present treatment group, is far from new to the psychiatric literature. It was the keynote of explanations of rape put forward by Walter Bromberg (1948) a generation ago. In his view: 'The neurotic mechanism operative in rapists is based upon an underlying inferiority feeling which is reflected in sexual attitudes. . . . Aggressive sexual psychopaths are driven to repeated sexual conquests in pursuit of the emotional security that successful masculine dominance brings.' Similar opinions are advanced in more recent writings. For example, Seymour Halleck (1971, p. 191) suggests: 'Many rapists are individuals who are plagued with doubts about their own masculinity . . . The rapist tends to see all women as seductive, depriving and dangerous. He frequently vacillates between perceiving them as frightening giantesses or as lesser beings. In his attacks upon women he both conquers his fears and confirms their inferiority.'

These explanations of rape are easy to understand, and they fit quite neatly many of the details quoted from our case histories. But the theory, like all psychodynamic theories, is necessarily an abstraction and a gross oversimplification of real life. Even among this small and select sample, other themes were apparent alongside the major features that have been emphasized. Depending upon individual social circumstances and personality development in other respects, the masculine inferiority feelings were revealed in different ways. Some of the men were persistently dominating and possessive towards every woman with whom they managed to form a relationship. Anxious not to fail in the job of occupying the man's place, they could not afford to give an inch. One man told me he would never open a window or fetch a cup for himself because he did not give his wife that much respect. Another man admitted that he would not let his wife have any social life because he did not approve of baby-sitters and thought she should stay with the children all the time. In contrast, other men felt crushed in marriage, unable to express their discontent for fear of losing their precarious hold on their wives.

A sense of inferiority often goes with a shy, submissive personality. Several of the men were in fact overly quiet and unassertive in their behaviour. One in particular was so extreme in this respect, invariably polite, never critical, never saying anything wrong, never objecting, never contradicting, that he was assigned a special treatment goal. Each week he had to find fault with the attitudes or conduct of three other members. He complied, but with much discomfort and reluctance. On the other hand, deep feelings of inferiority can co-exist with outwardly aggressive, assertive behaviour, and some members of the group were verbally, if not physically, highly assertive. Five members had significant records of non-sexual crimes, which shows that they were not afraid to challenge authority. They had little opportunity to go on doing so in the controlled setting of the institution and under the watchful eye of nursing staff constantly on the look-out for rule infractions, although now and then some of their comments in group discussions gave an indication of their attitudes. One man, with a history of non-sexual crimes, who had committed some violent acts while in prison, spent most of his spare time in the institution practising weight lifting. He commented once, in a tone of complete detachment, that in his opinion, keeping sex offenders shut away for years in jails like caged animals was likely to turn them into real criminals on release. Asked what sort of criminals, he said he was thinking of armed bank robbers.

Given the masculine inferiority complex, relatively minor aggravations served to release sexual aggression in these men. One form of stress mentioned very frequently was failure at work. When periods of unemployment or failure to secure pay rises or promotion meant that a man could not provide for the home according to his own ideas of what was right and proper, then he was liable to feel deeply ashamed or depressed. If a wife was working when he was not, or if she was earning more than he was, the husband would feel resentful, as if it were a slur on his manhood. It was sometimes clear that the husband fretted much more about these things than the wife. An old-fashioned belief in the strict division of male provider and female housewife was very noticeable, all as a part of the machismo ideal. Living up to the ideal was particularly difficult where educational attainments were not good and work career before marriage had been unstable.

Loss of control over emotions and impulses in the face of stress and frustration was the immediate precursor of most sexual attacks. Loss of control was most dramatic in those individuals who were ordinarily very restrained, but even among those who were socially aggressive or actually criminal, an increasingly serious loss of restraint was reported in each case prior to the final sexual outburst. In a majority of cases this loss of control was associated with intoxication, and not with just a casual drinking spree, but with the culmination of a long slide into definite alcoholism. These were cases where the drinking habits had progressed to the point where therapeutic intervention might well have been required even if the sexual outburst had not brought the situation to a crisis. This observation is at least as important practically as the identification of masculine inferiority conflict, since it points to a potentially treatable situation.

It has been suggested that sex offenders' problems are aggravated by the kind of females they select as wives or girlfriends. Some diffident males choose forceful, expressive women who do not require much initiative from a lover. Others choose excessively submissive, undemanding and sometimes much younger girls, whom they can successfully dominate and who seem to pose no threat to their self-image of masculine supremacy. When, in the course of time, the women begin to show dissatisfaction with the persistent imbalance of the relationship, the men feel threatened, betrayed and resentful. Abrahamsen (1960) reported the results of an investigation into the conduct and attitudes of wives of the rapists who were undergoing psychiatric treatment in Sing Sing prison. He found that on the surface these women behaved towards men in a submissive and masochistic way, but this was only a cover for their latent hostility and aggressiveness. Their husbands frequently complained of their frustrating sexual unresponsiveness. They 'unconsciously' invited sexual aggression, only to respond to it with coolness and rejection. They stimulated their husbands into attempts to prove themselves, but their cool and crushing response to these attempts only increased the husbands' doubts about their masculinity. In this respect they echoed the deceptively seductive behaviour typical of rapists' mothers. One of the main motives for rape 'might be tentatively described as a displaced attempt to force a seductive but rejecting mother into submission'.

In a small study in which wives of hospitalized rapists were interviewed Garrett and Wright (1975) came to a rather similar conclusion. Most of the wives were better educated than their offending husbands and considered themselves to have had better home backgrounds. They enjoyed visits to the hospital and felt that their husbands had improved. The investigators suspected that they were using the situation to enhance their positions of moral and social dominance over their unfortunate menfolk.

With one isolated exception, the histories of the members of the treatment group did not suggest that suffering at the hands of domineering or covertly hostile wives was an important contributory factor. Most of the group were or had been living as married men before coming to prison. Judging from their own accounts, and from talking to wives who still visited, there was no instance of an offender being driven to crime by his wife's behaviour. Marital tension, and failure of communication between husband and wife, certainly prevailed, but, contrary to what might have been expected, the wives seemed to play a relatively small part in producing these problems. These were men who would have found difficulty in sustaining an intimate heterosexual partnership with anyone. In fact, some of them had failed several times in attempts at a marital relationship with different women.

Some of these wives suffered as much, stood in as great a need of support and counselling and were, in a sense, just as much victims as the women their husbands had assaulted. One woman told of her horror when a posse of police banged on her door one evening, told her that her husband had been charged with several rapes, and wanted to know if she found that surprising. It was in truth totally unexpected. Her husband had not been allowed to phone her after his arrest, she had no idea anything was wrong, and the charges referred to incidents she knew nothing about which had taken place months before. The police proceeded to search and ransack her home but she never learned what they were looking for. Another woman, wife of a first offender, who had no idea that her meek-mannered, socially inhibited husband could be a rapist, rang the police in answer to a message. 'Yes, he's here. We're just going to charge him with rape.' She was so shocked she could not say anything. She heard the policeman's voice asking 'Are you all right, dear?'

Wives who decided to stand by their husbands had to contend with hostile relatives who pressed them to use the situation to obtain a divorce. One woman was told in no uncertain terms by her husband's mother that she should leave him. Another wife described how she had had to plead with her employer to be allowed to stay on at her job, which she needed more than ever now she had to support herself and her child on her own. There had been considerable publicity about her husband's case, and the employer felt she would be upset by people passing comments and that her work would inevitably suffer. She had to drive herself doubly hard to increase her performance as a saleswoman in order to prove that she could still do the job. Many of her acquaintances did pass comments, either remarking upon her foolishness in sticking to such a monster, or hinting that there must have been something wrong with her to have made him do such a thing.

The legal process was traumatic to the wives as well as the offenders. One wife tried hard to enlist the help of a private lawyer, but found the demands for large payments in advance too much. One lawyer suggested she should mortgage her home, but her husband would not allow that, and preferred to accept legal aid, because he could not stand the thought of his wife and child losing their home while he was in prison. At the trials, wives had to bear the curious public gaze and to look helplessly at their husbands in the dock. One wife who could tell how much her husband was suffering longed to be able to hug and comfort him. Another described how she found herself alone in a room with her husband's victim, who was trembling and clearly under great stress. She went down on her knees to her and begged the victim to understand that her husband was a sick man and had not done it in his right mind. In contrast, another woman found little sympathy for the victims when she saw them at the trial. They were flashily dressed young girls who joked and flirted with the court officials. At least one she knew to be a local prostitute. She could not see at the time why they should have complained. She realized when she thought about it that even promiscuous girls have a right to say no to sexual propositions they do not want.

The offence histories of some of the men in the group raised an important problem, namely the escalation of less serious forms of sexual deviance, such as clothes fetishism, peeping and exhibitionism, into more serious and violent assaults. Several offenders described such a sequence. One man who had pounced upon and injured a number of women in his later outbursts had been for many years before that a persistent exhibitionist, voyeur and transvestite. He was in the habit of loitering in the vicinity of ladies' lavatories observing the women going in and out. When he knew that no one was inside, he would sneak in himself, shut himself up in a booth and wait for a female to enter an adjoining cubicle so that he could spy on her while he masturbated himself. He had also been caught red-handed taking underwear from clothes-lines. On one occasion, having left his car to expose himself in the nude to passing women, he had been forced by the cold to give himself up, watched by jeering spectators, to some policemen who had set a guard on his vehicle.

It is widely believed (MacDonald, 1973) that a feeling of sexual inadequacy, resulting in anger against females on account of their supposedly dominating and demanding attitudes, is characteristic of exhibitionists. In fact, the masculine insecurity feelings and tortured relationships with women, which were so prominent among this group of rapists under treatment, are problems common to all types of sexual deviants. It is not surprising, therefore, that some exhibitionists and peepers should become more openly aggressive in the course of time, but it needs explaining why some do but most do not.

The members of the rapists' group differed from ordinary sexual deviants in several important respects. Many timid, inhibited, neurotic deviants are crushed by their ineffectuality with adult women. Their sex life is more or less limited to their deviant sexual ritual, which they find easier and safer than heterosexual assertiveness. In contrast, every man in the group had been married or had heterosexual affairs. Their socio-sexual performance may have fallen far short of their ideals of smooth male dominance, but at least they had come to some sort of terms with real women in the real world. Another distinctive feature of some of the rapists was their tendency to translate feelings of frustration into aggressive action, a trait more typical of the delinquent than the neurotic. In some cases this showed up in their criminal convictions for non-sexual offences. In other instances it showed in a fast, reckless living, excessive drinking, needless debts, sexual promiscuity and a striking gap between low career achievement and high intellectual potential. The causes of this gap could sometimes be seen in educational indiscipline and in readiness to walk out on employers who failed to meet their expectations. Two of the men had, for considerable periods, prostituted themselves to homosexuals as an easier way to make a living than legitimate employment. One of these, on first admission to the institution, defiantly quoted 'prostitute' as his main occupation.

Given their aggressiveness and their tendency to express emotional conflict in deviant actions, it becomes more understandable why these men could not contain their sexual frustration by means of a fantasy ritual without physical contact with a real woman. One man put it in a nutshell in the course of a group discussion. Responding to the suggestion that sexual fantasies of subjugating a woman are too commonplace to be really dangerous, he commented: 'They are dangerous for us because we have all proved we have the guts and the ability to act on them.'

The connection between sexual fantasy and sexual crime was discussed many times. Most of the men believed that deviant thoughts led more or less directly to deviant deeds, and they admitted having dwelt upon thoughts of attacking women for some time before actually doing so. An almost obsessional preoccupation with sexual fantasies was a not uncommon precursor of crime. Some of the group were still very worried by intrusive sex thoughts and by the deviant or aggressive content of some of their masturbation fantasies. One man volunteered to explore his sexual preferences by viewing pornographic slides. There were some pictures of women tied up or being choked by an assailant, but he did not rank these among the ones he found especially stimulating. He explained that if pictures of women being overpowered and their clothes ripped off had been included, he would have found those more erotic than the scenes of ordinary sexual intercourse.

The discussion of individual sex fantasies in group sessions might be expected to add to the salacious interest and to reinforce the deviant ideas, but the reverse seemed to happen. When the lonely, secretive sex thoughts were brought out into the open some of their force was dissipated, anxiety was relieved and perhaps the intensity of the sexual preoccupations was lessened.

The recitals of crimes committed, and the recitals of sexual fantasies, brought out forcibly the delight which some of these men took in the spectacle of women subjugated, forced into acquiescence, shamed and humiliated. It was a way for them to conquer their inadequacy, to overcome and take revenge on the domination of women. Cruelties inflicted in the course of sexual assaults seemed, in most cases, instrumental to the need to dominate. Pure sadism, in the sense of gaining erotic delight from the victim's physical pain, was not usually admitted. In fact, an involuntary reaction of pleasure on the part of the victim was more likely to please the offender. One man confessed that the height of pleasure for him was to imagine a woman he had forced against her will beginning to respond with an approaching orgasm. In describing one of his most violent assaults he mentioned that the victim had moaned as if she were enjoying it, although judging by his account it seemed much more likely she had been groaning in agony. Although the two motives were not easily distinguishable, the need to dominate and torture psychologically seemed more evident than the desire to cause pain or injury for its own sake. None of the men admitted to sadistic practices as part of their love-making with girlfriends or wives. They were brutal only with their crime victims.

The conclusion that rape is not usually a manifestation of sadism, in the strict sexual meaning of that word, agrees with the views expressed by Karpman (1954, p. 346), a clinician with a particularly wide experience of sex offenders. In his opinion, to respond sexually outside the framework of affection contravenes all our cultural conditioning, and it takes an abnormal individual to be able to do so. But lustful enjoyment of the victim's pain is not the main motive. 'If there be . . . pain in connection with rape, it is incidental, the primary aim is the overcoming of the victim.'

CHAPTER VII

Varieties of Sex Offender

The subjects in this study, a small group of prisoners undergoing intensive psychotherapy, although perhaps representative of a certain category of sexual criminal, were in many ways untypical of sex offenders in general. Their crimes were graver and more repetitive than is usual among offenders charged with rape or sexual assault. All of them were unhappy men with complicated, conflictual motivations. In some cases their offending behaviour was quite alien to their usual character. Their problems were suited to a psychiatric approach. In order to provide a background against which to view the significance of observations based upon such cases, it is necessary to consider briefly the scope and nature of sex offences in general and of rape in particular, in so far as these are revealed by national crime statistics and systematic offender surveys.

Many countries report an increase in the number of officially recorded violent sex crimes. A particularly steep rise in the incidence of rapes has been recorded in Canada. In 1975, 2,843 rapes were known or reported to the police and 1,016 persons were charged with rape. According to *Crime and Traffic Enforcement Statistics* there was an increase of 14.4 per cent in reported rapes in Canada in 1974 compared with 1973. The annual rate of rape offences per 100,000 of population was 5·0 in 1970, 8·1 in 1974. Although only 10·5 per cent of the total Canadian population is located in British Columbia, that province accounted for 20·5 per cent of the rapes reported in 1974.

The United States is well known for having a particularly serious rape problem, with an annual rate of reported forcible rapes of about 25 per 100,000 of total population. In some of the larger cities, such as New York, Los Angeles, Chicago and Detroit, the number of reported forcible rapes runs into thousands each year. According to *Uniform Crime Reports* the number of forcible rapes reported in the United States increased by about 10 per cent per annum during the period 1970 to 1974, but it has slowed down recently. The increase in rapes reported to the police in 1975 compared with 1974 was only 1·3 per cent, with a further increase of 1·1 per cent in the year

1976 compared with 1975. Nevertheless, the small rise in the total of forcible rapes reported for the country as a whole concealed substantial increases in particular cities. From 1974 to 1975 reported forcible rapes increased from 351 to 453 in Boston, from 434 to 547 in San Francisco and from 1,260 to 1,414 in Detroit.

In Britain the problem, in absolute terms, remains comparatively small, the total number of reported rapes for the nation as a whole being of the same order as that of the single city of Detroit. Nevertheless, the figures are rising fast. In England and Wales 1,094 rapes were reported to the police in 1976 compared with 784 in 1971 and 618 in 1965. Some areas have been worse affected than others. In London, that is in the Metropolitan Police District, reported rapes increased from 118 to 181 between 1974 and 1976.

Crude statistics of crimes known to the police provide an uncertain indication of what is really happening in the community. They are governed by the proportion of incidents actually reported, and of course rape cases are very often not reported. Victims may feel compromised or embarrassed, disinclined to become involved in investigatory proceedings or reluctant to appear in court and face the prospect of hostile public cross-examination. A change in the direction of greater public sympathy towards rape victims could result in more cases being reported to the police without there being necessarily any real increase in incidence. Reporting habits may well have changed as a result of administrative and legislative measures designed to facilitate the prosecution of rapists without causing the innocent victim avoidable insult or distress. For example, in the United Kingdom, the report of the Advisory Committee on the Law of Rape (Home Office, 1975) led to the enactment of a law to protect rape complainants from irrelevant public questioning about their previous sexual experience during the offender's trial.

The recent upsurge of public interest, and the numerous publications on the topic that have appeared, have contributed comparatively little to the limited store of hard, factual information about rape offences. Crime statistics reveal very little of the nature and circumstances of the incidents recorded (Goldner, 1972). The legal categorization of an incident does not always indicate what actually happened. Police practice in the recording and classification of offences can affect the statistics. Legally, rape requires penetration of the vagina by the penis, but inevitably there exists a grey area between violent sexual assault and accomplished rape. Whereas rapes increased in England and Wales from 784 to 1,094 between 1971 and 1976, in the same period indecent assaults upon females decreased from 12,400 to 10,901. Unlawful sexual intercourse with girls under 16 (a charge frequently used for incidents in which the girl's unwillingness to participate was not 100 per cent clear) also decreased from 5,060 to 4,313 in the same period. One can see how a minor readjustment in the classification of marginal cases could go a long way towards explaining an apparent increase in rape. It is not a safe presumption that sexual assaults are always less serious crimes than rapes. Some of the most brutal attacks admitted by men in the treatment group has led to convictions for sexual assault. In cases involving girls under age what is actually a forcible rape may lead to conviction for 'statutory' rape (i.e. the American category for intercourse with a girl below the legal age of consent) or indecent assault, because this avoids the necessity to prove the girl's unwillingness. From the victim's standpoint the degree of violence used during a sexual attack may be of more significance than whether the incident qualifies as legal rape. Some years ago the British criminologist F. H. McClintock (1963) carried out a survey in London of crimes of violence of all kinds, classifying them according to the circumstances of the offence, as revealed by police reports, instead of by the usual legal labels. By including in rapes all attacks on women accompanied by violence or threats he found that the number of serious sexual crimes was considerably increased. Moreover, although the crimes he classed as violent sexual offences at that time (1960) constituted only 6 per cent of crimes of violence against the person, he found that sexually motivated violence had increased in frequency over the previous decade more rapidly than other types of violence, such as family disputes, or fights in the vicinity of bars and similar public meeting-places.

Sex offences in general, and rapes in particular, cover a wide range of incidents involving very different individuals activated by very different motives. This variety accounts for the contradictory stereotypes which exist in the public mind and in penological writings, and the conflicting findings which attempts at systematic surveys of rape offenders have produced. Everything depends upon how the sample is selected. The prevailing patterns of aggressive sexual behaviour are governed by local cultural standards and social class mores, but the number and quality of incidents processed as crimes depend upon the readiness of victims to report assaults, the statutory definitions of sex crime, the administrative practices within the criminal justice system and the standards of evidence demanded by the courts. Finally, the types of offender likely to be encountered differ according to the point in the legal process at which the sample is taken.

In Canada, for example, men against whom complaints are made to the police will differ from those actually charged, differ still more from those ultimately convicted of rape, differ even more from the restricted selection of offenders committed to penitentiaries and differ yet again from the unfortunate few classed as dangerous sexual offenders and subject to indefinite detention. For instance, according to *Crime and Traffic Enforcement Statistics*, the total of alleged rape incidents reported in Canada in 1974 was 2,868, whereas the number of males charged was 1,002, of whom 84 were juveniles. In that year the number of males admitted to Canadian penitentiaries under sentence for rape or attempted rape was only 152, of whom 21 were under the age of 20.

From one viewpoint the man charged with rape seems little different from the average man, save that, in efforts to satisfy the desires and fantasies shared by many males, he has acted impulsively or over-enthusiastically and had the bad luck to encounter a woman who decided to report him. The late Dr Kinsey is said to have commented that the difference between a good time and a rape often largely depends upon whether the girl's parents happened to be awake when she returned home. According to one Canadian medical authority, experienced in the examinations of rape complainants in Edmonton (Ringrose, 1975), alleged rapes are often ambiguous affairs. They may involve young girls who become afraid of venereal disease or of discovery by their parents after a sex act has occurred, or 'it can be a woman having a casual affair who fears detection by her husband because of fluid stains on her garments . . .' or 'a woman with indignant friends' or 'a prostitute who was not paid'. Scepticism about the significance of psychiatric factors in rape is certainly widespread. One distinguished British criminologist laughed on hearing of the present inquiry. The reasons for rape seemed to him only too plain, although he understood that psychiatrists would find it necessary to unearth emotional complexes and blame the rapist's mother.

In their massive survey of American sex offenders Gebhard *et al.* (1965), of the Institute of Sex Research at Indiana University, point out some of the cultural influences which result in many men, who would not ordinarily be considered either sexually or morally deviant, becoming offenders. Society expects nice girls to put up some token resistance to sexual intercourse, perhaps murmuring 'No, no' or 'We mustn't'. As these authors remark (p. 177): 'Any reasonably experienced male has learned to disregard such minor protestations, and the naive male who obeys his partner's injunction to cease and desist is often puzzled when she seems inexplicably irritated by his compliance.' Some women enjoy being playfully overpowered and others find incipient guilt feelings assuaged by the thought that they were forced into it. All this leaves a good deal of scope for genuine misunderstandings by men who cannot, or perhaps will not, distinguish between decorum and genuine disinclination or appreciate that the roughness one woman finds titillating another finds repulsive.

Medea and Thompson (1974) are among the many present-day writers who argue that the sexual aggressor is usually a very ordinary man. They blame the conventionally accepted cultural roles of the two sexes for fostering attitudes that encourage otherwise law-abiding men to take advantage of any woman who puts herself into a position that allows him to rape her with probable impunity. Men are taught that sex is not a free exchange between two persons. To obtain sex, the man must persuade and seduce, or he must pay for it in some way, bribing with gifts, or undertaking to support a wife and family. The woman is supposed to guard her sexual treasure, reserving it for the husband who pays for it in the marriage contract. A woman who goes out alone enticingly dressed, who accepts lifts or drinks, or who allows herself to be taken out by a man she does not know well, is held to be fair game for sexual exploitation. She has dropped her guard and has only herself to blame if the man takes more from her than she wanted or expected. These widely held social values permit the driver who has forced a hitch-hiker into sexual intimacies to feel free of guilt and to think that, having got what he wanted at bargain price, he has been just that bit smarter and more manly than the average. In the opinion of these two feminist writers, the double standard, according to which a man's sexuality is something to be enjoyed and freely given when it pleases him, whereas a woman's sexuality has to be persuaded or forced out of her, promotes the kind of thinking that makes rape possible. Other sexist conventions contribute to the high incidence of rape. The identification of femininity with submissiveness and non-aggression robs women of the courage to put up a resolute resistance. Permissive fashions in dress and manner, promoted by men, give the rapist an excuse to say that his victim was 'asking for it'. Like the old-fashioned owner of black slaves, in his mind the rapist places certain women in a class whose rights to refuse him can be ignored.

Another feminist writer, Susan Brownmiller (1975), cites many historical examples showing that a woman's body has been traditionally regarded as the property of her father or husband rather than her own, a conception that readily leads to women being used as objects for barter or theft. In the course of warfare and political struggle between male groups, rape of the opponents' women, even where officially condemned, has often been exploited as a terrorist weapon or formed a part of the loot extracted by the victors. A modern example was the wholesale raping of Bengali women by West Pakistani soldiers during the war of 1971. The tragedy was compounded by the attitude of their Moslem menfolk. The victims, having been sullied, were no longer acceptable as brides or fit to remain as wives. Many became paupers, cast out by their families and left to the mercies of a precarious government welfare service that resorted to bribing reluctant men to take them in. During the Vietnam war, according to Brownmiller, in spite of the brothels organized by the military, rape of oriental girls by American GIs was pretty much S.O.P.—standard operational practice—in some units. During the slavery era in the south of the United States, white overseers or owners often forced their black females into sexual subjugation. The numerous mulatto babies so produced added to the economic advantage of the system, which depended upon rapid breeding once further importation of Africans came to an end. These examples seem to show that, given the right setting and opportunity, acts of rape are by no means alien to the so-called civilized male. In some American prisons, non-aggressive young men of puny physique submit to homosexual advances of a more established convict in order to gain protection from rape by all and sundry (Scacco, 1975). Brownmiller speculates that this may have been the original female motive for supporting the institution of monogamous marriage.

The theory that rape is a natural product of social systems, rather than a manifestation of individual pathology, receives some support from systematic studies of crimes reported to the police. It appears that a substantial proportion of rapes occur in the context of ordinary relationships between normal men and women. The offenders are mostly young and working-class, and their victims are likely to be the same, coming from the same neighbourhood and ethnic group. Amir (1971), in a study of 646 rapes recorded in police files in Philadelphia, found that a substantial proportion of offenders, about half in fact, were free of prior criminal record, and of those with a record the great majority had been convicted for non-sexual crimes such as burglary and robbery. Similar conclusions emerged from a study directed by Radzinowicz (1957), based upon English police records. Only about 9 per cent of identified rapists and attempted rapists, and about 13 per cent of men guilty of sexual assaults on females, were found to have any previous conviction for a sexual offence. In a small sample of males charged with rape or attempted rape over a twelve-month period in Toronto, Mohr (1965) found that any substantial violence was rare. In most cases only threats, slaps, or forceful removal of clothing was alleged. None of the victims showed visible injuries beyond slight bruising. In nearly all cases some social interaction between offender and victim had led up to the incident. The commonest sequence of events was a meeting in a bar or restaurant followed by acceptance of a ride in the offender's car, which was then driven either home or to a secluded place. Only 18·4 per cent of the accused were finally convicted, and then not necessarily for the crime of completed rape. About a third of the incidents had taken place in the home of either offender or victim. In the Philadelphia survey 55·7 per cent of the incidents had taken place indoors, at the residence of either offender or victim. In a survey of 200 rapes in Denver published by MacDonald (1971), the corresponding figure was 54·5 per cent. In the Denver study, 40 per cent of the victims were raped by a friend, relative, employer or casual acquaintance. In the Philadelphia study, 19 per cent of the incidents were categorized as 'victim-precipitated', in so far as the woman had apparently given preliminary consent to intercourse and then retracted, or else shown no strong resistance to the offender's sexual advances. In another study in Berkeley, California, Nelson and Amir (1975) found that a fifth of the total of reported rape incidents were attacks on girl hitch-hikers. The victims were often fatalistic in their acceptance of the risk of being raped by drivers and ready to submit once an attack had begun. Such figures highlight the fact that many rapes are not cases of strangers taking women completely by surprise. In reality, an even larger proportion of rapes than is suggested by the statistics probably belongs to the grey area between forcible wooing and forcible assault. These are the circumstances least likely to lead to an official report to the police, for the woman who has put herself in a so-called compromising position knows that she will find difficulty and embarrassment in establishing that she was not a consenting partner.

The group rapes perpetrated as masculinity-proving rituals by some motorcycle gangs, or occasionally in more respectable settings at stag parties, or in student dormitories, demonstrate the relative ease with which, under appropriate circumstances, even in civilian life, young males can be led to participate in sexual assaults. Group rapes form a much larger proportion of the totality of reported crimes than is generally realized. In Amir's study, 26·5 per cent of the victims were raped by three or more offenders. In nearly all these cases the circumstances were deliberately engineered in advance and the rape therefore premeditated, at least by the leaders of the escapade. Such incidents provide further evidence that rape is not an unthinkable, improbable activity committed only by extremely deviant individuals acting in isolation.

Rapists finally convicted and imprisoned represent a selected minority of the worst offenders. Prison samples regularly yield a different and more horrifying picture of the character of rape and rapists than do surveys based upon initial complaints to the police. Gebhard *et al.* (1965), who drew their sample from American penal institutions, found that among attackers of adult women or minors (that is, females aged 12 or more) over 90 per cent were convicted for some crime by the age of 30, and that over half of their crimes were sexual. Of those who were under sentence for attacks upon females of 16 or older, nearly a half had one or more previous convictions for a sex offence. A high proportion of their current crimes, 72 per cent, were attacks upon complete strangers. In two-fifths of the cases considerable force had been used and in another two-fifths serious threats for instance against the victim's children, were employed. The majority of the offenders agreed that their victims had put up an active resistance. McCaldon (1967), who examined rapists in Kingston Penitentiary, found that 84 per cent had used considerable force in the course of their attacks, and that a fifth had had previous convictions for sex offences. Among sex offenders against children in the same institution, two-fifths were found to have previous convictions for sex offences.

Follow-up studies of the subsequent conviction histories of convicted sex offenders have also yielded results that vary with the nature of the sample. The public, encouraged by selective reporting of the worst and most sensational cases in the media, has an exaggerated idea of the recidivist tendency of the generality of sex offenders, which is in reality quite low. For example, according to the report by Radzinowicz (1957, Table 53) 84 per cent of the 1,919 offenders studied, and 90 per cent of the aggressors against females of 16 or older, were not reconvicted of any sex crime during a follow-up period of four years in freedom. On the other hand, the report also pointed to the existence of a minority who persisted in sexual crime in spite of repeated sentences of imprisonment.

An unusually large and thorough survey of sexual recidivism carried out in Denmark by Christiansen *et al.* (1965) was based upon 2,934 sex offenders followed up in records for a period of not less than 12 years and up to 24 years. Little difference was found in the recidivism rates of different types of sexual crime. For the whole sample, nearly a quarter sustained a further conviction, but only about 10 per cent were reconvicted for a sex crime. Nevertheless, there were some persistent offenders. A history of previous conviction for sexual crime increased an offender's likelihood of sexual recidivism more than threefold.

A gloomier picture of the likelihood of recidivism emerged from a study by Frisbie and Dondis (1965) of the post-release careers of sexually aggressive patients discharged from Atascadero State Hospital, California. The sample was of course a highly selected one, since all these men had been committed for an indefinite period under a statute that required the offender to be 'diagnosed' a sexual psychopath and assessed as 'amenable' to treatment in a state hospital. A substantial majority were offenders against children or minors, often members of their own family. Men whose original offence had been sexual aggression against females unrelated to them and aged 18 or more tended to remain in the institution longer than other categories and to fare worse after release. The sexual recidivism rate of this group climbed to a cumulative total of 35·6 per cent over a five-year period, with sharp increases annually after the first six months. The recidivism rate of this group was three times greater than that of the men whose original offence consisted of sexual contact with female children or minors.

For most types of crime, offenders who have not been reconvicted in the first three years are unlikely to be reconvicted later. Reconvictions for sex crimes, however, often occur after long intervals of ten years or more. Christiansen *et al.* found that in his sample the total reconvicted for a sex crime continued to rise year by year for some 17 years. In fact the number of purely sexual recidivists was hardly any greater in the first six years of follow-up than in the second six years. In a recent British survey, Soothill *et al.* (1976) followed up for 22 years the subsequent conviction records of 86 men who had been found guilty of rape offences in 1951. Over this period 15 were reconvicted of a sexual offence, including 5 who were reconvicted of a further rape. Two of these 5 committed a further rape offence 16 or more years after their initial rape conviction. It follows that, unless a long span of time is taken into account, the risk of repeated sex crime may be underestimated. Owing to the secrecy surrounding sexual behaviour, and the difficulty of securing a conviction for rape, these long gaps between recorded offences do not necessarily mean that the recidivist has been of good conduct throughout the period of apparent freedom from crime.

As has been pointed out, rapists form only a small minority of the totality of convicted sexual criminals, only 3·0 per cent in the survey by Christiansen *et al.* Most of the crimes of male sex offenders consist of indecent behaviour with children or minors of either sex or acts of genital exhibitionism. According to the Radzinowicz report (p. 110), 82 per cent of victims of sex crimes were under 16 and the vast majority of offenders had made contact with them in an amicable manner without resort to intimidation or the offer of money. All the surveys seem to agree that the reconvictions of most sexual recidivists, at least in so far as their purely sexual crimes are concerned, are repetitions of the same kind of misbehaviour, the indecent exposers continue to offend by exposing, those who play sex games with small boys continue to pick up small boys, and those who make unwanted advances to young girls do the same again subsequently. The

Radzinowicz report sums it up (p. 179) as follows: 'There was no indication in any of the classes that persistent offenders progressed from less serious to more serious sexual offences. Generally there was a great similarity between the reported sexual offences.'

In spite of this statistical evidence to the contrary the myth still persists that the average sex offender is liable to progress to more serious crimes as time goes on. Men caught spying through bedroom windows, or exposing themselves to girls in the park, come under unjustified suspicion of being potential rapists. In point of fact, clinical experience with run-of-the-mill deviants, of the kind seen in psychiatric out-patient wards, shows that most of these unfortunates are timorous, socially inadequate males who experience difficulty in establishing relationships with adult women. Men convicted of acts of peeping or exhibiting themselves from a distance are pathetically non-violent and essentially ritualistic. They do not progress to acts of aggression and would probably run away if the victim came closer.

There are exceptions to this rule. Just as case histories of serious heroin addicts reveal that some of them have started with common-place marijuana smoking, so do case histories of rapists reveal that some of them, in their younger days, used to indulge in acts of voyeurism or exhibitionism (MacDonald, 1973). In their American survey, Gebhard *et al.* (1965) found that as many as one in ten of the exhibitionists in their prison sample had at some stage attempted rape or seriously contemplated doing so. They also found (p. 193) that of the total offences committed by men convicted of aggressive assaults upon adult females 21 per cent were for exhibition and 19 per cent for peeping. On the other hand, they pointed out that even in their prison sample escalation was not typical of the minor sex offenders. For example (p. 378), out of 41 offenders convicted of peeping, most of whom had been found guilty of the same act more than once, only 3 had also committed aggressive sexual acts.

The relatively high incidence of minor offences of a deviant nature in the histories of some rapists was noted also by Cormier *et al.* (1969) in a study of a small group of very serious or homicidal Canadian sex offenders. They suggested that systematic progression to ever more serious and sadistic crimes was a characteristic of the truly dangerous sex offender. This phenomenon of progression, because it does not manifest itself in the majority of the offenders who come before the courts or who are seen by psychiatrists, and is limited to the most serious cases, has tended to be neglected, if not actually denied, in criminological writings.

A true, progressive escalation occurs in some cases, but in others the progression may be more apparent than real. Sometimes offenders are convicted of minor crimes initially only because they were interrupted before they could put their intentions fully into effect. A prospective rapist peering through windows in search of a likely victim may be arrested at that stage and convicted of no more than peeping. Some offenders, especially the mentally subnormal, may expose their genitals as a crude form of sexual invitation or as a preliminary to further indecent acts. When a conviction career consists of indecent assaults interspersed with an occasional conviction for indecent exposure, the offender is unlikely to belong to the psychiatric category of compulsive neurotic exhibitionists.

One cannot proceed far towards understanding serious sexual assaults without some attempt at definition and preliminary classification. Legal labels like rape and indecent assault are unhelpful because they cover such a wide range of circumstances and take no account of the motives or characteristics of the participants. This book is concerned only with seriously aggressive assaults on women where the offender makes an obviously uninvited sexual advance, accompanied by actual violence or terrorizing threats, typically directed against a complete stranger who is actively resisting. This definition eliminates all those incidents, even though sometimes legally classed as rape, which consist of imprudent but non-violent over-persuasion of girls by young men behaving in ways only slightly less restrained than those of many of their peers who never come to official notice. It also eliminates the commonplace, non-violent offenders, including the vast majority of exhibitionists and sexual molesters of boys and girls, whose activities are more of a nuisance than a physical danger. It also excludes the situational offender, the man drawn into a sexually inviting situation who encounters an unexpected refusal and reacts by continued pursuit of his sexual goal with unacceptable forcefulness.

Serious sexual aggressors naturally predominate among men serving long terms of imprisonment for sexual attacks. Many of them have a record of repeated non-sexual as well as sexual crime. The immediate goal of their attacks being, apparently, heterosexual gratification, they are not usually considered deviant. Their problem seems to be lack of control over impulsive, unsocialized behaviour rather than any obvious peculiarity of sexual appetite. They are the sort of characters who take what they want regardless of social rules and undeterred by the distress caused to their victims. Sex crimes and property crimes are inextricably intermingled in those cases in which offenders have taken advantage of female victims encountered in the course of robbery and burglary. In short, the assaultative sex offender shares so many of the characteristics of other aggressively predatory criminals that he is virtually indistinguishable from them, and for that reason all too often considered of no particular psychiatric interest.

Gebhard *et al.* (1965), in their survey of imprisoned offenders, recognized three groups of heterosexual aggressors. The first consisted of 'statistically normal individuals who simply misjudged the situation'. This group was naturally small among prison inmates, and does not come within the definition of serious sexual aggressors. Gebhard *et al.* placed the majority of their sample in what might be called a 'criminal' or 'sociopathic' group. These were described as 'criminally inclined men who take what they want, whether money, material, or women, and their sex offences are by-products of their general criminality'. These hedonistic men pay little heed to social restraints, have frequent confrontations with the law, and treat women as functional objects for the provision of sexual pleasure on demand. They are not active women-haters, but they are apt to become aggressive with a woman if she frustrates their wishes. After heavy drinking they are liable to become even more selfish, unreasonable and potentially violent than in their sober state.

The sociopathic category has been identified by many observers. Guttmacher and Weihofen (1952, p. 117) refer to a type of rapist who is not primarily a sex offender: 'He is the aggressive, antisocial criminal who, like the soldier of a conquering army, is out to pillage and rob.' They cite as examples young men who, in the course of the same night's work of plunder, commit both burglaries and rapes.

Sociopathic hedonism and lack of restraint, although it may be the most prominent characteristic of a majority of imprisoned rapists, does not explain the behaviour of all sexual aggressors. It fails to explain why some men, at great risk to themselves, and notwithstanding the availability of wives, girlfriends and prostitutes, should go out of their way to seek out strange and unwilling women, all for the sake of brief sexual release under conditions of struggle and considerable discomfort. They may afterwards display anxiety and remorse about their conduct with an intensity quite unusual in a simple sociopath. Such offenders would appear to be driven by strong impulses that are not just urges for straightforward sexual gratification. Gebhard *et al.* must have become aware of these cases when they described a group of aggressors, smaller than the sociopathic group, who 'were suffering from personality defects and stresses which ultimately erupt in a sexual offense'. These men 'might lead non-criminal, even conventional, lives until they suddenly snap from hidden emotional conflicts'.

This group of conflict-ridden aggressors, or acting-out neurotics as some authorities prefer to call them, has been described by various writers. Guttmacher and Weihofen refer to rapists in conflict because they fail to live up to their own image of masculinity, whose crimes result from 'an irrational effort to deny the existence of homosexual urges', or from a 'deep-seated hatred focused particularly on women'. The same type was described in the Canadian study by McCaldon (1967) of convicted rapists in Kingston Penitentiary. Having first distinguished the sociopaths, who pursued their goals regardless of normal restraints, but usually with no more sadism than was necessary to achieve their object, he went on to delineate a group which he called 'defensives'. These were men acting desperately and irrationally to try to compensate for inner insecurity. They were true misogynists who expressed their hostility to women by overpowering, devaluing and dirtying their victims. Their crimes were acts of symbolic virility, by which they strove to compensate for a felt inadequacy. At the same time their attacks served as revenge against the female sex for having in the past so often tantalized and frustrated them with unfulfilled expectations of warmth and love.

The concept of rape as a form of overcompensation for feelings of inadequacy receives some support from the results of personality testing. Fisher and Rivlin (1971), working in California, applied the Edwards Personal Preference Schedule to 100 men convicted of forcible rape and compared their responses with those of a control group of non-sexual offenders. The rapists appeared more self-critical, less self-assured and more dependent than the other offenders. The investigators considered the findings consonant with the idea of rape as an expression of hostility by a man who feels weak, inadequate or dependent.

Most of the members of the treatment group in the present study could be described as belonging to the relatively unusual category of manifestly unhappy, conflict-driven rapists who themselves recognized a need for psychiatric help to understand and control their turbulent emotions. Nevertheless, some of them also displayed aggressive, antisocial and criminal habits more characteristic of sociopaths. For descriptive purposes one may conveniently contrast the ideal type of unrestrained, care-free sociopathic rapist with the compulsive, guilt-ridden, acting-out neurotic, but such a clear dichotomy does not exist in real life. Many offenders exhibit a mixture of sociopathic and neurotic features, with one or the other predominating. It would be wrong to dismiss a rapist as hopelessly unamenable to the psychiatric approach because his resistance to antisocial impulses appears weak or because he comes from a criminal subculture. Sociopathically inclined individuals are not always immune to irrational inferiority feelings and urges to over-compensate. Indeed they may give expression to such impulses all the more readily because their powers of self-control generally are weak. Hence even the more criminal types may sometimes benefit from the lessening of frustration that may be brought about through coming to a better understanding of the irrational and compulsive element in their behaviour. Writing off offenders as hopelessly unamenable to psychiatry on account of their sociopathic attitudes is a dangerous procedure. Since the assessment depends upon a presumed absence of feeling, and absence of desire to conform, mistakes can be made when offenders hide their true feelings behind a protective smoke-screen of toughness and hostility to authority.

To conclude this brief review, one can see now that the treatment group in this study was made up from a relatively unusual type of offender, but one that experienced clinicians have long since recognized. For want of a better term they might be described as 'compensatory aggressives'. Their importance is out of proportion to their numbers, first because their crimes are serious and persistent enough to require drastic intervention, and second because their problems appear potentially treatable by psychotherapy.

CHAPTER VIII

The Treatment Process

The group had two main therapeutic tasks. The first was to achieve greater self-understanding through discussion of the intimate details of each man's past. The topics discussed included the traumatic incidents of childhood that may have affected the men's attitudes for the worse, the discontents and miseries that had soured their hetero-sexual relationships, and the bitter feelings that had culminated in sexual attacks. By gaining insight into the way past injuries continue to produce hostile feelings and inappropriate conduct in the present, it was hoped patients would come to realize the changes they needed to make, and would develop a determination to act accordingly.

The second therapeutic task was to learn to cope with immediate realities in a sensible and self-controlled manner. Observations by nursing staff and group members of how each man was behaving, on the ward and in the institution at large, were reported back to group meetings. This enabled assessments to be made of the extent to which the improved self-awareness spoken about in the group had taken root and was being translated into action in daily life.

These treatment procedures were based on the assumption that the offender's crime was a sick act, alien to his own better judgment and conscious ideals, to which he had been driven by emotional urges that he could not, at the time, fully comprehend or control. This assumption was continually reinforced by the case histories presented in the group, which attributed relatively little importance to the element of sexual gratification, but showed that crimes had been committed during states of emotional turmoil and had been swiftly followed by considerable guilt and remorse. Doubtless it was in part a function of the selection process that group members conformed so solidly to this pattern, for many ordinary rapes are primarily pleasure-seeking acts which the offenders do not view as any more shameful or deviant than, for example, stealing goods when the opportunity arises. To many tough, hard-living, predatory males the borderline between forceful seduction and legal rape is far from clear, especially if the female involved is seen as a 'no good' character or as 'asking for it'. Girls of the kind chosen by young delinquents for 'gang bangs' are often far too compromised to complain afterwards of having been raped, even had they a mind to do so. Girl hitch-hikers who decline lifts from women in the hope of enjoying amorous adventures with male drivers are said to have only themselves to blame if the consequences exceed their desires. Rapists who think along these lines, and have no particular regrets, save for having been caught, would not find their way into this kind of therapeutic group because they would be most unlikely to be considered by a psychiatrist as suitably motivated for psychotherapy. Moreover, the situational rapes committed by these uninhibited offenders do not compare with the desperate attacks upon unsuspecting females which most members of the group had committed.

Even in this group some members, particularly those accustomed to a criminal life, occasionally described sexual misconduct in terms more suggestive of casual indulgence that had not seemed very wrong at the time, than of serious emotional conflict. One man, for instance, told how he used very frequently to pick up young Indian girls in his car and then seduce them, forcibly if necessary, or with threats to make them get out and walk, but none of them resisted very much or reported him to the police. It was not these incidents, but some much more serious attacks committed later that brought him to prison and made him realize that he had by then lost control and needed psychiatric help.

Another and less secure assumption underlying the present treatment programme was the belief that observation of behaviour in the institution could be used to judge whether fundamental changes in a patient's personal outlook had taken place, and whether these were sufficiently stabilized to prevent a reversion to old habits after release. Admittedly, striking changes sometimes occurred that were not only clear to everyone but were of a kind likely to alter a man's whole life for the better. For example, at the start of treatment, a man might be sulky, suspicious and rebellious towards the nurses and explosive-tempered in his dealings with other inmates. Over a period of time he might become more equable, more confident in his relations with staff and fellow patients, able to stand frustrations without exploding and able to put across his feelings and point of view without losing his temper or giving offence. Another man might start off by being uncommunicative, socially isolated, always answering politely, but never giving away his real feelings, never standing up for his rights, meeting frustrations silently and without complaint, but at untold cost in unexpressed tension and bitterness. In time, he might learn to open up, to talk freely to nurses of both sexes, to assert himself appropriately, to say no or to disagree when occasion demands. Such changes seem clearly beneficial, likely to make life after release run more smoothly, and hence to lessen the risk of further outbursts of sexual aggression.

Unfortunately, so long as observation remains limited to behaviour inside the institution, it is impossible to demonstrate that improvements will last after release. Surrounded by a wire fence, cut off from sexual relationships, kept away from intoxicants, relieved of responsibility for earning a living, with a daily time-table mapped out for them like infants, these patients had no opportunity to test their new-found confidence against the harsh realities of life outside. Prison restricts and frustrates, but it also protects inmates from social rebuffs, sexual rejections, humiliations at work and many other stresses that free men must be prepared to face. Changes made while inside the institution do not prove that a man will maintain the same equilibrium when faced once more with all the old stresses with the added burden of an ex-convict-sex-offender label to carry.

No system has succeeded fully in reconciling the needs of treatment with those of justice and security. Justice demands fixed terms of detention as a punishment for past crimes. Penal authorities are charged with a responsibility to protect the public from criminals for the duration of their sentence. They cannot risk relaxation of security, or permit trial periods of freedom, for offenders whose criminal history suggests that they are potentially dangerous. The medical treatment model, on the other hand, calls for some flexibility in the time spent in custody according to the offender's progress towards emotional reorientation. Even more important, a realistic treatment programme concentrates on readjustment to the community rather than adjustment to artificial institutional life. The most critical phase of treatment starts when the offender begins to face life outside once again. That moment is the testing time for treatment gains made during incarceration. It is also the moment when emotional conflicts are liable to be reawakened and help is most needed and most likely to be effective. In concrete, practical terms, the psychiatric approach calls for release by easy stages while the offender is still under supervision and still an active participant in a treatment programme. Without this essential provision treatment schemes are not being given a fair chance and should not be blamed if they fail to prevent recidivism.

The group operated under a penal system which made virtually no concession to the goal of integrating treatment effort with the processes of discharge. A man could remain two years or more in the group and attain, in the judgment of the staff, a state of mind that made further offending unlikely, but if he had still a long time to go before the end of his sentence, or if he were under indeterminate detention from a life sentence or from categorization as a dangerous sexual offender, he could not begin any sort of phased release, however gradual. Instead, he would have to return to the penitentiary and lose contact with the treatment team. If the same man had served more of his sentence, and was approaching or actually at the point of eligibility for consideration for parole, he still could not be tested on day passes in the community while remaining under treatment. The restrictive policy of the Centre, which counts as a maximum security institution within the penitentiary service, would not permit it. Instead, he would have to apply for transfer to another penitentiary institution in the hope of being sent to a prison where privileges such as day passes or working outside are permitted in selected cases. He would still lose contact with the treatment team, and of course at the very time when he most needed their support.

This reversion from a treatment milieu to a prison setting, and especially to the setting of a large penitentiary where sex offenders not in protective custody face a constant physical threat from hostile inmates, is hardly conducive to the maintenance of improved attitude changes. Not only will the former patient lack help at the time of release, but by then the beneficial effects of group therapy may have been counteracted by the necessity to readopt the self-contained, unconfiding and exploiting attitudes that men must have to survive in prison. In spite of the intensive nature of the group effort, and the optimistic appraisals of changes achieved by some patients, this defect in the treatment scheme, attributable to the rules of a penal system not having been designed with psychiatic treatment in mind, cannot but lessen confidence in these patients' future prospects. The scheme has not been in operation long enough for the treatment team to be able to report what happens when former group members who have graduated from treatment to prison are eventually released. At the time of writing, most of them are still in prison.

Following their latest conviction, the cases of several members of the group had been referred, on the basis of their conviction record, to a special judicial hearing, as a result of which they were placed in the legal category of Dangerous Sexual Offender (Greenland, 1977). The effect of this is to convert the previously fixed sentence into a completely indeterminate period of detention. If the offender is ever to come out of prison alive, the parole authorities must take the initiative and the responsibility for discharging him. In view of widespread public criticism of sex offenders being given parole, and the fact that parole policy so easily becomes an issue in political controversy, any such decisions must be peculiarly difficult. Out of 82 persons committed as Dangerous Sex Offenders since 1949, and alive in December 1975, 65 (79.3 per cent) were still in custody. In the United States the statutes that permit indeterminate detention of selected sex offenders have been the subject of so much criticism that many jurisdictions have repealed them. The criteria for determining dangerousness were themselves dangerously unclear. Although the declared purpose of such legislation may have been to secure appropriate treatment, this was not always available. Custody tended to become interminable owing to the absence of firm guidelines for release. In Canada it appears that British Columbia is the only province that has used the DSO law for any significant number of cases. Without knowing the details of the evidence presented, or the nature of the psychiatric testimony relied upon, it is impossible to comment upon the merits of particular cases. From a therapist's standpoint, however, the men so designated were not necessarily worse, or manifestly more dangerous, than other members of the group, but the effect of being so labelled increased their pessimism about the result of the treatment. It seemed to these offenders that the authorities had little confidence in the elaborate and expensive psychiatric treatment provided, and a great reluctance to put it to the test by releasing anyone.

The difficulties of trying to apply a pure treatment philosophy in a penal setting manifested themselves in many different ways. In their autobiographies and in their discussions the group were much more open about their crimes and their motives than is usual among sentenced prisoners, but that is not to say they were completely without reserve. They were conscious of being under surveillance by a staff who were paid by, regulated by, and owed primary loyalty to the penitentiary authority. They realized full well that the opinions, assessments and reports by nursing staff and by the psychiatrist were made use of by transfer boards, which governed their prison placements and affected their status and privileges, and also by the parole hearings, which determined their release dates. Remarks were made which indicated considerable soul searching on the part of some of the patients, who found difficulty in knowing how much they dare reveal, especially about their current anxieties and fantasies. One man told how his confessions to a social worker had been used against him when he was declared a 'dangerous sexual offender'. After that experience it was a struggle for him to bring himself to trust anyone again. Another said openly that his dislike of the policing aspect of the nurses' role in the institution prevented him from conversing with them on an ordinary, friendly basis. From time to time he and others vented their feelings of resentment at the psychiatrist's coercive powers. They had little faith that enthusiastic psychiatric reports would advance their release, but they feared that less than enthusiastic reports would count heavily against them. As one man put it, he would agree to any useless advice, whether to take Antabuse or to stand on his head, in order to satisfy the doctor and gain a favourable report. The body counts every few hours, repeated ward tours by the nurses, occasional room searches, the sight of larger watch-towers under construction which were to house armed guards, and all the other apparatus of high security, dismayed and discouraged some of the patients. One man pointed out with much feeling that he was expected to trust the staff, without the slightest trust being shown him in return. Another man felt that the nursing staff were so expectant of 'manipulation' by inmates that they could not recognize or give credit when a patient was sincere.

Laying bare one's worst thoughts to critical scrutiny by a group is no easy task at best, but some of the patients, after an initial period of caution, managed to overcome the added fears of recrimination induced by the penal setting. For some men, this was in itself a very considerable change. One man said that before he came to the group there was no way in which he could bring himself to disclose the full truth about himself and his crimes. He felt that if people only knew all the bad things he could tell about himself, they would want to lock him up and throw away the key. At a much later stage he admitted that the idea of covering up some feelings still lingered. 'I want to get out of being confined, but I have to be careful that this feeling of wanting to be free doesn't interfere with treatment. I've done some sick things in my time, and I don't want to risk doing them again.'

Aware of the temptation to keep an eye on the gate and cover up disapproved feelings, both patients and staff were peculiarly critical of suspected insincerity. Expressions of sweet reasonableness, or of ready acquiescence in the doctor's interpretations, could be dismissed as so much garbage if they appeared inconsistent with a man's attitude or behaviour outside the group. Because of the limited scope for rebellious acts within a total institution, small rule infractions which, to an outsider, might seem childishly trivial, assumed a special significance in the eyes of both nurses and patients, presumably because they could be taken as indications of a something less than whole-hearted dedication to the group goals. If someone got up late on Sunday, or left a dirty cup lying about, or delayed dealing with a correspondence course lesson, or obtained a pair of slippers from another inmate without going through official channels, the matter was liable to be aired at length and with much feeling.

In spite of all these pressures towards conformity, the group was far from being brain-washed yes-men. Playing safe by phoney protestations of goodwill or slavish adherence to the rules was not the usual reaction. Most of the group revealed their true feelings only too clearly on occasion, in outbursts of anger, in sulks, in defiant denials of the obvious, in open resistance to advice or in argumentative contradictions of the interpretations put upon their conduct. One member, constantly under criticism for his solitary habits, equally constantly insisted that he chose to be that way, that he preferred to be independent, that it was no problem for him, that he liked to think things out on his own and that he could perfectly well act differently if he saw any benefit in doing so. Another man insisted, almost as emphatically, that he was the best judge of his own progress, that the inferiority feelings that had led to his crimes were cured, and that soon he would be ready to leave and would ask for a transfer regardless of the opinions of the psychiatrist and the group on the matter. Confrontations of this sort, accompanied by considerable emotional tension, not always restricted to the man on the hot seat, were fairly frequent and appeared to be useful in promoting psychological insight.

Some degree of reluctance to conform to the demands of the group, and some episodes of disturbing behaviour, had to be tolerated. Emotionally disturbed persons cannot always control themselves, and their outbursts provided valuable insights into personality defects and emotional problems. But some forms of behaviour were too disruptive to be allowed to continue for long. Walking out of group meetings, refusing to get out of bed, slashing oneself with a table knife, spitting out medication after pretending to swallow it, lying to staff or indulging in swearing and tantrums were among the hundred and one examples of troublesome behaviour that invited rejection from the group. Deciding the point at which to draw the line and ask for expulsion was one of the most exacting of the therapists' tasks. It was complicated by the fact that the system required any inmate transferred out of the institution without completing a recommended course of treatment to be returned to the prison where he had been before admission. This could amount to a severe punishment because of the expected adverse effect it might have upon parole release date. According to taste, the situation could be regarded as a helpful circumstance, promoting cooperation and increasing motivation for treatment, or as a counterproductive form of coercion engendering unhelpful attitudes of suspicion among the patients. Some of the patients, certainly, reacted to the challenge in destructive, negative ways. Anti-authoritarian characters were stimulated to test how far they could go. When finally the inevitable rejection came, it served to confirm their worst fears, so that when they left the treatment programme they did so feeling more bitter than ever about society and the system. Other patients, finding staff criticism and periods spent on the hot seat too uncomfortable, tried to obtain some relief from pressure by threatening to demand their own transfer against the wishes of the treatment staff. This continual threat of a return to prison if treatment went wrong was, on the whole, detrimental, and partly to blame for the high proportion of men who left prematurely. Some of them felt impelled to ask for their own transfer in a pathetic attempt to demonstrate their courage and defiance, others did so to avoid the prospect of ultimate rejection and the presumed adverse effect of an actual dismissal upon their hopes of early parole.

In spite of these hindrances to the honest expression of feelings, especially bad feelings, nursing staff, patients and the psychiatrist were often unanimous in their views about a particular man's progress. They could agree on whether he seemed to be fully committed to the treatment ideal or was still holding back, whether he was putting up a genuine struggle to understand his own emotional reactions and whether, in his everyday relationships within the institution, he could now deal with people more easily and avoid an emotional explosion when something frustrating occurred. All these judgments were largely intuitive, and unanimity might be the result of a common bias. When, as sometimes happened, opinions conflicted there was no external criterion to settle the issue.

This last point became very obvious in the course of discussions in the group, and also among staff members outside the group, concerning some of the patients who were due to leave. These patients had been in the programme longer than the two years or so considered optimal, or else their parole eligibility date was approaching. In the latter event, transfer to a less secure prison, where day passes might be permitted, was believed to be in the inmate's best interests, so that he would have a chance to impress the parole board with his readiness for release under supervision. In these cases, if there was any disagreement about the advisability of terminating treatment, or if members of staff had differing views as to whether the report on the man's response to treatment should include a favourable comment about his prospects after release, it was very much a case of one person's opinion against another's. There was one man, for example, who had become more tolerant and understanding in his expressed attitudes towards women. He claimed that this change in his emotional outlook had been accompanied by a change in his sexual fantasy, which had previously run to themes of violence. He said he no longer obtained pleasure from erotic thoughts of a sadistic kind. Since his problem in dealing with women on an intimate level had never revealed itself at all obviously in his ordinary social relations, there was no striking change in his outward behaviour to be seen. Accordingly, some persons could not believe that a significant change had taken place, while others were prepared to accept it.

Unsatisfactory as it may be to base predictions upon subjective impressions of personality and attitude change, especially in a restricted penal setting, therapists have nothing else available. Compared with arrangements in some penal treatment centres, the therapists had the advantage of unusually prolonged and intensive observation in an atmosphere considerably more liberal and more committed to a therapeutic ideal than, for example, that of the typical prison. Although, from some points of view, the therapists' lack of decisive involvement in the release process was unfortunate, it helped inmates to speak their minds more candidly than they might otherwise have done. One may contrast the situation with that described by Roberts and Pacht (1965) in Wisconsin, where both diagnosis and treatment took place in the state prison. All convicted rapists were required to undergo a psychiatric examination. If they were then committed for treatment their subsequent release on parole depended upon a favourable recommendation by a Review Board. The psychiatrist and social worker on the Board evaluated the sexual psychopathology, personality and social prospects of each offender in the light of his case history, and his therapist's reports. Inmates were warned that any matter brought up in therapy might be made known to the Board. These conditions must have reduced self-revelation and freedom of discussion. In their report the psychiatrists admitted that it was so, but argued that on the whole the system worked to good effect.

There are three main reasons to justify scepticism about the value of the group treatment programme in British Columbia: absence of firm evidence that the attainment of insight into motives for sexual aggression will prevent recurrence, lack of any means for testing behaviour beyond the confines of the institution, and the barriers to frank communication and assessment within a penal setting. These grounds for scepticism would not amount to much if it could be proved by a follow-up study that the programme really achieved the prevention of further crimes after release.

Unfortunately, for reasons only too familiar, the preventive value of this programme is not likely to be proved for a very long time, if at all. If offenders serving long or indeterminate sentences are kept in custody until they are so old that further sexual aggression becomes a physical impossibility we shall never know if their treatment would have prevented crime during the age of risk. Relatively few rapists released from prison are reconvicted for serious sexual crimes. In order to show that treated sexual offenders run a significantly smaller risk of reconviction a substantial number of cases would have to be followed up for many years. A small-scale programme such as this could never hope to furnish sufficient cases to build up the necessary statistics. Furthermore, it would hardly be fair to evaluate the effectiveness of treatment from a scheme operating under the handicaps that prevailed at the time of this study, with patients returning to prison on completion of their treatment and no organized system for providing continuity of psychiatric attention during the critical phase of release back into the community. Finally, even if, long after the working lifetime of those presently concerned with the programme, sufficient numbers accumulate to demonstrate a lower reconviction rate for treated than for untreated offenders of similar age and criminal history, this would still not amount to proof. The difference might be due to the way the treated cases were selected in the first place, by weeding out the recalcitrant, the unintelligent and the poorly motivated. Treating only those with good prospects guarantees impressive results. To prove the effectiveness of treatment like must be compared with like, treated cases must be compared with others, assessed as equally eligible for inclusion, who did not receive treatment.

The necessary comparisons are unlikely ever to be made. Lawyers, administrators and psychiatrists dislike assessing cases for suitability unless all those selected actually receive treatment. The fact is conveniently overlooked that facilities are always so limited that only a fraction of potentially suitable cases can be accommodated. Ethical scruples can present an insurmountable barrier to scientific evaluation. These scruples are rarely heard in connection with any demand made in the interests of security, but suddenly they become paramount when a request is made in the interest of furthering knowledge for the benefit of all.

In the present state of the art, a treatment effort such as the one described is largely an act of faith. The therapists believe in it, superficial indications suggest that it helps and, though it can be painful at times, the patients want it, but the security of scientific proof of effectiveness is missing. However, in human affairs, especially in matters of social policy, many decisions have to be taken without benefit of rigorous scientific testing. Having observed the work at close quarters, weighed the pros and cons as critically as possible, using common sense and intuition where scientific assessment is not available, we reached a personal conviction that important and relevant changes in attitude were being made by these patients. There were some men in the group whose improvement was so plainly evident to all observers that we should have gladly recommended their release under continued psychiatric supervision had that course been open, despite a lively appreciation—and some practical experience—of the difficulties and responsibilities of making recommendations for parole. But clearly, no effort should be spared, in spite of all the methodological problems, to secure more objective evidence of effectiveness.

Comparisons with other Treatment Programmes

There might be less reason for optimism about the beneficial effects of the present treatment system were it not for the fact that promising results have been reported from comparable schemes at other centres. Group therapy for sex offenders at the Regional Psychiatric Centre, although instituted under a very different legal framework, was originally modelled on a sex offender treatment programme directed by Dr. G. J. MacDonald which has been in operation in Washington State, U.S.A., since 1966. A law passed in 1951 permits the prosecuting attorney in the superior courts in that state to charge any defendant under trial for a sexual offence with 'psychopathy'. The trial proceeds and sentence is pronounced but its execution deferred or suspended. The allegation of sexual psychopathy is then considered, and if it is sustained the offender may be committed to an indefinite period of detention in a state hospital until recommended as 'safe to be at large'.

Statutes of this sort have earned a bad reputation. All too often the labels 'psychopath' and 'treatment' have been exploited to legitimize long periods in custody, under conditions far from therapeutic, for men whose offending behaviour would never have warranted such a severe punishment under an equitable system of justice. In California, programmes for cases defined as Mentally Disordered Sex Offenders have been criticized for relying upon psychiatric assessments of dangerousness that may have little validity. The decision to release, in so far as it depends upon recommendations from therapists, depends upon observations of the patient's conformity to hospital rules, cooperativeness in groups, acceptance of guilt and personal responsibility for his crimes, absence of dangerous sexual fantasies, length of time spent in the institution and circumstances at his home at the moment of the proposed discharge. These criteria may be the ones most readily available to therapists, but they are not necessarily the ones most directly relevant to the risk of re-offending (Dix, 1975). According to one limited follow-up study which compared cases thought to have been successfully treated with others considered not amenable to treatment, there was no difference in the treated cases in terms of subsequent arrests for sex crimes (Dix, 1976). In Washington State, however, the courts have taken advantage of the presence of an active treatment centre at Western State Hospital to put their sexual psychopath statute to constructive use. They commit the offender in the first instance to a 90-day observation period at the hospital to confirm that he is an 'unsafe' psychopath and to ascertain whether he is suitable for the treatment available. If the treatment staff consider the offender too great a risk, or insufficiently motivated to change, he is reported to be unamenable and the court orders reversion to an ordinary correctional sentence.

Offenders accepted for treatment and committed by the courts return to the hospital for a minimum period of twelve months. If they progress satisfactorily they are brought back to the court with a recommendation for conditional release. If this is granted a phase of gradual release begins, during which the offender spends increasingly long hours working outside the hospital until such time as he is considered safe to live on his own in the community, but reporting back as an out-patient. He remains subject to supervision by the hospital, and to the other terms of his conditional release, until the court finally discharges him. Offenders who fail to respond after commitment to the hospital are returned to court as still 'unsafe', but unsuitable for further treatment. The court has the power to release them on its own authority or to order the balance of the judicial sentence to be served in an ordinary correctional institution.

The Washington State system has distinct advantages over the customary arrangements for treating offender patients. The staff have effective control over the selection of potentially treatable cases and a means of relinquishing responsibility for those who, after selection, fail to respond satisfactorily. Decisions to begin a phased release, and decisions to discharge altogether, have to be ratified by the courts, so that public interest in the matter can be seen to be safeguarded. Active treatment continues throughout the critical period of gradual return to life outside the institution. The statutes provide for prolonged loss of liberty, but in practice the offender patients pass through the hospital programme within a reasonable period of time, in most cases regaining at least conditional liberty sooner than they would have done under the prevailing prison sentence tariff. This gives inmates a practical reason for cooperating to the utmost.

The treatment methods used at Western State Hospital have been described in various monographs and annual reports issued by the Department of Social and Health Services (MacDonald and Williams, 1971). Guided self-help is the key principle, with intensive use of group psychotherapy in place of the traditional casework approach. Offenders participate to the full in running their own programme, the longer-experienced guiding the newer members and monitoring their progress. Patients have ample opportunity to mix with each other and with staff and visitors. Their attitude and behaviour in all these interactions is constantly under scrutiny and open to critical discussion at daily group sessions. Each offender has to write a detailed autobiography and submit to cross-examination on its contents at group meetings. Frankness about past offences and present sexual fantasies is demanded of every inmate. Attempts to cover up, or to play 'con games' with staff or fellow patients are swiftly put down. Married patients are required to take part in group counselling together with their wives. Patients are helped to recognize the selfishness and hurtfulness of their offences, to try to understand the pressures which provoked their sexual misconduct, and to accept their need to change their habits and their responsibility for doing so by their own efforts. Promotion through the treatment system, and the privileges that accompany each step forward, have to be earned by positive cooperation, by a show of self-control and by appropriate concern for others. When a generalized improvement in social relationships and in self-confidence has been achieved, the resolve and the ability to give up antisocial sexual practices are expected to follow.

After the gradual release phase has begun the offender can be recalled at once if he neglects work or family responsibilities, forms undesirable associations, lapses into excessive drinking or shows any other signs that he is at risk of re-offending.

The successful social adjustment and improved sexual habits of patients recently under treatment give reason to believe in the benefits of the programme, but no systematic study of long-term results has been published. It is known that re-arrest rates for offenders who have completed the course of treatment is significantly lower than that of sex offenders in Washington State who have served ordinary prison sentences, but the difference may not be entirely the effect of treatment, for high-risk cases and recidivists tend to be rejected as unamenable. About a hundred patients pass through the sex offender programme each year, so it should be possible to demonstrate the impact of treatment even without a strictly matched control group. For example, the total of sexual recidivism among offenders passing through courts which make frequent use of the facility could be compared with that from courts which rarely commit for treatment. Unfortunately, the staff at Western State maintain, with good reason, that the immediate problems of administering treatment leave them no time for proper follow-up research.

The apparent success story of the Western State project cannot be fairly compared with the treatment effort described in this book. In the first place, most of the patients are less serious offenders than the members of the Canadian group. Many are guilty of nothing more than sexual exhibitionism or indecent liberties with minors. Reiatively few have a previous history of imprisonment or of non-sexual crimes. Some have committed violent sexual assaults or forcible rapes comparable to the offences of the Canadian group, but they are in a small minority. In view of the milder character of these offence histories the judicial authorities in Washington State are being something less than reckless in following psychiatric advice and authorizing the release under supervision of men who have apparently responded well to one or two years of in-patient treatment. In the Canadian setting, with offenders having years of imprisonment still to serve, it would be a practical and political impossibility to instigate a similar release policy. Cruel as it may seem, the only solution, in the present climate of opinion, may be to limit intensive psychiatric intervention to men whose sentences afford a reasonable prospect of release into the community on completion of treatment.

Another major difference between the two treatment projects is the greater freedom and scope for self-determination given to the patients at Western State. They are not faced with gun turrets or obtrusive security checks. The prevention of escapes and the protection of inmates from each other is effected more by personal contact and moral persuasion than by physical restraint. This policy is made feasible by careful initial selection, by the high morale and optimism of the participants, by the extensive use of a 'buddy' system (which enables patients to police each other and to dissuade the more impulsive members from foolish acts), by cramming every waking hour with intense activity and by making sure that every individual accepted for treatment is fully committed to the communal effort and to the principle of collective responsibility. Desirable as all this may be in the interests of psychiatric treatment it would be difficult to duplicate in a traditional high-security institution where a distinctive section of staff, with no responsibility for treatment, has charge of security.

Of all the distinctive features of the Western State project, probably the most important is the successful integration of the crucial phase of gradual release into the treatment process. Before being placed on work release by the court, patients are given a detailed plan to which they must adhere. For the first month they must attend all scheduled afternoon or evening meetings at the hospital. In subsequent months attendance requirements are steadily reduced, but patients must still stay most nights at the hospital. On transfer from work release to outpatient status, the patients are set individual goals, such as work training, savings, control of drinking or constructive use of leisure. Their progress in these directions is evaluated when they report back at monthly out-patient meetings. The hospital is fortunately positioned in an area where work is available, but nevertheless the programme depends upon unusually close collaboration between the medical and the judicial authorities, and by the maintenance of good relationships with the surrounding community, upon whose employers and social agencies the patients' rehabilitation depends.

In countries like Canada, where parole authorities control release, an equally close collaboration might, in principle, be established, but in practice therapeutic assessments come low on the list of factors governing release policy. Public opinion, as reflected in comments in the media and in political speeches, acts as a powerful deterrent to the early release of sex offenders, however desirable on therapeutic grounds. At Western State, the therapists have probably been wise to spend a considerable amount of time and thought on public relations and on keeping representatives of the media well informed about what they are doing. But sooner or later in any such treatment programme, however successful it may be in general, among the hundreds of patients passing through the system one is sure to re-offend in a dramatic and dreadful way that attracts banner headlines and a storm of unthinking protest. It is greatly to the credit of those responsible for the Western State programme and its public relations that when, after the scheme had been in operation for some ten years, a storm of this kind broke out they were able to weather it successfully.

The programme for sex offenders at Rahway, New Jersey, an account of which has been published by Brancale et al. (1972), has much in common with the projects at Western State and at the Regional Psychiatric Centre. Like the State of Washington, New Jersey operates a sex offender statute, originally enacted in 1950, which requires sex offenders in certain legally defined categories to be sent to the State Diagnostic Center for a period of observation not exceeding 60 days. If, in the opinion of the psychiatrists, an offender's sexual misconduct appears to be repetitive or compulsive, or if violence was used, or if the victim was under 15 and if the psychiatrists recommend specialized treatment, then the court must commit the offender for treatment, either to an institution or as an out-patient. The duration of custody cannot exceed the maximum sentence for the crime, but unlike other convicts the committed sex offender cannot earn a reduction of sentence through good behaviour. A specialist review board examines each man's progress reports every six months, and has the power to recommend release, but the final decision is taken by the state parole board.

Brancale et al. (1972) examined the use of the sex offender statute over a twenty-year period and found that 28·8 per cent of sex offenders sent to the Diagnostic Center were considered to require specialized treatment, and that about two-thirds of this 28 per cent were committed to institutions. Of the offenders sent to institutions, about a third served their maximum term. About 5 per cent of those passing through institutions on a sex offender commitment were detected in a further sexual offence after release on parole and were accordingly returned as parole violators.

In the New Jersey system, men committed under the sex offender statute spent an initial period at a classification centre, after which they were distributed, according to their needs, between various penal and treatment institutions. Some went to a special treatment unit, accommodating a hundred sex offenders, at Rahway. The unit, at the time of the report, was sited in a prison, but operated to some extent autonomously, utilising an active programme of group therapy.

The treatment at Rahway was based on much the same principles as those that inspired the project at the Regional Psychiatric Centre. In the light of many years experience in probing motives for sex offences, using hypnosis and narcoanalysis, Brancale and his colleagues concluded that many sex crimes were 'merely the surface manifestation of internal psychological motivation'. Some crimes they considered situational, 'largely socially determined' and 'of little psychiatric significance'. Other crimes, especially rapes, were committed by 'socially uninhibited' personalities, 'often influenced by alcohol', as part of an overall antisocial tendency, which frequently included prior criminal activities. But 'close to one half' of sex crimes were thought to be of 'neurotic' origin, that is springing from underlying psychological problems, not necessarily of a specifically sexual kind. For instance, men with pent-up feelings of frustration and resentment in their relations with their wives or girlfriends might suddenly explode in 'some acute assaultive sexual behaviour on an unknown female' without themselves realizing the origin of their aggressive impulses. This type of offender would be likely to benefit from group treatment directed towards improving insight and self-control.

Brancale et al. mention some of the all-too-familiar obstacles to active treatment in a penal setting. The offenders' natural distrust of clinical staff responsible for their compulsory commitment, the resentment aroused in other prisoners when despised sex offenders receive preferential attention, and the resistance of older staff to changing traditionally aloof, authoritarian attitudes in favour of active participation in therapy. They found, as have others, that group therapy had more impact upon offenders than individual interviews, especially when conducted in a more directive fashion than is customary in standard psychotherapy. They instructed the men, instead of considering their crimes as isolated events, to review the feelings and problems that had led to these acts. They also found it necessary to hold sex education sessions, since many sex offenders were 'grossly misinformed or sexually naive or both'.

A special feature of the Rahway programme was the emphasis on catharsis, emotional release. To this end selected inmates participated in special marathon sessions at which discussions would carry on until one or more of the members were provoked into an emotional outburst of crying or cursing. Others in the group, both staff and patients, would then focus upon the affected members individually, helping them to ventilate the painful feelings and memories that had produced the crisis. The whole process was recorded on videotape and later played back as an aid to further exploration and under-standing. This technique, clearly very demanding upon all concerned, appears to be an extension of the 'hot seat' phenomenon of ordinary group sessions, when everyone's attention focuses upon one member who seems on the brink of some new and critical emotional insight.

Brancale suggests that the emotions released by this special technique, the validity of which appears confirmed by the beneficial attitudinal and behavioural changes subsequently noted by relatives and custodial officers, point to a psychodynamic explanation of some rapes and aggressive sexual assaults. The anger revealed in these acts is a cover for deep feelings of hurt which the offender cannot express openly because any such show of weakness would conflict with his concept of a proper manly attitude. This interpretation is essentially identical with the concept of 'hurt masculinity' advanced earlier as an explanation of some of the behaviour of members of the Canadian treatment group.

None of the treatment schemes so far mentioned has included any convincing evaluation of long-term outcome, such as might be obtained from a comparison of follow-up statistics of treated cases with those of a reasonably equivalent control group. A study virtually unique in this respect was reported by Peters *et al.* (1968). They followed up a sample of sex offenders who had been undergoing out-patient group treatment in Philadelphia General Hospital while on probation. The sample included some assaultive offenders, but most were homosexuals, exhibitionists or paedophiles, and therefore not comparable with the much more serious offenders in the Canadian treatment group. The men were required to attend for at least 12 weeks. Some of them did not become much involved and left at the earliest permitted date, but the median duration of stay in the groups was 21·5 weeks. A series of 92 patients passing through the group treatment scheme was compared with a control sample of

75 sex offenders who received ordinary supervision on probation but no group therapy. The treatment and control samples were alike in most important respects, such as the proportions who were first offenders or who had a previous conviction for non-sexual crime, but the treatment group had a higher incidence of previous convictions for sex offences and hence a greater expectation of recidivism. In spite of this, the incidence of re-arrest during a two-year follow-up was strikingly lower among the treated group than among the control group, 3 per cent as against 27 per cent for all crimes, 1 per cent as against 8 per cent for sex crimes.

It seems scarcely credible that a short-term and not particularly intensive course of group therapy could have been responsible for so large a difference, and certainly this one short report will not in itself convert many sceptics to a belief in the effectiveness of psychotherapy for sex offenders. Nevertheless, the Peters study points the way to the feasibility of follow-up evaluations. It could turn out that, unlike other forms of benefit from psychotherapy, which are notoriously difficult to demonstrate, improved control of sexual conduct is easier to substantiate once sufficient cases are available for statistical processing.

Discussion of treatment has so far been limited to group psychotherapy, since this is the most versatile and widely used approach. It fulfils a variety of needs. In men whose crimes have severed many of the human contacts they once enjoyed, participation in a group restores a feeling of acceptance and belonging. Confrontation with others similarly placed forces offenders to face up to their own weaknesses and peculiarities, but at the same time the group offers hope of overcoming their problems. Listening to the experiences and reflections of others in a group may help even those who can never themselves express their emotional conflicts in words. They may gain just sufficient insight into their own behaviour to appreciate the situations of danger which they must strive to avoid. But group treatment is no universal panacea. Some offenders stand in greater need of simple sex education than of emotional delving. Others are by nature or habit incapable of analysing motives or relating verbal discussion to real-life action. Others again are too set in their ways, too unwilling to accept individual responsibility, or too hostile towards their captors to benefit from a process that makes such heavy demands upon their cooperation and trust.

G. G. Abel (1976) and his collaborators at the University of Mississippi, struck by the gauche and inappropriate behaviour some rapists display when they have to deal with women socially, advocate coaching in heterosocial skills as a method of treatment. As they aptly put it, 'unless they can carry out the preliminary conversation, flirting and other dating skills antecedent to a relationship, [offenders] will not have the opportunity to become involved sexually with the female (except by rape).' Realistic treatment programmes for sex offenders, including those at the Regional Psychiatric Centre, generally provide some education in heterosocial skills for those in need. This may include didactic instruction in methods of sexual arousal and sexual intercourse, intimate discussions with therapists or other patients about successful techniques of courting females, and actual practice in the preliminaries of 'chatting up' and 'dating', using nurses, secretaries or other female staff as subjects.

The restrictions of closed institutions, and the necessarily artificial quality of heterosocial rehearsals, when of a couple one is a patient and the other a staff member, impose severe limitations on what can be accomplished along these lines. Even so, the effort is worthwhile. Several members of the Canadian treatment group spoke warmly and gratefully of the help they had derived from opportunities to share friendly conversations and some social activities with female staff. Abel and his colleagues have gone some way towards systematizing and evaluating these educative enterprises. Videotape recordings were made of sexual deviates and normal males while they were attempting to make social approaches to a female assistant. Subsequent analysis of the videotapes served to identify details of gesture, voice tone, conversation flow and emotional expression that distinguished the normal males from the inept deviants. From these items a heterosocial scale was constructed which proved useful in assessing the individual rapist's disabilities and in registering any improvement following training. It seems a reasonable assumption that a man whose previously defective heterosocial skills have been demonstrably improved by corrective education will more easily find normal and satisfying sexual outlets after release. But just how much reduction in sexual recidivism may be expected as a result of these methods has yet to be established. In any event, sex education alone is unlikely to suffice in many cases, for lack of skill is more often a contributory factor than a major cause of a man resorting to sexual assault.

Some rapists experience no difficulty in obtaining access to wives or other consenting women, but because of their strong sadistic interests they remain dissatisfied with these conventional outlets. They obtain maximal sexual arousal only when taking a woman by force against her will. Abel et al. (1975) have developed a method of identifying the stimuli which such aggressive sexual deviants find most exciting. They had sexually deviant and normal males attached to a plethysmograph registering changes in penial volume, while they played to the subjects tape-recorded descriptions of sexual scenes or projected slides showing sexual situations. Unlike the normal males, who preferred scenes of mutually enjoyable love-making, some rapists registered the highest erotic arousal whenever any form of sexual violence was portrayed. Other rapists produced maximal responses when the female in the scene was a girl younger than any legitimate sexual partner. Identification of these deviant interests, sadistic or paedophiliac, indicated both a motive for the rape and a focus for treatment.

Where the offender's primary problem lies in the unacceptable nature of his sexual preferences, this can sometimes be modified with the aid of the techniques developed by behaviour therapists. The oldest of these, the aversive methods, depended upon exciting the subject with a presentation of his preferred sexual scene, then administering a painful shock. Frequent repetition of the sequence would 'decondition' the subject, producing an aversion in place of an inappropriate attraction, leaving the man free to develop other more acceptable interests. In recent years therapists have concentrated on methods less disagreeable to the subject. In the method known as 'fading', the subject is required to masturbate while watching a projected picture of his favourite sexual object. As climax approaches the therapist substitutes a modified slide so that, at the moment of orgasm, the man is watching a somewhat more socially acceptable scene. Repeated association of orgasm with the new sexual stimulus gradually influences the man's sexual interests in the direction of the therapist's manipulations. Even without these elaborate arrangements and apparatus men can be trained to use their imagination, aided perhaps by appropriate items of pornography, to conjure up sexual fantasies of an acceptable kind during masturbation. At Western State Hospital, for example, private rooms were made available to offenders for the purpose of masturbation, but with the proviso that they report their fantasies truthfully and allow them to be discussed at group sessions. This eclectic combination of behaviourist techniques with psychotherapeutic discussion is a more realistic treatment strategy than either method used separately. It calls for therapists who are free from dogmatic professional commitment to the exclusive use of methods derived from their particular theoretical training.

Surgical castration is still sometimes advocated as treatment for aggressive or otherwise dangerous sex offenders. Since castration is also a harsh punishment and a method of social control, its justification on medical grounds is always suspect. Legal statutes of undisguisedly punitive intent, such as those enacted in Nazi Germany in 1933, which provided for the compulsory castration of certain categories of convicted sex offenders, infringe the basic human rights of prisoners, and run counter to contemporary penal philosophy. On the other hand, offenders themselves occasionally plead for castration to relieve them of an intolerable burden of sexual temptation which they fear may lead them to irretrievable disaster. If these men are correct in their belief that this is the surest way to protect both themselves and the community from their otherwise uncontrollable impulses, should they not be allowed to have their wish granted? It is, after all, less destructive than the urge to be executed which occasionally foils attempts to reprieve condemned men, as in the recent case of the American murderer Gary Gilmour.

The results of castration of sex offenders are known from extensive follow-up studies which have been summarized by Sturup (1972), who was himself for many years responsible for operating a law enabling detained sex offenders in Denmark to petition for medical castration and thus to secure a relatively early release. Under the Danish system, castration was sanctioned only for a minority of the most serious offenders, aggressively assaultive men and persistent child molesters, who were thought unlikely to be helped by purely psychological methods.

Surgical removal of the testes reduces drastically the level of circulating androgens upon which sexual desire and sexual potency partially depend. In most cases, the urgent, imperative quality of sexual desire is lost, and so also in the course of time, though it may take many months or even years, is the ability to produce erections and effect penetration. Although the intensity and intrusiveness of sexual fantasies and sexual interests diminish, the direction of a man's sexual urges do not change. Following the loss of their sexual drive some therapeutic castrates become depressed, but the majority were calmer and happier afterwards, and glad they had opted for surgery. Men who had feared that life without sex would turn out to be hardly worth living found that other interests developed to replace their sexual preoccupations. The insertion of cosmetic plastic fillings into the scrotal sac, to prevent obvious shrinkage, and so avoid an embarrassing physical stigma, was an important part of the treatment technique, and helped the patients to preserve confidence in their continuing male image. Physical changes, such as skin softening, altered distribution of body fat and a temporary 'menopausal' phase characterized by hot flushes, were less extreme and less troublesome than might have been expected.

It is rare for a castrated offender to repeat a sexual offence. Sturup quotes a 2 per cent recidivism rate for serious and potentially persistent sex offenders, which is certainly much less than would have been the case without surgery. One has to bear in mind, however, that the Danish patients received prolonged after-care, with a great deal of counselling and practical help in resettlement into the community, so the good results may not have been solely due to surgery. The operation does not afford absolute protection. Sturup himself cites one published case of a sadistic rapist who repeated his crime after castration. As one knows from the experience of rapists who fail to complete the act of intercourse with their victims, or of paedophiles whose ritual does not include any attempt at intercourse, impotence does not in itself prevent violent sexual molestation. Sturup always explained to his patients that they would be able to control themselves better, but that they would still need to take care to avoid sexually provocative situations.

Since the discovery that cyproterone acetate can be used to neutralize the action of naturally circulating androgen, the use of surgery to quell unwanted sexual drive is theoretically no longer necessary. The drug is not available for medical administration in all countries, owing to varying regulations for safety clearance, but derivatives of progesterone can be used, if necessary, with much the same result. Dosage has to be continued regularly, and the full effect may take a long time to develop, but when it does the reduction in libido is dramatic. The effect can be monitored by determination of the diminishing testosterone level in plasma, and by failure to produce erections in response to erotic material or during masturbation. One advantage of this treatment over castration is that androgens from all sources, including the supra-renal glands, are neutralized, whereas some castrated men still retain significant amounts of natural androgen. The drug is useful for the temporary control of inconveniently overactive sexuality, and has been found helpful, for instance, in reducing unwanted manifestations of sex among the institutionalized subnormal. As therapy for the dangerous sex offender, especially if used with a view to the release of men who would otherwise be kept in custody, it has the serious limitation that it depends upon continued administration, and hence the continued cooperation of the offender. The castrated patient cannot so easily renounce his commitment to a sexually quiescent existence, unless, of course, he manages to persuade some misguided therapist to administer substitute androgen.

We have described the promising responses of one small sample of offenders to a form of group treatment suitable for men who can cooperate in an exacting therapeutic regime. We have briefly reviewed other programmes and mentioned other methods, some of which might help offenders for whom a group, such as that at the Regional Psychiatric Centre, would be inappropriate. Aggressive sexual offenders present a wide range of social and psychiatric problems, and although we believe many cases would benefit from treatment, we propose no single cure-all solution. In the end, it remains a matter of clinical judgment what approach to use in a particular case, but some rational classification of offenders would make the choice easier.

As Clifford Allen (1962) points out, the diverse forms of conduct covered by the legal term rape are extraordinarily difficult to classify for psychiatric purposes, and the existing literature provides very little authoritative guidance. Rape occurs when a man inserts his penis into the vagina of a woman, other than his wife, without her consent, by means of force, threat or trickery. Rape incidents range from relatively minor deviations from accepted conduct to grossly aberrant and sometimes dangerously homicidal behaviour. Moreover, some gross sexual attacks are technically not rapes, perhaps not even attempted rapes. Allen himself suggests four categories of offenders:

(1) the sexually and psychiatrically normal;
(2) the sexually deviated who are psychiatrically normal;
(3) the sexually and psychiatrically deviated;
(4) the psychiatrically deviated who are not sexually abnormal.

The type (1) offender leads a normal sex life and does not usually transgress the accepted rules of courtship and love-making. He breaks out of his conformist pattern only under special circumstances, usually when, under the disinhibiting effects of alcohol, he loses his temper with a woman who unexpectedly refuses him, or pursues the object of his desires in a clumsy way that leads to subsequent complaint. The sexually deviant, type (2) offenders, rape because they obtain particular erotic pleasure from obtaining intercourse under duress and in painful conditions. They are sadists who depend upon the victim's reactions of pain or terror to obtain sexual arousal. Type (3) offenders combine unusual sexual urges with a character defect that diminishes their self-control. This type includes men with excessively strong sexual libido who, because of their personality problems, fail to obtain sufficient satisfaction from wives or prostitutes. It includes antisocial, if not actually psychopathic, characters who pursue predatory sexual interests without regard to social rules or to the wishes of their sexual partners. It also includes men, like those in the present treatment group, with abnormal attitudes towards women arising from their own inferiority complex. Harbouring irrational grudges they seek psychological satisfaction from degrading and humiliating women. For them, sexual aggression is both erotically pleasurable and an effective weapon of revenge. Type (4) consists of those who would not behave in a sexually deviant fashion but for some gross psychiatric abnormality. They include mentally subnormal offenders whose social skills are inadequate to permit them to obtain sexual satisfaction without offending, as well as deluded schizophrenic offenders who do not properly appreciate what they are doing. Among the totality of rapists type (4) forms a small minority. Even in a selected sample referred for forensic psychiatric examination those with gross psychiatric abnormalities (organic, subnormal, schizophrenic) amount to only about 10 per cent. The majority are personality deviants, usually of the antisocial type. The 'crazy rapist' is largely mythical (Henn *et al.*, 1976).

These four categories encompass most of the types of rapists that have been recognized by other authorities. For example, they correspond fairly closely with the clinical classification derived from experience with serious sexual offenders committed to the Bridgewater Treatment Center in Massachusetts (Burgess and Holmstrom, 1974, Ch. 2). Allen's type (2) offenders, the sadistic men who require some physical violence to achieve sexual excitation, are called by the Bridgewater group 'sex-aggression defusion' cases. They remark upon the relative rarity of the extreme form of sadism that leads to lust murder, noting that sadistic rapists are sexually excited rather than angered by struggle, and that after intercourse is over they usually cease to be aggressive.

The Bridgewater workers subdivided Allen's sexually and psychologically deviated offenders (type 3) into three groups. The first and most readily recognizable are the 'impulse' rapists, the ones variously named by other authorities amoral delinquents or impulsive, predatory, antisocial criminal types. The second group, corresponding to the men described in this book, are those with an aggression complex who use rape as a weapon in their hostilities against women. Finally, they describe the sexually motivated offenders who are trying to compensate for feelings of masculine inadequacy by acting out a fantasy of successful, forceful seduction. These tend to be passive, inhibited characters, inept in sociosexual skills, whose assaults appear to others out of character and unexpected. They do not develop the determinedly hostile stance of the aggressive group, their motive is more predominantly sexual, and they usually give up or run away if faced with much resistance.

Although Allen's classification is the best to be found in the psychiatric literature, it has obvious limitations. Boundaries are ill-defined and the overlap between groups is considerable. For instance, as Allen himself points out, the so-called normal offenders of type (1) may not be so normal as they seem at first sight. Mild intoxication will not convert an otherwise conformist character into a potential rapist unless, in his sober state, he is experiencing conflict and frustration in his efforts to establish satisfying socio-sexual relationships. Type (2) offenders, men with no disorder other than sadistic sexual interests, are unusual. The sadist who cannot rest content with the wide range of love play permissible between like-minded couples is likely to be deviant in personality and in attitude to women as well as in his erotic tastes. Type (4) offenders also overlap with other groups. Only a small minority of mentally subnormal or psychotic individuals commit sexual assaults and those who do so are sometimes affected by much the same attitudes and conflicts as other types of rapist.

In spite of its imperfections, this simple classification serves to highlight contrasting treatment needs. Type (4) cases, men with classic psychiatric syndromes, need conventional treatment before it can be decided whether their sexual problems are mere secondary by-products which will disappear when the primary condition is brought under control. Type (1) cases, who are free from any gross personality disorder, would nevertheless obtain benefit from practical advice and counselling, but preferably as out-patients or probationers, rather than in the contaminating environment of a closed penal institution. For type (2) offenders, with a major problem of deviant sexual interests, suitability for techniques of behaviour therapy will be a first consideration, but this should not exclude simultaneous psychotherapy. Type (3), the largest category among imprisoned offenders, will mostly require group psychotherapy of one kind or another. Some may need preliminary individual therapy to establish trusting relationships before they can be brought to participate in a group effort. Regrettably, there will always remain a residue not amenable to any psychotherapeutic approach. The size of this residue varies with the skill and patience of the therapists, but it also greatly depends upon the atmosphere of the institution in which treatment is to be attempted.

We should like to end on a note of cautious optimism. The relevance and feasibility of psychiatric approaches to imprisoned sex offenders have been amply and repeatedly demonstrated. Given the range of methods, there is no excuse for a therapeutic defeatism. Owing to practical and methodological problems, results, in terms of long-term reduction in sex crime recidivism, may be difficult to establish conclusively but there are strong indications of a substantial level of success awaiting to be documented by those in a position to organize the necessary follow-up studies. Attempts to show the effect of psychiatric treatment upon recidivism in non-sexual crimes have so often yielded no evidence of any reduction that penal authorities have become sadly disillusioned with the treatment philosophy. As a consequence, new penal codes in certain states of America seek to fix sentences in direct proportion to the nature of the crime, and to abolish discretionary early release on parole. One reason for this policy is to avoid the coercion of prisoners into participation in expensive and possibly futile treatment programmes by the prospect of early release as a reward for cooperation. Whatever one may think of the justification for this trend as regards the generality of adult prisoners, it does not fit the needs of aggressive or dangerous sex offenders for two main reasons. First, because, in the absence of some effective treatment intervention, for purposes of community protection there is no alternative to very long sentences. These are both expensive for the community and destructive to the individual offender. Second, because we believe treatment is effective in reducing the risk of recidivism in at least some types of sex offender. If a long and immutable sentence is fixed before the offender's response to treatment is known, this in effect robs the community and the offender of all hope of the benefit which psychological and psychiatric methods can sometimes bring.

Three requirements appear to us essential for the successful treatment of serious sexual offenders. (1) A maximum sentence, in proportion to the seriousness of the offence, beyond which the offender cannot be detained. (2) A flexible policy for earlier release and adequate supervision and treatment thereafter, with release decisions guided by therapeutic recommendations, but preferably subject to scrutiny by judicial authority. (3) A treatment setting separate from the ordinary prison, with a specialist staff in complete control of the regime and of the selection of cases suited for the treatments available.

The systems of treatment available to sex offenders at the Regional Psychiatric Centre in British Columbia have developed further since this report was written. The limitations that have been pointed out do not detract from the potential importance of the pioneering projects that have been initiated or of the rapid progress made during the hospital's brief history. The ideal models for treatment suggested here are goals which will not be attained without the collaboration of numerous authorities. One hopes that this Centre, and other facilities with similar aims, will find the support their task requires.

References

ABEL, G. G. *et al.* (1975), 'Identifying specific erotic cues in sexual deviations by audiotaped descriptions', *Journal of Applied Behaviour Analysis*, **8**, 247–60.

ABEL, G. G., BLANCHARD, E.B. and Becker, Judith V. (1976), 'Psychological treatment of rapists', in Walker and Brodsky (eds.).

ABRAHAMSEN, D. (1960), *The Psychology of Crime*. New York: Columbia University Press.

ALLEN, C. (1962), *A Text Book of Psycho-Sexual Disorders*. London: Oxford University Press.

AMIR, M. (1971), *Patterns in Forcible Rape*. Chicago: Chicago University Press.

BRANCALE, R., VUOCOLO, A. and PRENDERGAST, W. E. (1972), 'The New Jersey program for sex offenders', in Resnik, H. L. P. and Wolfgang, M. E. (eds.).

BRODSKY, S. L. (1976), 'Prevention of rape: Deterrence by the potential victim', in Walker, M. J. and Brodsky, S. L. (eds.).

BROMBERG, W. (1948), *Crime and the Mind*. Ch. 4, Sexual Psychopathy. New York: Lippincott.

BROWNMILLER, Susan (1975), *Against Our Will*. New York: Simon Schuster.

BURGESS, A. W. and HOLMSTROM, L. L. (1974), *Rape: Victims of Crisis*. Bowie, Md.: R. J. Brady.

CHAPPELL, D., *et al.* (1974, 1977), 'Forcible rape: bibliography', *Journal of Criminal Law and Criminology*, **65**, 248–63, **68**, 146–159.

CHRISTIANSEN, K. O. *et al.* (1965), 'Recidivism among sexual offenders', *Scandinavian Studies in Criminology*, Vol. 1. London: Tavistock.

CORMIER, B. M. and SIMONS, S. P. (1969), 'The problem of the dangerous sexual offender', *Canadian Psychiatric Association Journal*, **14**, 329–35.

DIX, G. E. (1975), 'Determining the continuing dangerousness of psychologically abnormal sex offenders', *Journal of Psychiatry and the Law*, **3**, 327–44.

DIX, G. E. (1976), 'Differential processing of abnormal sex offenders: Utilisation of California's mentally disordered sex offender program', *Journal of Criminal Law and Criminology*, **67**, 233–43.

FISHER, G. and RIVLIN, E. (1971), 'Psychological needs of rapists', *British Journal of Criminology*, **11**, 182–5.

FRISBIE, Louise V. and DONDIS, E. H. (1965), *Recidivism among treated sex*

173

offenders. California Mental Health Research Monographs No. 5: California Bureau of Research and Statistics.

GARRETT, T. B. and WRIGHT, R. (1975), 'Wives of rapists and incest offenders', *Journal of Sex Research,* 11, 149–57.

GEBHARD, P. H. *et al.* (1965), *Sex Offenders: an Analysis of Types.* New York: Harper and Row.

GIBBENS, T. C. N., WAY, C. and SOOTHILL, K. L. (1977), 'Behavioural types of rape', *British Journal of Psychiatry,* 130, 32–42.

GOLDNER, M. S. (1972), 'Rape as a heinous but understudied offense', *Journal of Criminal Law, Criminology and Police Science,* 63, 402–7.

GREENLAND, C. (1977), 'Psychiatry and the dangerous sexual offender', *Canadian Psychiatric Association Journal,* 22, 155–9.

GUTTMACHER, M. S. and WEIHOFEN, H. (1952), *Psychiatry and the Law.* New York: Norton.

HALLECK, S. L. (1971), *Psychiatry and the Dilemmas of Crime.* Los Angeles: University of California Press.

HENN, F. A., HERJANIC, M. and VANDERPEARL, R. H. (1976), 'Forensic psychiatry: Profiles of two types of sex offenders', *American Journal of Psychiatry,* 133, 694–6.

Home Office (1975), *Report of the Advisory Committee on the Law of Rape* (Heilbron Report). London: Stationery Office, Cmd. 6352.

KANIN, E. J. (1969), 'Selected dyadic aspects of male sex aggression', *Journal of Sex Research,* 5, No. 1. Reprinted in Schultz, L. G. (1975).

KARPMAN, B. (1954), *The Sexual Offender and his Offenses.* New York: Julian Press.

McCALDON, R. J. (1967), 'Rape,' *Canadian Journal of Corrections,* 9, 37–59.

McCLINTOCK, F. H. (1963), *Crimes of Violence.* London: Macmillan.

MacDONALD, G. J. and WILLIAMS, R. A. (1971), *The Western State sexual psychopath law: A review of twenty years experience.* Fort Steilacoom, Washington State: Dept. of Social and Health Services.

MacDONALD, J. (1973), *Indecent Exposure.* Springfield, Ill.: Thomas.

MACDONALD, J. (1971), *Rape Offenders and their Victims.* Springfield, Ill., Thomas.

MEDEA, Andra and THOMPSON, Kathleen (1974), *Against Rape.* New York: Farrar, Straus and Giroux.

MOHR, J. W. (1965), *Rape and attempted Rape:* An examination of the nature of offences under S. 135 and 137 of the Criminal Code of Canada. Toronto: Forensic Clinic, Toronto Psychiatric Hospital.

NELSON, S. and AMIR, M. (1975), 'The hitchhike victim of rape: A research report', in Drapkin, I. and Viano, E. (eds.), *Victimology,* Vol. 5, 47–64. Lexington, Mass.: Lexington Books.

PETERS, J. J. *et al.* (1968), 'Group psychotherapy of the sex offender', *Federal Probation,* 32 (3), 41–5.

RADZINOWICZ, L. (ed.) (1957), *Sexual Offences.* London: Macmillan.

RINGROSE, C. A. D. (1975), 'Sociological, medical and legal aspects of rape', *Criminal Law Quarterly,* 17, 440–5.

ROBERTS, L. M. and PACHT, A. R. (1965), 'Termination of in-patient treatment for sex deviates', *American Journal of Psychiatry*, **121**, 873–80.

SCACCO, A. M. (1975), *Rape in Prison*. Springfield, Ill.: Thomas.

SCHULTZ, L. G. (ed.) (1975), *Rape Victimology*. Springfield, Ill.: Thomas.

SOOTHILL, K. L., JACK, Anthea and GIBBENS, T. C. N. (1976), Rape: a 22 year cohort study, *Medicine, Science and the Law*, **16**, 62–9.

STOLLER, R. J. (1968), *Sex and Gender*. New York: Science House.

STURUP, G. K. (1972), 'Castration: The total treatment', in Resnik, H. and Wolfgang, M. (eds.), *Sexual Behaviors*. Boston: Little, Brown.

WALKER, Marcia J. and BRODSKY, S. L. (eds.) (1976), *Sexual Assault*. Lexington, Mass.: D. C. Heath.

Index of Authors

176

Index of Subjects

Age, xi, 3, 38, 43, 122, 134–5
Alcohol, xii, 11–12, 15, 19, 28–9, 33, 34, 41–2, 44, 55, 59, 61, 62, 68, 70–2, 75, 80, 85, 91–3, 100, 101, 102–3, 104, 109, 112, 117ff., 130, 162
Autobiographies, x, 3, 51, 159

Bridgewater Treatment Center, 170
'Buddy' security system, 160

Castration, 166–7
Catharsis, 163
Compensatory aggression, 146
Criminality, non-sexual, 11, 12, 18, 24, 39, 40, 73–5, 77, 79–80, 97, 103, 126, 130, 143–4
Cyproterone acetate, 168

Dangerous Sex Offender status, xii, 150–1
Drugs, 45, 92, 117–18

Eneuresis, 16, 52, 56, 69
Escalation of crimes, 50, 130, 142
Exploitation of women, 137–8

False
  accusations, 114–15, 136
  protestations, 152–3
Feminist views, 137–8

Gender role, 9
Group
  rapes, 139, 148
  treatment, 1, 3–7, 158–9, 162–4
Guilt feelings, 9, 20, 22, 27, 29–30, 36, 48, 49, 51, 66–7, 74, 76, 84, 100, 105, 108, 110–13, 117, 120, 121, 144

Hitch-hikers, 84, 93, 96, 108–12, 137, 139, 148

Homosexual
  assault, 35, 37, 78, 80
  experience, xii, 41, 69, 78–9
  prostitution, 37–8, 78–80, 130
Hospital setting, ix–x, xi, 1, 5, 149, 159–61

Impotence and inadequacy, 8, 34, 36, 41, 42, 47, 54, 76, 79, 102–3, 104, 115–16, 117, 119, 122, 125
Incest, 24, 26–7, 46, 74
Indecent exposure, 141, 160
Inferiority feelings, 23, 27, 30, 34, 35, 40, 45, 50, 56, 65, 72, 86, 89, 102, 125–7, 145
Injured victims, 117, 118, 120, 130, 137–8

Marriage, 28–30, 34, 45, 49, 54, 55, 62–4, 76, 82–3, 86, 87, 88–91, 95–6, 99–100, 105, 126–7
Masculine image, 8–9, 25, 26ff., 31, 45, 65, 83, 85, 89, 104–6, 125–7, 144, 163, 170

New Jersey treatment scheme, 161–2

Parental
  brutality, 9, 10–11, 12, 13, 16, 19
  rejection, 11, 12, 13, 14, 15–16, 18, 21, 25
Parole, 6, 80, 85, 151, 154–5, 161, 172
Patients' evaluations, 3–4
Physical inferiority, 18, 30, 40, 47, 60, 72–3, 87
Plethysmography, 165–6
Probationary period, 3, 158
Psychiatric disorders, 5, 169
Publicity, 161

Rape
  definitions, 107, 134–5, 169

177